The Agency of Eating

Contemporary Food Studies: Economy, Culture and Politics

Series Editors: David Goodman and Michael K. Goodman
ISSN: 2058-1807

This interdisciplinary series represents a significant step toward unifying the study, teaching and research of food studies across the social sciences. The series features authoritative appraisals of core themes, debates and emerging research, written by leading scholars in the field. Each title offers a jargon-free introduction to upper-level undergraduate and postgraduate students in the social sciences and humanities.

Kate Cairns and Josée Johnston, *Food and Femininity*

Peter Jackson, *Anxious Appetites: Food and Consumer Culture*

Philip H. Howard, *Concentration and Power in the Food System: Who Controls What We Eat?*

Terry Marsden, *Agri-Food and Rural Development: Sustainable Place-Making*

Emma-Jayne Abbots, *The Agency of Eating: Mediation, Food and the Body*

Further titles forthcoming

The Agency of Eating

Mediation, Food and the Body

Emma-Jayne Abbots

Bloomsbury Academic
An imprint of Bloomsbury Publishing Plc

B L O O M S B U R Y
LONDON · NEW DELHI · NEW YORK · SYDNEY

Bloomsbury Academic
An imprint of Bloomsbury Publishing Plc

50 Bedford Square   1385 Broadway
London   New York
WC1B 3DP   NY 10018
UK   USA

www.bloomsbury.com

BLOOMSBURY and the Diana logo are trademarks of Bloomsbury Publishing Plc

First published 2017

British Library Cataloguing-in-Publication Data
A catalogue record for this book is available from the British Library.

ISBN: HB: 978-1-4725-9854-7
        PB: 978-1-4725-9853-0
        ePDF: 978-1-4725-9856-1
        ePub: 978-1-4725-9855-4

Library of Congress Cataloging-in-Publication Data
A catalog record for this book is available from the Library of Congress.

Cover design: Adriana Brioso
Cover image: *Abstract Figures in Red* (2001), Diana Ong © Getty Images

Series: Contemporary Food Studies: Economy, Culture and Politics

Typeset by Deanta Global Publishing Services, Chennai, India

To find out more about our authors and books visit www.bloomsbury.com. Here you will find extracts, author interviews, details of forthcoming events and the option to sign up for our newsletters.

To Dad,
with love, always

Contents

Acknowledgements   viii

Introducing the agency of eating   1

1   Eating bodies and bodies of eating:
Theoretical foundations   13

2   Eating at home: Kinned, shared and acquired bodies   35

3   Eating away from home: Displaced and
(re)rooted bodies   57

4   Eating heritage foods: Proximate and
distanced bodies   79

5   Eating 'Global Food' and its alternatives: Anxious,
obscured and active bodies   101

6   Eating for self and society: Responsible, acceptable
and abject bodies   123

7   Eating futures: Reflections and directions   143

Notes   157
Bibliography   160
Index   176

Acknowledgements

Over the course of writing this book I have been blessed with support, encouragement, feedback and friendship from a host of individuals. My foremost thanks go to my 'co-conspirator' on the topic of eating, Anna Lavis. An incidental conversation at a Goldsmiths Christmas party has led to a collaboration that has not only produced a conference, two edited collections and a research network, but also has significantly shaped the way I think about food, the body and eating. I am a better academic for our discussions and I worry she is not acknowledged enough in the following pages. Many thanks also to the SOAS Food Studies NKUMI group comprising Harry West, Jakob Klein, Lizzie Hull, Johan Pottier, Anne Murcott, Sami Zubaida and James Staples. Their critical, yet always constructive, comments, insightful questions, and close reading of various chapters helped cohere my thoughts and clarify my writing. I enjoy our lively conversations enormously. Thanks are also due to Ben Coles for commenting on an early stream of consciousness that masqueraded as a draft chapter and for asking me what I meant by eating. By suggesting we co-write the next book, Ben further gave me the motivation to finish this one.

I am grateful to Mike Goodman for his input at the development stage, and to David Goodman and an anonymous reviewer for providing comments on the first full draft. In addition, I benefited from feedback from participants at the anthropology and UVBO seminars at the University of Oxford and the indigenous food conference at Humboldt University, Berlin. Part of the book was drafted during a short stay in Oxford and my thanks go particularly to Karin Eli and Stanley Ulijaszek. My thinking on materialities was further informed by two 'Food Stuffs' workshops at UWTSD and my gratitude is extended to all the workshop participants and especially to my two co-conveners, Louise Steel and Katharina Zinn. Further thanks are also due to my students, particularly those in the 'Material Worlds', 'Body, Culture and Society' and 'Political Anthropology' modules for their thoughtful questions, feedback on draft chapters, and engaged discussions.

UWTSD provided practical support in the form of a two-term sabbatical, as did the RAI/Sutasoma Trust and Wenner Gren Foundation, which funded my doctoral and postdoctoral fieldwork, respectively. The Wenner Gren also funded the later Food Stuffs workshop. At Bloomsbury, Clara Herberg and Jennifer Schmidt have been instrumental in getting this book to press and have been a wonderfully supportive team with which to work.

The original ethnography contained in this book would not have been possible without the support, friendship and collaboration of a whole range of individuals in Ecuador, who are too numerous to name individually here. The warmth of the community in Jima and their readiness to open their doors and share their lives with me is beyond compare and I am truly grateful for their hospitality and generosity. Particular thanks go to Maria, Teresa, Marcelo and Zoila, who were my guides through the Cuenca foodscape and who did so much to make me feel at home. My gratitude also extends to the privileged migrants who openly shared their hopes, dreams, fears and experiences with me. Closer to home, my thanks go to Margaret Birt for her never-ceasing support and to David Harries and Philip Brocklehurst for their never-ceasing supply of gin and laughter. And finally, a very special thanks to Gemma, Lizzie, Leonie and Kasia, who are the most beautiful, amazing, creative and inspiring group of women I could ever hope to meet and the best friends anyone could wish for.

Introducing the agency of eating

This book explores how eating, as an embodied experience, mediates and is mediated by the relationship between food's matter and meaning. My first aim is to tease out how the human eating body, the material stuff of food, and cultural knowledges about food (and the individuals and institutions who produce such knowledges) all dynamically interplay to shape social understandings of what and how we should – and should not – be eating. I am particularly interested in where power lies in such interactions and how it is enacted in and through bodies: I therefore raise the questions 'Do eaters absorb knowledges and values about foods as they are eating them?' 'Does this bestow authority to those who encourage us to eat certain foods or position themselves as food "experts," such as food activists, doctors, or even family members?' and 'Can eating contest these political relations and produce new knowledge?' Asking these questions leads me to consider what agency – meaning the power to affect change (Bennett 2010) – looks like in relation to food and eating and I consider 'Who has agency – the eater or experts?' 'Can agency be located in the matter of food itself?' 'Is agency to be found in the interactions between eaters, food and knowledge-(makers)?' 'Is agency distributed across a food's network or does it coalesce around certain individuals, institutions or even objects?' and, most importantly, 'In what ways can eating be an expression of agency?' This book can, then, be largely read as addressing the political dynamics and power relations of eating.

Incorporating eating bodies, the material stuff of food, and knowledges about food into the same frame leads me to examine how matter and meaning interact, and my second aim is to interrogate how this gets played out in the reality of everyday life. My interest and overall approach to this question is, in part, influenced by the recent turn to 'new materialisms' (Coole and Frost 2010; see also Bennett 2007, 2010) and Actor Network Theory (ANT) (Latour 2005; Law and Hassard 2004), in the sense that I am open to the possibility that non-human 'things' – such as foods – can produce affect and effect and be attributed with agency. Nevertheless, as an anthropologist schooled in political economy and the argument that humans give meaning to objects, I find a wholesale adoption of the 'agency of objects' thesis unsatisfactory. I cannot discount the structures and inequitable distribution of political and economic power within the contemporary food system. Nor can I gloss over the cultural politics of food and the role certain actors and institutions play in shaping what people eat and the values and beliefs they hold about food and bodies. To do so would do an injustice to the wealth of food studies scholarship that has painstakingly drawn attention to these dynamics in considered and robust ways, as well as potentially bypassing the lived reality of people's experiences of food. However, this is not to say that established political economic approaches to food cannot be enhanced by a (re)turn to materialisms – food is, after all, political, symbolic *and* material. Hence, a path that attempts to draw these two seemingly estranged perspectives together in a workable framework is required. What follows is my attempt to do so.

For me, as I hope will become clear as this book unfolds, the affects and effects of eating stem, in part, from the beliefs, values and symbolic meanings that humans attribute to foods. And such beliefs, values and meanings derive, again in part, from the social relations that produce knowledges about food, the economic structures through which food arrives in our shopping baskets and to our plates, and the political dynamics that result in particular social actors having greater cultural authority to talk and be heard than others. Food studies scholarship, especially that within the anthropology of food, has, however, arguably privileged the meaning of food and its political economy to the detriment of its materiality (Abbots 2016a; Abbots and Lavis 2013; Holtzman 2009). Holtzman writes, for instance, that food has often been mobilized as 'a sort of triviata that provides a window onto something more important' (2009: 54) and that it is this very tendency to 'disaggregate' food from the study of food that elides the 'very simultaneity as material, social, and symbolic that makes food food' (ibid.: 55). Accordingly, I have argued with Anna Lavis (Abbots and Lavis 2013) that food is both matter *and* meaning and, to fully encompass this multifaceted nature, we need to move beyond questions about what food means and symbolizes, and also ask what food *feels* like when we encounter it through our bodies. In short, food is not just good to think with (Levi-Strauss 1969), it is also good to eat; and we need to start attending to this far more if we are to better understand food in all of its cultural, social, political, economic and material glory.

One of the core messages of this book, then, is that while food is a productive lens through which to explore broader social and political relations, food should also be treated *as food*. Food is worthy of attention as its own object of enquiry, not just as a window into social life. I thereby respectfully disagree with the notion that food is better to think with than to eat. One of the most interesting things we can do with food is to eat it, and we forget this at our peril. Yes, food gives us a window to 'society': it is imbued with symbolism; we look at it, talk about it and think about it; we give meanings to it; involve it in ritual processes; perform with and through it; express our aspirations and social position with it; castigate and celebrate people with it; withhold, distribute and offer it; and create social bonds and boundaries with it. *But we also eat it*. And in this book I encourage food studies scholars to remember this oft-ignored, yet rather commonsensical, fact. Moreover, as I aim to show, interrogating how eating brings the matter of food – its very substance – and its meaning – its socially produced knowledges – together can give us a deeper insight into the dynamics that make meaning meaningful and the material matter.

In sum, I argue, and look to demonstrate over the coming pages, that matter has the agency to create affect and effect not because of some inherent quality, but because of the social meaning that humans imbue into that matter. Whereas meanings are powerfully resonant because they come to us entwined with a material substance that produces a visceral embodied response. Matter and meaning are thus inherently as one – they are two sides of the same coin.

Teasing out the intersections between matter and meaning and the ways this dynamic mediates, and it mediated by, eating requires two things: First, that bodies and the embodied experience are brought to the fore and treated as critical subjects of enquiry and second, that an examination of these, often somewhat abstract and conceptual, processes and practices are grounded and elucidated through rich ethnographic examples. This relationship between eating bodies, food knowledges and power has been productively interrogated – at times ethnographically – by scholarship inspired by Foucault's (1978, 2001, 2002a) work on biopower (see for example Rose 2007; Wright and Harwood 2009) and framing my thinking through this lens would have been, in many ways, the obvious path to tread. I do not wish, however, for the following discussion to be categorically 'Foucauldian', although there are clear symmetries as I explore how power and knowledge are exercised and produced in and through bodies. I discuss some of these studies and how my own approach draws upon and extends them in the following chapter, but I want to note here that I treat this scholarship primarily as an anchoring influence as I attempt to draw Foucauldian insight on power/bodies into dialogue with ANT takes on mediation and the agency of the non-human.

Similarly, I do not approach the body as an abstracted concept but rather look to take the embodied experience of eating and the senses into account. I discuss the differences in approach that come with treating 'the body' in its abstract, social constructionist (or non-representational theory) sense and by attending to embodied encounters in the following chapter, but needless to say I move between these two treatments of bodies as I shift between conceptual understandings of how 'the body' is constructed and ethnographic experience. The sensate, feeling body is thus central to my discussion and I align with the recent 'turn' to viscerality and food, which has been particularly productive in geography, gender studies and obesity and fat studies (cf Colls 2007, 2012; Colls and Evans 2009, 2013; Hayes-Conroy 2014; Hayes-Conroy and Hayes-Conroy 2008, 2010a,b; Longhurst, Johnston and Ho 2009; Longhurst 2012), as well as anthropological and sociological (and beyond) work on embodiment and embodied politics (cf Carolan 2011; Csordas 1990, 1994), and writings on affect and the senses (cf Anderson 2011; Sutton 2001).

I hope it will become evident over the following chapters what a focus on the body and embodiment can contribute to our understanding of the politics of eating, and I could say here that these insights are so nuanced and complex that they cannot be effectively summarized in one sentence in an introduction. Nevertheless, I have attempted on occasion to write such a sentence or respond neatly to the incessant question(s) directed to me, particularly by those with a more political economic leaning: 'But what does a focus on the body bring to the study of food?' After various contortions to try and answer this question in a manner that legitimized the centrality of the body, I arrived at a far shorter and simplistic retort: 'Why shouldn't we be thinking about the body?'

It is, in many respects, extraordinary that discussions of food and eating require such a justification. Surely we should be questioning why accounts of food and eating omit the body? This is not to deride the insightful and sophisticated research that has detailed and productively analysed food preferences and practices without recourse to the body, but instead note that the requirement for a justification for why bodies are important to studies of eating – an inherently bodily practice – is suggestive in itself. For me, this is indicative of the long-established and prevailing ethos within much of food studies scholarship – we have spent so long using food to think with that we have tended to forget that we eat it (with the notable exceptions I highlight in the ensuing chapters). I am not attempting to circumnavigate difficult questions with semantics here, but rather subvert and question them, and the theoretical and disciplinary purviews that give rise to them. A focus on the body should not be an anomaly or an out-of-the-ordinary event. On the contrary, I make a plea here for the sensate, feeling body to at the very core of critical food studies across disciplines.

The other question I have been frequently asked over the course of writing and talking about this book is 'What do I bring to this subject as an anthropologist?'

Initially I rallied against such a question – we are, after all, researching and writing in a post-disciplinary world, and I draw on literature that interests me, paying little heed to the discipline from which it originates. Critical food studies is, first and foremost, a fertile ground for interdisciplinary conversations and throughout this book I engage with scholarship variously framed as anthropology, sociology, geography, cultural studies, political ecology, education, fat and obesity studies, and gender studies, to name but a few. But such a disciplinary question is cause for reflection, and an anthropological approach does, I suggest, bring an additional element to these discussions – that of ethnography.

A deep appreciation of the richness of ethnographic detail, despite debates as to its place and problematic nature (see Clifford and Marcus 2010), remains at the heart of anthropological enquiry. This is not to say that ethnography is exclusively anthropological (or that anthropology is exclusively ethnographic) or that other disciplines do not base their discussions on robust primary data. But a significant proportion of the work I discuss on the agency of material substances and the non-human has remained at a somewhat abstract and conceptual level (cf Bennett 2010), and this, like all abstract concepts, does not fully accord with the realities of everyday life. There is a disjuncture between ontological imaginings of what material 'stuff' can theoretically do and the lived practical experience of encountering it. Likewise, it is possible to theorize notions such as 'distributed agency', but whether this equates to any sense of political empowerment for individuals subjected to a consolidated agri-food regime is debatable (cf Goodman 2016). And, in parallel, we can consider how 'the body' is socially and discursively constructed through food, but this may be far removed from the embodied feeling food provokes. As an anthropologist, I focus on the ethnographic detail and look to tease out ways in which we can explore these theoretical questions of new materialisms as they play out in real life, in order to better understand their limitations and potential in explaining social and political dynamics.

As has undoubtedly become clear, I have a rather magpie approach to theoretical perspectives, schools of thought and disciplinary frameworks. And I chart a rather tricky course throughout this book between myriad perspectives, many of which do not obviously align or neatly dovetail. It is not my intention to make that which jars, accord. Instead, I adopt the approach, as I have done previously with Anna Lavis (Abbots and Lavis 2013; Abbots, Lavis and Attala 2015), that productive conversations take place at the very edges of disciplines and theoretical schools, and that it is in exploring these jagged intersections that we can prise open new possibilities and ways of thinking. There is a risk here, of course, that I satisfy no one: the political economists may not see my arguments as sufficiently politically economic, and my thinking may not go far enough for the new materialists. But I am not looking to reconcile the irreconcilable or work from the safe confines of a coherent framework. On the contrary, every perspective has something to offer; therefore none can be unreservedly satisfactory. Acknowledging the multifaceted character of food – recognizing that it is political, symbolic and material – requires a fluid approach that involves stitching elements of seemingly estranged perspectives together to better account for food's myriad dimensions.

Methodological approach

Throughout the book I draw on both my primary ethnographic data, collected during long-term fieldwork in the Ecuadorian Andes, and the secondary literature. As such, I pair syntheses of existing scholarship with insights gleaned from my own original data. The secondary literature frames key debates and research directions that my ethnography then illustrates and elucidates. I also use my primary data to critically reflect upon existing scholarship and extend conceptual arguments, and I pay particular attention to the ways in which the more abstract theoretical points play out – or not – in the everyday lived experience of my research participants. My ethnography, therefore, is a mechanism through which analytical concepts – which at times are in danger of floating away from the messy reality of life – are grounded in the voices and embodied experiences of individuals eating and being-in-the-world.

I could, in moments throughout the book, be accused of playing 'fast and loose' with the secondary literature. This is intentional, and I handle existing scholarship in two ways. First, I take the more orthodox approach of summarizing and engaging with the arguments presented. Second, I read between the lines and look beyond the main argument to discern what is implied but not developed, and to explore how the data presented can be framed in a different manner. In short, I look to tease out the implications of existing research by revisiting the data presented. This data is, of course, already subjective and partial and I have no way, or interest, of ascertaining its veracity. All I can do is work with what it is in front of me, and this involves a process of reinterpretation and extrapolation, as I pay heed to footnotes and cursory observations and the detail of research participants' actions. In so doing, I may run counter to a writer's intended argument and overarching approach – the way they have viewed their data – and when this occurs, I endeavour to make clear the distinction between the argument which is presented and my reworking.

My primary ethnographic data was collected during a total period of twenty months of fieldwork in the Ecuadorian Andes and was obtained through the established anthropological approach of blending a range of methods, including participant observation, focus groups and group discussions, formal and informal interviews, online questionnaires and discussions, photo elicitation, casual chats, and serendipitous conversations. Additional data came from an array of material and discursive objects, such as newspaper clippings, blogs, cooking pots and pans and, most obviously, food. Following Jackson's (1989) influential work on phenomenological approaches and Jenkins's (1994) emphasis on practice and the discord between verbal accounts and physical performance, I paid attention to the embodied experience and physical practices of my participants in addition to their words. Consequently, I spent large proportions of my time corporeally engaged with food preparation, cooking and eating, with a number of my participants teaching me the correct method of preparing certain dishes and ways to enjoy eating them. My focus on these physical actions not only encouraged my appreciation of the skills involved, but also ensured I observed the embodied mechanisms through which cultural knowledge and meanings about food are produced and transmitted. My methodological approach thereby combines physical and oral performance and the interplay between these two modes of communication.

To supplement these observations and recordings, I draw occasionally on my own embodied experience, autoethnographic insights and fieldwork diaries. Autoethnography carries the dangers from, at best, deviating from participants' voices (Aull-Davies 2008) to, at worst, being akin to self-serving 'navel gazing'. But it can also arguably better reflect the blurred lines between insider and outsider, and researcher and researched (see Reed-Danahay 1997) – especially in contexts where long-term immersive fieldwork is being conducted. Considering one of my key lines of enquiry is embodied experience and the subjective, visceral encounter between bodies and foods, it would, perhaps, seem remiss if I did not occasionally draw upon my own body and eating experiences to better illuminate the processes to which I am referring, especially given recent work on eating that has used such approaches to excellent effect (cf Longhurst 2012; Murray 2009; Sexton 2016: see Chapter 7 for a fuller discussion). Being mindful of the criticisms this method can justly warrant, I am cautious, however, of overusing it and have adopted an approach whereby I use autoethnographic insights sparingly and ensure they are contextualized by being situated alongside my participants' voices.

Although it presents ethnography, in no way should this book be read as a monograph of the eating practices of people living in the region where I conducted my fieldwork – the greater Cuenca region in the Southern Ecuadorian Andes. And, although I write in the ethnographic present for consistency, the data contained in the following chapters was collected in the past and I have no intention of reifying that which I describe in aspic. Practices and processes change, and all I can provide is a partial snapshot of the time and place I recorded. Some of the ethnography I present here has been discussed on previous occasions, but I do onto myself as I do onto others and have taken this opportunity to revisit my data, explore avenues I previously glossed over and remodel my arguments through a different analytical frame. To put it crudely, my ethnography carries a 'for illustrative purposes only' warning. That being said, it may be helpful at this stage to provide a little ethnographic context about the people and region from which my data was collected.

The greater Cuenca region of Ecuador

Known colloquially as 'the Athens of Ecuador', the greater Cuenca region is renowned for its pre-Inca ruins, Spanish colonial architecture and a rich tradition in literature and the arts, with the city of Cuenca being designated a UNESCO world heritage site. The landscape outside the city's sprawling suburbs contains multitudinous rural and semi-rural villages, hamlets and communities, which have historically relied on small-scale agriculture. The village of Jima, where I conducted my rural fieldwork, is approximately an hour and half's bus journey, along the Pan-American Highway and poorly surfaced mountainous roads, from Cuenca city. Connections between the city and village are strong, however, and there is constant movement between the two, not uncommonly for food provisioning, among other activities. I also conducted urban research in the city and its immediate suburban environs.

While ostensibly an agricultural region, with additional income from tourism, the local economy has been transformed following national economic crises and the collapse of the rural economy in the late 1990s.[1] Extensive and sustained, often undocumented, migration to the United States, and to a lesser extent Europe, has resulted in significant political economic, social and cultural changes across the region, not least because of its gendered nature, with many men 'opting' to leave – especially in the earliest migratory phases. As a result, some of the rural communities, Jima included, effectively have become 'villages of women', which has far-reaching consequences on agricultural production, food practices, and consumption preferences (Abbots 2011, 2012a,b, 2014a,b), as well as in other areas of social organization and political dynamics. As Whitten writes, the region is 'the locus of massive, predominantly male migration to the United States and Spain and the inflow of remittances that serve to transform the livelihood of the poor' (2003: 10).

Compounding these changes in the countryside has been the not inconsequential flow of remittances, which have led to in the emergence of a newly wealthy migrant-peasant class who are orientated towards being 'modern' and socially mobile (Abbots 2011, 2012b, 2014a,b). Such orientations are made manifest in this group's shifting eating practices, although there are also, as I show in the following chapters (especially 2 and 3), concerted attempts to maintain the cultural integrity of some dishes. The majority of my Jimeño participants are drawn from this social group and are also, not surprisingly given outward male migration, women.[2] Although these individuals reside in the *campo* (countryside) and would be deemed lower class in the region's complex class structure,[3] any assumptions about them being members of 'the peasantry' would be misleading, as small-scale agriculture becomes increasingly marginalized and households shift towards being units of consumption instead of production (cf Jokisch 2007).

In addition to outward migration, the region has also witnessed increasing levels of inward migration, primarily from the United States, and my second tranche of participants are drawn from this community. 'Privileged migrants', as I classify them, are predominantly, although not exclusively, white and retired, and have relatively comfortable incomes in comparison to much of the local population. Most, as I discuss in the following chapters (especially 3, 5 and 6), come to Cuenca looking for a change in lifestyle and a 'simple life', with a number of them being encouraged by the positive press the region receives. Cuenca was named 'The World's Best Retirement Haven' by International Living magazine (International Living 2010), not least because of the lifestyle it affords. To maximize these benefits, privileged migrants tend to coalesce in the city and its suburbs, where there is an increasing array of cosmopolitan food spaces, including global fast food chains and local restaurants, focused towards middle-class sensibilities (Abbots 2014a). While small in number, this group of people, who are by no means coherent or homogenous, are significantly shaping the local foodscape and engage, as I demonstrate in the subsequent chapters, readily with discourses of good – and bad – food.

Overview of chapters

The first chapter lays out the theoretical foundations for what follows and explicates how I conceive the intersections between bodies, foods and knowledges. I ask what eating is and why and how it should be treated differently from other forms of embodied food practices, and introduce my model of the eating body, indicating how I address tensions that arise between 'the body' and 'embodiment'. I further introduce my approach to the (re)production of knowledges that shape, and are shaped by, eating. The multidirectional flows between these three elements – of eater, food and knowledge – are considered through two key concepts that are ethnographically elucidated through the book – *bounded vitalism* and *bio-authority*. The theoretical foundations for these concepts are presented in this first core chapter, as I look to tread a path through ANT-inspired work on materialities, the agency of the non-human and mediation, Foucauldian perspectives on knowledge and biopower, and Bourdieusian approaches to cultural intermediaries.

Chapter 2 focuses on family relations and the domestic household, and examines the ways in which bodies are socially and corporeally kinned through the sharing of the substances of food. Rereading classic ethnographic studies of kinship and commensality, I explore how intimacies and proximities are fostered through the symbolic meanings and materiality of food. As such, I expound how individuals are socially and corporeally made as kin. Much of the discussion centres on my experience of eating roast guinea pig (*cuy*) in the Ecuadorian Andes, and I tease out the ways in which this dish is understood to act upon and acquire the eater's body. Further attending to the ways in which matter and meaning intersect, I consider how agency is distributed across cuy's assemblage, as well as how it coalesces around the bio-authority of the cook. This bio-authority can be both upheld and contested through an eater's desire or rejection of food, and I destabilize notions of commensality as a mechanism for social cohesion by showing how eating in a domestic setting can be fraught. I close this chapter by reflecting on the gendered politics of these household dynamics.

In Chapter 3, I explore the multiple ways in which migrants construct their personhood, belonging and social relations by eating both the foods 'from home' and those they encounter in their new environment. Developing the themes of how the eating body is a critical mediating site through which notions of sameness and otherness are produced, agency expressed and bio-authority bestowed, I address how eating together and sharing substances across space can produce coterminous kinned bodies and redraw, uphold and blur gustatory boundaries. Place comes to the fore in this chapter as I discuss how eaters use food to root themselves to home, especially through their sensory experiences and visceral encounters. My purpose here is to draw attention to the embodied experience of eating in migratory environments: I demonstrate how a closer examination to this oft-overlooked material encounter can deepen insights into how migrants' affective relations are maintained, reinforced and ruptured to places and people who are physically distant, as well as being created and disturbed by those in proximity. I argue that social, cultural and corporeal boundaries are transgressed, constructed and reaffirmed through migration, which allows for new hybridized identities to be forged and new spaces of bodily belonging to be opened up. This process can give rise to tensions and conflict as much as it can produce social cohesion.

Chapters 2 and 3, then, attend to the ways in which eating materially and symbolically performs relations between bodies that are both embedded in place and distributed across space. They also demonstrate how eating can produce proximity and distance, and sameness and otherness, as it produces, destabilizes and erodes social and bodily boundaries. Chapter 4 continues and extends these arguments, and engages with the notions of real and imagined places integral to them, in the context of local food festivals and nationalized food. Bio-authorities come to the fore in this chapter, as I interrogate the local and national agents and institutions that select and iconize foods as being particular to a locale or traditional to culture. Contending that the discourses, objects and events of food heritage can be understood as bio-authorial encounters, I tease out how matter, bodies and knowledge are entwined in seemingly politically benign celebrations of eating 'our food' and argue that such celebrations provide a mechanism through which citizenship is inscribed into bodies – a process that can obfuscate the construction of otherness and alienate as much as it can include and cohere. This chapter further explores how such encounters discursively charge and bound the vitalism of food, and I emphasize the oft-neglected role of affect, the senses and the embodied experiences of food heritage encounters.

In Chapter 5 I extend my investigation into the ways relations of distance and proximity are enacted through the intersections of bodies, foods and discourse by focusing on globalized and seemingly place-less foods. In so doing, I return to the theme introduced in Chapter 3 of how eating brings bodies together and fosters intimacies across geographical distances, as well as continuing to address the processes that, conversely, produce social distance through corporeal proximity. As in the preceding chapters, I explore these questions through the conceptual lens of how matter and meaning are entangled, agency is distributed across food's assemblages, bio-authority coalesces around particular actors, and the vitalism of food's matter and its assemblage is bound. This chapter further attends to questions of food anxiety and the ways they are produced by obscured and unknown production networks, with the focus being (much like in Chapter 3) on the ways such worries are viscerally experienced. This leads me to consider the measures taken by eaters to reassert control over their bodies and the substances they ingest, particularly through those foods that are semiotically marked and politically framed as 'alternative', in this case fair trade and Slow Food. Such markers, I suggest, act as mediating symbols that bind a food's vitality and shape its assemblage, and thereby inform the ways it is experienced in the body.

Chapter 6 is the final ethnographic chapter, and it builds upon earlier discussions by accounting for the ways in which the self and 'other' are constituted through notions of abject and acceptable bodies. Drawing together organic and genetically modified foods (GMO) foods, food waste and obesity through the thread of 'responsibilized eating', I continue to elucidate the entanglements between matter and meaning and examine how the vitalism of food is bound by social, cultural and political dynamics. Doing so draws out those bio-authorities who identify and define abject and irresponsible eating, and hence I further my argument that eating creates distance and proximity between bodies. In addition I work to dissolve false discursive boundaries between reflexive eating loaded with agentic capacity for change and unreflexive 'problematic' eating. The themes of trust, risk and anxieties also continue to emerge in this chapter, as does the concept of care, which was touched upon in all previous chapters, especially 4 and 5. I conclude by calling for more attention to be paid to the bodily experiences of organic and GMO food, food waste and obesity, arguing that this can bring deeper, eater-orientated, insights to our understanding of political economic structures and relations.

The book concludes in Chapter 7 with my reflections upon emergent research directions, with a particular focus on the areas that are opened up through the concepts of bio-authority and bounded vitalism. I discuss the methodological challenges and opportunities afforded by a study of eating, as well as ANT-inspired work on the non-human, suggesting that autoethnography and radical interdisciplinary work between the human and natural sciences could be potential ways forward. I close with a renewed call for a focus on the body and for critical food studies scholars to treat food as food.

Chapter 1

Eating bodies and bodies of eating: Theoretical foundations

Introduction

This chapter outlines the key concepts and theoretical influences found in the following pages. I first examine what eating is and explore how it arguably differs from other embodied experiences with food, and how this implicates varying definitions of agency. I thus introduce the model of the eating body I adopt throughout the book and briefly explore the tensions that emerge from writing about 'the body' in a more abstract sense, while also attempting to account for people's subjective embodied experience. This leads me to consider questions of materiality, as I attend to how eating draws human bodies and the very stuff of food together in unpredictable and incidental ways that are viscerally felt. I am cautious, however, of losing sight of the political and economic relations that inform such entanglements between the bodies of humans and the stuff of food, and hence I introduce another dimension – that of food knowledges and meanings. The multidirectional flows between individual eating bodies, the matter of food, and knowledges are examined through two key concepts that are expounded and illustrated in the chapters that follow: *bounded vitalism* and *bio-authority*.

Bounded vitalism and bio-authority are the principle theoretical foundations running throughout this book. In developing and using these concepts, my aim is to tread a path between two seemingly incommensurable literatures that have been critical, albeit in differing ways, to illuminating the processes and practices of eating. These are Latourian actor network inspired work on materialities, the agency of the non-human, and mediation, and Foucauldian perspectives on knowledge and biopower. I move constantly, therefore, between the micro – what the stuff of food does in the human body – and the macro – how social and political dynamics potentially constrain what foods go into our bodies, the meanings we give to particular foods and the value we bestow on certain knowledges and their sources. In so doing, I draw attention to the ways that food is both matter *and* meaning, and indicate how these dual aspects are at the heart of food's affect. But first, what do I mean by eating?

What is eating and why does it matter?

Eating – due to its sensual, visceral nature – is a strategic place from which to begin to understand identity, difference and power.

(Hayes-Conroy and Hayes-Conroy 2008: 462)

While the relationship between food and bodies has been subject to myriad academic investigations, eating, with some notable exceptions (Lupton 1996; Mol 2008; Probyn 2000), has largely been an elusive object of enquiry. Scholarship often appears to address eating, but scratch beneath the surface and we find that discussions of food either stop at the plate and outside of the body – as in established paradigms that address food's political economy, social relations and/or symbolic meanings – or have focused on food inside the body from the perspective of medical anthropology and sociology. The momentary process of getting food inside from the outside has, then, been largely under-conceptualized (Abbots and Lavis 2013: 1–3). This is perhaps because eating is an object that keeps disappearing and is methodologically difficult to observe (Murcott 2013). Such methodological difficulties should not, however, prohibit a critical and conceptual examination of how eating draws in, upholds, negates, appropriates and transforms political dynamics. Eating is the act in which the affects and effects of food on the body are fully realized. It is through eating that the body engages with both the materiality and the meaning of food. 'Glossing over' eating risks overlooking such moments of engagement and the micro-practices of contestation and acceptance inherent within them.

Eating is not, of course, the only form of embodied encounter individuals have with food, although it is the focus of this book. Producing, selecting, preparing, cooking and serving food all indisputably involve the body. Inevitable questions thus emerge as to whether eating differs from these other embodied interactions, why it should be distinguished as a particular object of enquiry, and, perhaps more importantly, how it can illuminate the power dynamics of agency and food knowledges in ways that other practices cannot. Questions also arise regarding the definition of eating. This may seem somewhat self-evident; we all eat, after all, and intuitively know what eating is and when we are doing it. But where in the body does eating take place? And does this matter? Is eating a process of ingestion, that is, of taking food into the mouth, chewing it, tasting it and swallowing it? Or should it be defined as digestion and our focus orientated towards how food is broken down and absorbed into the body? Or perhaps the object of our attention should be metabolic processes and the transformation of food into life sustaining energy? To add to this complexity, eating can also extend beyond the confines of the body and does not necessarily have to involve placing food into the mouth at all. As Lavis (2016) elucidates in the context of anorexia patients' engagement with visual images of food, individuals can eat with their eyes and media representations can invoke embodied responses associated with eating, such as salivation. Similarly, Holtzman's (2016) discussion of how his Japanese informants can gain satisfaction from sweets by visually admiring their aesthetic qualities gives us call to reflect upon what it means to consume a food.

In short, eating can be all or any of these approaches. Throughout the following chapters I adopt this more open definition as I tease out the ways that eating, and the networks of relations it produces, can take multiple forms. Rather than assuming what eating is, then, I examine how it can be conceptualized and understood in myriad ways.

Definitions aside, it is evident that, at its most fundamental level, eating is unique to other forms of embodied interactions with food in that it draws food into the body and ensures its survival. While other food practices transform its material substance – and make and unmake material substances as food – no other practice ingests and digests food, thereby transforming its matter within the corporeal boundaries of the body (Fischler 1988; Mol 2008). As Korsmeyer notes:

> Eating is a liminal activity, occurring at the threshold between 'inside' and 'outside' the body…. As such it represents both opportunity and danger, and so it stands to reason that it would be freighted with significance that bears upon values and the relative worth of different ways of life. (2005: 5)

Eating thereby sculpts and produces bodies as food is fragmented, metabolized and biologically incorporated. Food's 'solidity is thus broken down and rendered into fragments that both pass through, and become, the eater's body' (Abbots and Lavis 2013: 1). Fischler refers to this process of sending 'food across the frontier between the world and the self' as 'incorporation' (1988: 279), whereas Mol in her essay *I eat an apple* refers to a process of 'transubstantiation' (2008: 30) that blurs the semipermeable boundaries of eater and eaten. Mol explains that, prior to eating, the human body and an apple are two discrete entities but upon ingesting, and in turn digesting, these two bodies become one. She ponders:

> For how to separate us out to begin with, the apple and me? One moment this may be possible: here is the apple, there am I. But a little later (bite, chew, swallow) I have become (made out of) apple; while the apple is (a part) of me. (ibid.: 30)

As such, eating not only makes human bodies in ways that other embodied food practices do not, but it also incorporates other bodies – that of food's matter – into the eater's body. Indeed, eating is 'a series of mutual transformations in which the border between inside and outside becomes blurry' (Bennett 2010: 49).

I wish to extend Mol's thesis by exploring how eating can incorporate knowledges about foods, and the political dynamics that produce them, into the eating body. By knowledges I am referring to understandings, conceptions and meanings of food. Just as Mol's apple is broken down, transformed, incorporated, rejected and reconstituted by eating, so too, I argue, are the knowledges and social relations in which a particular food is situated. As Jessica Hayes-Conroy argues, it is in visceral experiences of food that 'molecules and meaning, or matter and discourse, collide' (2014: 17). Eating, then, as I have argued with Anna Lavis, goes beyond 'a way of placing oneself in relation to others' (Goody 1982: 37) and actively, accidentally and haphazardly makes (and unmakes) those relations and others in the co-production of coterminous bodies (Abbots and Lavis 2013). As we stated; 'in the act of placing food in the mouth, landscapes, people, objects and imaginings not only juxtapose with and fold into one another, but are also reconstituted and reordered' (ibid.: 5). I am now taking this statement more broadly than our original intention to include foods' attendant knowledges. This is in order to stress that food does not travel alone but instead comes to us entangled within multiple relations, symbolic meanings and myriad understandings. These intangibles, I suggest and aim to demonstrate in the following chapters, *are made to matter*, in the sense that they are materially and viscerally experienced, by eating. The eating body can thus be conceived as a culmination of matter, knowledge and social relations. Eating makes the knowledge-power dynamics of food materially manifest, and as such opens up the possibility for such dynamics to be inscribed upon, and contested by, the eating body.

The human eating body

My starting point when conceptualizing the eating body is the premise that, instead of being a fixed biological entity, the human body is a social construct in a continual process of being made, both by the self and others (Csordas 1990, 1994; Lupton 1996; Turner 1996). This is not to deny that all humans have biological urges but instead work from the understanding that social relations and cultural values shape the way biological drivers are fulfilled. In other words, we all have the need to eat in order to survive, but how and what we choose to eat, the forms of bodies that are produced, valued and desired – as well as those deemed problematic and repugnant – the way we approach food, even the way we taste it, are socially and culturally contingent. Bodies are therefore multiple; not just in the sense that different body shapes and sizes are subject to varying cross-cultural valuations, but also because the same physical body can present itself and be read in myriad ways (Mol 2002). The relationship between the body, self and society is dynamic and in a constant state of flux. These dynamics can be considered through a range of lenses and in their now-classic essay Scheper-Hughes and Lock (1987) identify 'three bodies', which I explore below: the individual body, referring to the lived experience of the self; the social body, meaning the ways in which the human body can be a natural symbol that represents society, nature and culture; and the body politic, which relates to how bodies are regulated and controlled.

Self and society: Constructing the consuming body

Focusing on the individual body draws attention to how people conceive and construct the self, both as independent individuals and as social beings, while also recognizing the varying forms that selfhood and personhood can take (Morris 1994). Food practices, as Lupton (1996) explains, are central to this construction, particularly in a Western consumerist context in which self-discipline and control are valued and made manifest by slim bodies (see also Abbots and Attala 2014; Coveney 2006; Mennell 1996). The body, then, becomes a project that is seen to be constitutive of the self (Shilling 1993). This assertion, together with the premise that bodies are in a constant state of flux and uncertainty – what Turner calls 'the sensitive self' (1996: 21) – gives rise to an interest in how bodies consume. Or, in short, how commodities, including food, are used to construct bodies and bodily subjectivities. A model of the consuming body thus emerges that shows us how contemporary capitalist society dislocates and disembeds bodies from 'traditional' cultural institutions, such as religion, while concomitantly providing the means and objects to (re)construct and present the body (Falk 1994; Turner 1996). As Turner concludes, the 'social dislocation of the body means that the body has been more exposed to the playful manipulation of consumerist culture' (1996: 6). Human bodies are thus conceived, in this historical moment, as being more prone to social influence and intervention – by both the self and by others. The following chapters build on this conclusion by working to understand how this process is played out through eating and exploring the ways by which such interventions and influences are navigated by the eating body.

The ways in which bodies are made through the everyday interactions of self and society have been further illuminated by accounts that demonstrate how social values and relations are inscribed upon the body. Whether it is Mauss' (n.d. [1934]) 'techniques of the body', Bourdieu's (1990) *habitus*, or Butler's (1993) account of how gender is constituted through 'normative constraints', bodies are evidently socialized into particular ways of being. This not only indicates the interplays between the individual body and the body politic, a point I develop below in my discussion of biopower, but also highlights how the body can symbolically reflect society. This notion of body as a metaphor for society was advanced by Douglas (2002) who concluded that 'just as it is true that everything symbolizes the body, so it is equally true that the body symbolizes everything else' (2002: 122). In contemporary industrial society, particularly in biomedicine and nutritionism, this metaphor has found its form in the idea of the body-as-machine (Scheper-Hughes and Lock 1987), which suggests the body can be 'fixed' through biomedical practices and the regulation of inputs (food) and outputs (energy). Running in parallel, we also see the historical emergence of self-control and restraint being valued in reference to appetite and eating and the association between thinness and health (Abbots and Attala 2014; Lupton 1996; Mennell 1996).

The politicized body

Douglas (2002) further argues that the vigilant protection of bodily boundaries could be interpreted as symbolic measures to protect society. As social groups perceive external threats and risks, they survey and control the bodies of its members, particularly those of women through ritual practices centred around bodily fluids and the maintenance of purity (see McClintock 1995, for example). The boundaries between individual bodies and the body politic are thus blurred and what goes into (and out of) bodies becomes a cause for concern, as it reflects the state of the social body and the condition of the individual body. Consequently, the body politic looks to assert control over its population of individual bodies. But it is not only political agencies that police bodily boundaries, as I show particularly in Chapter 6's discussion of obesity, abject bodies and notions of responsible eating, individuals police themselves as much as they are policed (cf Guthman 2011; Murray 2009; Wright and Harwood 2009).

Further questions emerge as to where the boundaries of the body lay as they stretch and merge into others, as seen by Mol's discussion of eating an apple. Bodies are rendered semipermeable (Mol 2008) as objects, people and knowledge cross corporeal boundaries and become 'incorporated' (Fischler 1988) into an eaters' body. But just as the eating body draws others inwards, so too does it extend outwards. The boundaries of the body are therefore not as fixed as first appears, but are rather more mutable and bleed into the bodies of others. This questioning of taken-for-granted assumptions about corporeality has been led by Haraway who, albeit in a non-eating context, points to the 'leaky distinction' (1990: 193) between human and animal and between human-animal and machine. In so doing, she draws our attention to the political possibilities that this breakdown of dualisms and transgressions afford. The resulting shift away from the body as a discrete entity to one that touches upon and 'interfaces' with other humans and non-humans provides the foundation for the model of the eating body I invoke in the following chapters, as I am interested in how individuals and cultural authorities look to make and mould bodies, both their own and others, at the point of intersection between the corporeal body, the stuff of food and knowledge.

Towards an embodied food politics

The model of the eating body that I develop throughout the following chapters is thus: continuously being made and unmade; fragmentary and fluid with permeable boundaries; embedded within and co-productive of social networks that extend to other human and non-human bodies, including food's matter and knowledges; subject to regulation, both by the self and others; and a site of political action and power. This model, however, is only half the story as it only concerns 'the body' in its abstracted and socially constructed form. Human bodies are also feeling and sensing 'things' that phenomenologically engage with the material world. A paradox consequently emerges between treating the body in its abstract form and engaging with embodiment as the immediate lived experience of being-in-the-world (Csordas 1994: 10). As Turner surmises, there is a danger that, as the body becomes an analytical object, 'the lived body drops from view' (1996: 28); a perspective reiterated in Csordas' calling for an embodiment paradigm:

> Using the term 'body' without much sense of 'bodiliness' ... carries the dual dangers of dissipating the force of using the body as a methodological starting point, and of objectifying bodies as things devoid of intentionality

and intersubjectivity. It thus misses the opportunity to add sentience and sensibility to our notions of self and person, and to insert an added dimension of materiality to our notions of culture and history. (1994: 4)

In essence, this critique serves to remind us that any model of the eating body must also account for its facticity and the ways in which eating is an experience through which people materially and viscerally taste, smell, feel and sense food (see Abbots and Lavis 2013; Goodman 2016; Longhurst, Johnston and Ho 2009). As Carolan reminds us, even in scholarship that claims to be about bodies, we struggle to 'hear from actual bodies, in terms of how they think and feel' (2011: 9).

The (re)turn to the visceral and its interplays with political dynamics has been particularly illuminated by Hayes-Conroy and Hayes-Conroy (2008, 2010a,b, 2013), who have trail-blazed an approach that seeks to recognize the ways in which bodies are viscerally affected or effected by food while also attending to the social relations and categories, such as race and gender, that inform, and are reflected in, such sensory experiences. In so doing, they are attentive to how political economic dynamics influence embodied engagements with food and, in turn, how affective relations shape food politics (see Chapter 6 for a fuller discussion). As Jessica Hayes-Conroy states, 'We must struggle to understand how social disenfranchisement and physical tastes both reinforce and resist each other' (2014: 3). This argument resonates with that of Probyn, who writes that 'eating is a powerful mode of mediation' (2000: 12) that continually 'interweaves individual needs, desires and aspirations within global economies of identities' (ibid.: 13). In accord with Mol (2008), Probyn articulates ways in which eating can destabilize bodies and blur boundaries as each eating body becomes situated in and constituted through a network of relations with others. She thus presents a fluid feeling body, with eating conceptualized as a practice that 'places different orders of things and ways of being alongside each other, inside and outside inextricably linked' (ibid.: 32).

Probyn draws the material and visceral experience of eating into dialogue with broader political and social relations. In parallel, Carolan's (2011) account of 'Global Food' illuminates how the individual body is orientated – or in his words 'tuned' – towards a preference for certain foods and tastes, that is, those produced by agri-industry. Broader political economic dynamics are thereby played out in and through the eating body; this can enable 'Global Food' to be contested, as bodies are 'retuned' towards more sustainable, by Carolan's definition, alternatives (see Chapter 5). Although adopting different perspectives, Carolan, Probyn and the Hayes-Conroys all work, then, to understand how subjective embodied experiences and political dynamics are entangled. They thereby raise the possibility that the body and its visceral experience is potentially a site of resistance to, as well as being subjected by, political relations. It is this platform on which I build in the following pages, as I work to illuminate, through ethnographic interpretation, how matter and meaning interplay, and how the embodied experience of eating both mediates and is mediated by social and political dynamics.

The matter of food's agency

Attending to embodied encounters and the material substances of food has consequences to the way agency – meaning the capacity to affect change (Bennett 2010) – is conceived. Specifically, it takes us away from the notion that agency is located exclusively in humans, or even in a thing, towards a model in which it is situated in interactions between bodies, the material world and discourse. Agency thus becomes understood as *relational*, continually produced through dynamic interplays and interactions, and *distributed* across ever-shifting heterogeneous networks of people, matter and knowledge. This model is most clearly seen in work invoking ANT – as laid out by Latour (2005), Callon (2005), and Law and Hassard (2004) – which challenges binaries between nature and society and assumptions about the agentic capacity of non-humans. David Goodman (1999) expounds the value of such an approach in relation to agro-food studies. Critical of approaches that have objectified nature and, incidentally or intentionally, glossed over the materiality and agency of non-human actors, he argues that dichotomizing society and nature is 'disabling – analytically, politically, and ethically' (1999: 33), whereas accounting for the 'hybrid co-productions of natures-cultures' (ibid.: 28) better reflects agro-food's political reality. Goodman centres on 'episodic events', such as food scares, which he contends results in the revealing and renegotiation of the relations between actors within a food's network. It is this analytical value that an attention on 'events' brings that I adopt and extend here through the concept of '*encounters*', albeit with a focus on the everyday and mundane – which can be just as illuminating as the spectacular.

We further see how such an approach to agency plays out in relation to eating by returning to Mol's (2008) apple. She explains that while an individual can bring muscles under his or her autonomous will, he or she cannot do the same with the internal organs. The metabolic processes of eating – the ways in which the body responds to particular foods – lie outside an eater's control and remain unmastered. As such, agency lies with the matter of food and its ungovernable interactions with the substances of the body. It is distributed. Yet the eater is not rendered entirely without action as he or she selects and prefers certain foods over others and deliberately and incidentally, as suggested by DuPuis' (2000) account of organic milk and Not-in-my-Body politics (see Chapter 2), co-creates the networks in which he or she is entangled. The critical point here is that the individual eater is just one of innumerable material and immaterial, human and non-human actors.

Jessica Hayes-Conroy confirms this point, writing that 'a person's individual ability to effect change is necessarily mediated through a complex and not fully controllable material-discursive world' (2014: 27). What is of interest to me, and what I tease out over the course of the following chapters, is how both individual eaters and cultural authorities of food, such as the family, local food activists and the state, look, if not to control the uncontrollable, then at least to enact constraints across food's networks. In essence, I am interested in how interactions between bodies, foods and knowledge are shaped and mediated, and how their vitalism is bounded. In so doing, I pay heed to Michael Goodman's (2016) distinction between ontological agency and political agency and his concern that a focus on matter and the visceral can elide political economic structures. I build on this argument through the concept of bounded vitalism.

Bounded vitalism

In developing and presenting bounded vitalism, I draw upon Bennett's work on *Vibrant Matter* (2010). She challenges the framing of objects as passive and inanimate – or in her words 'dead' (ibid.: ix) – arguing instead that they are things with an agentic capacity to affect and produce effect in human and non-human bodies (2007, 2010). She demonstrates this in the context of food by exploring how fat acts to create different cognitive effects and shifts in mood. Bennett is keen to stress, however, that this process should not be seen as mechanical causality with predictable results, but as emergent causality, meaning that different fats have different effects in different bodies at different times (2010: 41–2). This points to the ways that food's vital matter is relationally situated within a broader assemblage that incorporates other objects, knowledges, and social interactions and meanings. For example, Bennett draws on Nietzsche's argument that the material vitalism of German beer comes alive in relation to certain newspapers, anti-Semitic politics and Wagnerian music. The matter of food, then, co-acts with human meaning, emotion and knowledge.

While running somewhat contra to Bennett's overarching conclusions, as I interpret them, her discussion also shows that the vitality of food's matter is, at least in part, imbued through human understanding and action. A critical reading of the examples she presents on food's matter suggests that vitality is not inherent, but is instead co-produced through the relations between eating bodies, discourse and things. I am not denying matter's agentic capacity, but rather arguing that it remains a potentiality, dormant, until invigorated through social and embodied human interaction. In short, food's matter is *made to matter* by human practice and relations (cf Evans and Miele 2012; Goodman 2016). In an archaeological context, Stockhammer (2016) refers to this process as 'effectancy', which he describes as the 'three-fold changeability' of objects: the shifting perception of objects; the change in the materiality and function of objects through their life courses; and the transformative influence of human engagement with objects. He thus draws attention to transactions and interplays between meaning, matter and embodied practices, and allows for both the efficacy of things and human action while also ensuring their distinctiveness.

In light of these conclusions, questions arise regarding what or who makes food's matter vital and how these processes unfold. For me, some of the answers to these questions, as I expound below, lie in the interrogation of the knowledges that are co-produced and mediated through the interactions between food's cultural authorities and the other bodies that are invigorated by eating. This further suggests that the vitalism of food's matter, its efficacy, is bound by the assemblage in which it is situated – assemblages here include not only other objects, but also knowledges of foods and bodies, and the political relations between individual eaters and food's authorities. Such boundedness further indicates that vitality does not have infinite possibilities, but is instead constrained by political and economic structures, as well as human imagination and (embodied) experience. The vitality of matter is, therefore, not everywhere the same but contingent on its relationalities: just as eating gives knowledges and meaning its materiality, so knowledge bestows vitalism to food's matter.

What I am keen to explore here is how political influence is enabled and enacted through the relationalities between human bodies, matter and knowledge. I am not trying to quantify nor qualify the extent of the influence of a specific cultural authority on food; to do so would be contrary to my argument that such relations are continually being reproduced, circulated and shifted through multidirectional flows between myriad actors. Nevertheless, I am aiming to elucidate how, in the assemblages of food, certain human actors can be seen to be 'vectors' (Delueze and Guittari 2004), in that they attempt to define the form an assemblage takes, however momentarily. In short, they look to shape what we know, what we do not know, and what is accepted as 'truth' about certain foods. Or, following Carolan (2011), they 'tune' bodies to specific tastes (see Chapter 5). Or, in the language of Bennett (2007, 2010), they create the vitality of the matter of food.

Moving beyond Bennett's arguments, I contend vitalism is not premised on food's inherent agency, just as much as 'truths' about food are not inherently true. Instead, I argue, foods' vitalism, understandings about such vitalism, and the sources of those knowledges are socially constructed. Furthermore, knowledges are not constituted through a top-down dissemination of meaning but are instead co-produced by the relationalities between eating bodies, matter and discourse. This co-production should not be taken as equating to social parity, however, as some actors are granted greater cultural authority to imbue food's matter with meaning than others.

Assembling knowledge: Bourdieu's intermediaries and Latour's mediators

The recognition that a food's knowledges and meanings – and, in turn, aspects of its vitalism – emerge from interactions across a wide network of human and non-human actors, and that agency is hence distributed, moves us away from the Bourdieusian model of tastemakers that has been prevalent in much discussion of cultural intermediaries, particularly within economic sociology (Smith Maguire 2014). In *Distinction* (1984), Bourdieu argues that tastes, though experienced as natural, are instead socially learnt and are a mechanism for the reproduction of class differences and social stratification, with notions of 'good taste' – which the lower classes look to emulate – coalescing around the groups of higher social standing. Cultural intermediaries, who Bourdieu identified with the occupations of the new petite bourgeoisie, work to manipulate tastes and, in so doing, establish the authority and legitimacy of their social position as information experts. This argument, not unexpectedly considering Bourdieu's broader project (see Smith-Macguire 2014), draws attention to the class dynamics of cultural intermediation. But it is also limited in the ways that political authority – the ability to shape tastes – is restricted to specific social actors (and professions). Bourdieu firmly locates cultural intermediaries in the 'cultural industries' and at the juncture between economy and society (Matthews and Smith-Macguire 2014; Nixon and Du Gay 2002). It is these individuals who facilitate the flow of information between producers of goods and knowledge and consumers. As such, cultural intermediation is 'the process of *moving* "cultural" information around' (Piper 2015: 248, my emphasis).

This framing of cultural intermediaries is, however, problematic when viewed alongside models of distributed agency and Actor Network Theory, as it cannot account for the ways that knowledge is co-produced through interactions between multiple human and non-human actors. Knowledge and information is not just moved around, but is instead dynamically created and transformed through everyday engagements. As McFall states, mediation is 'spread across a network, not situated in a middle of a line connecting production and consumption' (2014: 49). Latour spells out this position in his critical distinction between intermediaries and mediators; intermediaries 'transport meaning' (are movers) whereas mediators 'transform, translate, distort, and modify' (2005: 39) and are active producers. Mediators are multiple in number, are 'endless' (ibid.: 40) and fluidly interconnected. In short, mediators make other mediators do things (ibid.: 217). Hence the outcomes are unpredictable and innumerable, as mediation sets off a whole series of uncertain chain reactions: 'Every mediator along any chain of action is an individualized event because it is connected to many other individualized events' (ibid.: 216). Mediation, thus, is not located in a particular social group or profession but instead takes place across a whole 'crowd' (Callon 2005). Latour draws our attention to the transactions across this crowd, to the work of the net rather than the network (ibid.: 143).

Through this lens, eating can be seen as a form of mediation in that it is a transaction between multiple bodies – including human eating bodies, the matter(s) of food and its meanings(s) – and the more self-evident Bourdieusian cultural intermediaries that comprise a food's network. Knowledge, then, both mediates and is mediated by food's matter and the bodies that consume it. In other words, eating bodies, foods and knowledges all are enmeshed in a continuous process of making and remaking, forming and reforming.

A note on assemblages

I want to expound here what I mean by assemblage, which is a term I use throughout the book, and especially how I see assemblage relating to agency. As Anderson et al. (2012) detail, assemblage can refer to a fixed and unified form that enables a classification of related phenomena. But it can also be used to denote a more dynamic and fluid process of merging, coming together, making and maintaining connections. This second definition is more open and allows for a range of diverse actors: heterogeneity replaces homogeneity, and networks develop along accidental and ephemeral rhizomes rather than being a stable organism (cf Delueze and Guittari 2004). In forwarding this, more ANT affined, definition of assemblage, Anderson et al. highlight the notion of assemblage as *agencement*. Although the translation of agencement has been disputed, this form of assemblage thinking can account for distributed agency, as it allows an empirical focus on the ways in which human and non-human actors come and are held together in (temporary and unstable) compositions (see also Bennett 2005; Collier and Ong 2005). In essence, it concentrates on the transactions and interplays – the work of the net – as opposed to the form an assemblage (or network) takes. There is fluidity to this momentary fixing, however, and Anderson et al argue that 'assemblage thinking' enables us to consider how different things and practices become entangled in one assemblage, while also taking on other forms and moving beyond to interact with other assemblages (2012: 7). There is change and disruption as well as flows and interactions. Assemblage thinking therefore

> allows us to foreground on-going processes of composition across and through different human and non-human actants; rethink social formations as complex wholes composed through a diversity of parts that do not necessarily cohere into seamless organic wholes; and attend to the expressive power of entities. (ibid.: 6)

Thinking of assemblage 'as an ongoing process of agencement through which form emerges and may endure' (Anderson et al. 2012: 11), while in concert with my model of knowledge-making through everyday interactions between bodies and foods, does not fully account for the political dynamics and structures that inform and shape an assemblage and bind its possibilities. Nor does it allow for the ways in which assemblages are subjectively experienced through existing political relations. In essence, the models of distributed agency invoked are arguably *too* egalitarian and do not recognize that vitalism can be bounded and assemblages limited. I am not advocating here a reversion to a static model of a food's assemblage with fixed boundaries, but rather wish to raise the possibility that the form an assemblage takes is perhaps not, in lived reality, as incidental as it appears conceptually. This takes us back to Michael Goodman's (2016) distinction between political and ontological agency; we can theorize fluidity and a lack of structures, but when we look to lived experiences those structures can feel very real and rigid for some.

Every human and non-human actor in an assemblage may act as a mediator, in that their interactions produce knowledge. But, as Bourdieu (1984) shows us, it does not necessarily follow that all actors are created equal: existing social structures and learned experience put some in a position to influence the knowledge-making process more than others. This brings me back to the value of ethnography and one of the key aims of this book. The conceptual models discussed thus far are inspiring and illuminating insofar as they encourage us to think beyond ethno- and human-centric perspectives. For the value of such ontological insights to be fully realized, however, they have to be balanced with, viewed alongside, and juxtaposed against lived experience. Otherwise they risk remaining mere abstract models and intellectual exercises, divorced from political realities and the experience of economic and social conditions.

Bourdieusian and Latourian approaches to mediation appear, at one level, incommensurate, just as much as models of distributed agency that stress that all human and non-human actors have agentic capacity seem irreconcilable with perspectives that emphasize how humans imbue meaning into objects. But I wish to suggest – and aim to demonstrate throughout the following chapters – that the concept of bounded vitalism helps us tread a delicate path between these divergent perspectives by recognizing the power dynamics that bestow authority and add credence to some voices. These dynamics limit possibilities while opening up others: in essence, they shape a food's assemblage. This concept concomitantly allows for the agency of the human and non-human and acknowledges their potential to (re)shape an assemblage, as well as taking into account the political economic constraints that inform such (re)shaping. As such, I constantly move between the political reality of lived experience and its potentiality.

I can only offer a glimpse of a food's assemblage as it appears at a particular moment as it is, by its very nature, constantly shifting and taking new forms. To this end, as I discuss below, I focus on *encounters* between multiple bodies in order to emphasize the fleeting fluidity and often incidental forms in which eating bodies, foods and knowledges transact. But let me first surmise my model of mediation that underpins much of what follows. Mediation is the process of the co-production of knowledge, and the imbuing of such knowledge with value and meaning, which occurs through the haphazard interactions between human and non-human bodies that form a particular assemblage in a specific moment in place and time. Bodies are both mediators and mediated. Mediation can, as such, reaffirm not just the legitimacy and political authority of the knowledge (re)created and valued, but also that of its source. This process can set the boundaries of a food's assemblage, as well as opening up spaces for the contestation of authority and the emergence of new mediators that, in turn, reshape an assemblage's form.

Knowledge of bodies: Foucault's biopower

In order to further interrogate the interplays between matter and meaning and the binding of vitalism, I also look to Foucauldian models of biopower, particularly the concept of biopedagogies as elucidated by Wright and Harwood (2009). Foucault presents us with a model of power in which it is conceived as being continuously produced and everywhere engendered through a capillary network of relations. Power is productive and relational, instead of being held and asserted by some over others in a hierarchized form (Foucault 1977, 1980, 2002a). This opens up the possibility for spaces of resistance, change and contestation. Agency is decentred, which 'allows new possibilities for resistance and the dispersal of agency and change in organizations and society' (Caldwell 2007: 3). The acquisition, mobilization and valorization of knowledge plays a pivotal role here as people are categorized in ways that facilitate, primarily state, intervention into their private lives through a range of normalizing mechanisms (see Foucault 1978, 2001, 2002b,c). Foucault (1978, 2002a, 2003) conceived this shift from sovereign power – the power to take life – to biopower – the power to preserve life – as two poles that blur into each other. Disciplinary techniques centred on the individual body, as epitomized by Bentham's Panopticon (Foucault 1977), and regularizing targeted populations. The body is implicated in both poles, becoming a 'political space' (Wright 2009: 7) that is shaped by, and resists, particular life – or bio – lessons. Biopower, then, in the words of Rose,

> brings into view a whole range of more or less rationalized attempts by different *authorities* to intervene upon the vital characteristics of human existence – human beings, individually and collectively, as living creatures who are born, mature, inhabit a body that can be trained and augmented, and then sicken and die. (2007: 54, my emphasis)

Authorities and their political relations to both individual and collective bodies thereby come to the fore, together with the dynamics between these relations and the production and application of knowledge. This is further elucidated by Rabinow and Rose who expound three key aspects of biopower: 'One or more truth discourses ... and an array of authorities considered competent to tell the truth'; 'strategies for intervention upon collective existence in the name of life and health'; and 'modes of subjectification, through which individuals are brought to work on themselves, under certain forms of authority, in relation to truth discourses' (2006: 197).

I wish to suggest that the '*array* of authorities' is of particular import here, both in light of my discussion of multiple mediating bodies above but also, following Rose (2001, 2007), in recognition that the nature of biopower has changed since the eras Foucault was addressing. As Rose (2001) points out, the state is no longer the only agency with an interest in preserving life, as we witness its attempts to free itself of responsibility, an increasingly heterogeneous society, the intensification and consolidation of capitalist interests, and the subsequent shifting of responsibility for health and well-being onto individuals – a theme I discuss at length in Chapter 6 (see also Guthman 2008a, 2011).

Through this lens, an individual can be seen as an active partner who engages with multiple authorities to manage his or her own body. In the context of food this has been commonly explored in relation to obesity (Wright and Harwood 2009), and while I discuss this topic in Chapter 6, I also move beyond this by considering the ways in which an eating body relates to 'an array of authorities', including the family (Chapter 2), and the state and local food activists (Chapter 4). Rose (2001, 2007) redefines this dynamic between responsibilized individuals and authorities as 'pastoral power' – a relational power that involves 'bidirectional affective entanglements' (2007: 74) that 'take[s] place in a plural and contested field' (ibid.: 73). This resonates with my notion that mediation takes place within, and forms, foods' assemblages, as it allows for the agency of an individual eating body while also accounting for how specific actors acquire cultural authority by being 'considered competent to tell the truth' about food. As I show in the following chapters, forms of pastoral power constrain the assemblages of food and bind its potential vitalism, as they open up – and limit – the possibilities of what is known and believed about food.

(Bio)pedagogies

Another way of considering this process is through the associated concept of biopedagogies (Wright and Harwood 2009), which I prefer here over pastoral power as it better reflects the specific teaching and learning interventions, and the co-production and mediation of knowledge, which I elucidate over the following chapters. Biopedagogies are defined as 'disciplinary and regulatory strategies that enable the governing of bodies in the name of health and life' (Wright 2009: 8; see also Truninger and Teixera 2015), and the 'the art and practice' of teaching of 'life' (Harwood 2009: 21). Put simply, they are the lessons that individuals learn about how to treat and comport their body or, in this context of the current discussion, the lessons in what we should (and should not) be eating. Wright and Harwood further explain that analytically interrogating such lessons offers a way of empirically 'getting at' the relationships and processes of the oft-concealed knowledge-power-*bios* dynamic that becomes inscribed upon, and internalized within, the eating body. Biopedagogue thus brings the body into view in ways that the terminology of political or cultural authority or intermediary does not, as well as emphasizing the political dynamic inherent in the teaching of eating. There is intent and action invoked in the concept of biopedagogue that is just not present in the more passive Bourdieusian notion of cultural intermediary. The term further highlights that knowledge is made (and transformed) through interactions, not solely moved around, and infers that the attempted inscribing of food knowledges by some onto the bodies of others – and its contestation – is a practice of power.

The argument that knowledge is co-created through embodied relations aligns with recent scholarship on pedagogies, which, in treating pedagogy in its broadest 'public' sense (Giroux 2004), attends to the 'relational cultural practices through which knowledge is produced' (Wright 2009: 8; also Harwood 2009: 21). This work demonstrates how pedagogical practices are material, affective and embodied (see, for example, Hickey-Moody, Savage and Windle 2010). Developing this thread through the concept of food pedagogies, Flowers and Swan (2012, 2015a) have further pointed to the 'proliferation and intensification' (2015a: 2) of formal and informal, institutionalized and unplanned, food education sites, as well as the mechanisms that draw together myriad teachers and learners in both public and domestic settings. Arguing that pedagogy can be an effective concept that opens up the politics of production and mediation of knowledges about food, they call for attention to be paid to the everyday situated practices through which such teaching and learning occurs. This can shine a light on both the self-evident and obscured political dimensions of food politics. Pedagogy, thus, Flowers and Swan argue, is a term that sufficiently encompasses a range of food education sites, processes and practices, and types of human and non-human teachers, while concomitantly signalling the hierarchies and enactments of power (and resistance) that are made present by an intent to change eaters' behaviour.

Questions subsequently emerge, as Michael Goodman (2015) suggests, regarding which social actors have the cultural, political and economic resources to construct, circulate and counter food pedagogies – or even be situated in pedagogical relations in the first instance. Yet, while these (political economic) questions of Goodman's potentially illuminate the *who* of food pedagogies, they detract from the *how* and pay scant attention to the ways that pedagogical relationalities are produced, experienced and contested through the body. This limits the possibilities for non-human actors to play a pedagogical role, which Hickey-Moody, Savage and Windle (2010) remind us to be critical. Goodman attempts to open this framing up a little in writing that 'food pedagogies are about the *visceral* and *affective* … as well as the *political economic*' (2015: 236 original emphasis), but does not develop this or offer any clues as to how these often incommensurate aspects can be drawn together. In the following pages, I pick up where Goodman stops by forging an analytical frame through which the productive interplay between visceral/matter and political economic/meaning can be better understood through close ethnographic reading.

Mobilizing biopedagogy as a lens, then, provides a method through which certain human actors' influences on the processes of mediation can be discerned. Or more accurately, it offers a way into better understanding *how* their influence is constructed and enacted through their engagements with other mediators – including human bodies, the matter of food, and knowledge. My point here is that biopedagogues need to be understood not in isolation, but as relational and politically influential 'bodies' that make other mediators do things (cf Latour 2005) – a process that also makes and legitimizes their own political authority (Bourdieu 1984). A focus on biopedagogues thereby helps elucidate the three key questions running through this book: *how* a food's assemblage takes a particular form; *how* the vitalism of food and knowledge is made to matter and becomes bounded; and *who* is behind such processes.

Bio-authorial encounters

While adopting the arguments underpinning the concept of 'biopedagogue', I prefer to use the term *bio-authority* in the following pages. For me, this implies a stronger political dynamic than biopedagogue, in that it suggests a social bestowal of legitimacy. It also better encapsulates the influence of both Foucault and Bourdieu on my thinking. Moreover, some of the food encounters I discuss in the following chapters, while producing knowledge, are not explicitly designed to do so whereas others are. Bio-authority allows me to make the distinction between these contexts, and I use the term biopedagogue only when a food encounter is clearly orientated as a learning experience, as in the case of some food festivals (see Chapter 4).

I use the term 'encounter' purposefully here. The definitions of biopower and biopedagogy made by Rabinow and Rose and by Wright and Harwood both highlight the multiplicity of actors, with the former stressing 'an *array* of authorities' (Rabinow and Rose 2006: 197, my emphasis) and the latter attending to '*multiple* pedagogical sites' (Wright 2009, my emphasis).[1] Little attention is paid, however, to how these multiple authorities/sites come together (or not) and perhaps more importantly – following the thread of 'assemblage thinking' (Anderson et al. 2012) – to the *moments* in which they temporarily take form and are subjectively experienced. I therefore explore, while recognizing that the practices of knowledge production, discipline and regulation are constant and continuous, how certain *encounters* – moments in time and space – emerge. These encounters are pauses when bio-authorial relations become more evidently manifest to the eating bodies subjected to them, a food's assemblage takes a particular shape, and its vitalism is bound. Biopolitical processes, I argue, are brought to the fore – empirically, experientially and conceptually – in such moments. A food festival (Chapter 4), a family meal (Chapter 2), a migrant's visit to a 'home' grocery store (Chapter 3), even a doctor's appointment (Chapter 6), are just some examples of the encounters discussed.

Framing these eating events as 'encounters' does four things. First, it encapsulates how eating is contingent on multiple interactions between food's matter, human bodies and knowledges that are emanated and animated by bio-authorities in a particular place and time. It accentuates the fluidity, context specific and partial characteristics of the production and mediation of food knowledges and the facticity of their temporality. Second, it makes a distinction between eating as mindful political action, as for example in the context of alternative food networks, as explored in Chapter 5, and the more incidental and quotidian practices through which food's knowledges and authorities are made and mediated through the body . While acknowledging that the personal can be intensively political, I am cautious here, returning to Goodman's (2016) warning regarding the blurring of political and ontological agency, of overstating the change that individual eaters can effect through their eating preferences – or even assuming their desire to do so. The term encounters accounts for action and agency without assuming intent.

In a related third point, 'encounters' further emphasizes that the mediating moments and formation of food's assemblages are often incidental and haphazard, rather than planned and patterned. As Anna Lavis and I, drawing on Deleuze and Guittari (2004), have previously argued (Abbots and Lavis 2013), the connections between multiple actors made by eating are rhizomatic and constantly folding and unfolding along 'multiple entryways and exits and its own lines of flight' (Deleuze and Guittari 2004: 23). Similarly, Probyn notes that 'bodies are assemblages; bits of past and present practice, openings, attachments to parts of the social, closings and aversion to other parts' (2000: 17–18). Bodies are fluid entities that are dynamically made and unmade through eating, which simultaneously makes and unmakes social relations and interdependent bodies. Drawing on Probyn, Lavis and I used the term encounters to convey this sense of eating as 'constant movement' (Abbots and Lavis ibid.: 3) and as openings and closures, formations and ruptures. It is this understanding and use of the term that I build upon here. Finally, framing eating as a bio-authorial encounter between multiple bodies allows for both the relational co-production of knowledge and the ways in which some knowledges have more authority than others. It reflects the multidirectional flows between bodies, matter and meaning, and accounts for the spaces, in line with Foucauldian conceptualizations of productive power, that enable the contestation (and acceptance) of authority. 'Encounters' further allows for the ways that rhizomatic 'lines of flight' can open up spaces through which agency can escape and take form.

'Encounters' thereby draws attention to the moments of possibility in which eaters can 'talk back' (Barnes 2015) and the 'episodic events' through which roles and relationalities are renegotiated and revealed (Goodman 1999: 28). This, in turn, takes us away from a top-down, intermediary-led image of food-body knowledges and leads us towards a more co-constitutive model of knowledge production, while also keeping in view the ways that not all knowledges (and knowledge-makers) have political parity. In short, it ontologically allows for distributed agency, while also recognizing that some actors have more political agency than others.

Concluding remarks

In this chapter I have introduced the theoretical argument that eating can be understood as a bio-authorial encounter through which food knowledges are produced and mediated through interactions between food's matter and eating bodies; I have also contended that the vitalism of such matter is bounded and given meaning by social practice and political dynamics. These two concepts – bounded vitalism and bio-authority – are the conceptual lynchpins for what follows, as I explore how matter and meaning are entangled through an analysis of multiple ethnographic examples. The answer to what constitutes eating appears rather straightforward, but I have indicated that this is not the case: we can consider eating in myriad ways and as being located in different parts of the body. I have thereby steered away from predetermined limited definitions of what eating is, preferring instead to tease out how eating can be conceptualized through the ethnographies that follow. I have, however, presented a working model of the eating body – one that is in a continual process of being made, is fragmentary with permeable boundaries, and embedded in networks of relatedness with human and non-human bodies.

Perhaps most importantly, I also treat the body as a site of political dynamics – it is both subjected to the bio-authority of others and a locus for resistance and contestation. The eating body is intrinsically active. It is further critical to recognize that 'the body' is not just an abstracted social construction, but also a sensing, feeling entity. I have indicated my debt to work that has drawn attention to embodiment and visceral experience, and in the following chapters I work, in different ways, to consider the subjective corporeality of eating as I zoom in on the individual encounter between bodies and food and then open out the lens to account for wider social dynamics in which that encounter is situated. In constantly shifting my analytical gaze between the micro and the macro, I am better able to account for the dispersal of agency across a food's assemblage, as well as recognizing the way political agency can coalesce around certain actors – agency here being defined as the capacity to cause affect and effect.

I have briefly presented my path through ANT-inspired work on the agency of the non-human and mediators, Foucauldian perspectives on knowledge and biopower, and Bourdieusian accounts of cultural intermediaries. Consequently, mediation is considered as a productive transaction between bodies, matter and knowledges, which shapes and is shaped by a food's assemblage – assemblage meaning a fluid, dynamic and haphazard process of merging and making connections. A focus on eating, then, can tease out the productive multidirectional flows between individual eating bodies, the stuff of food, and knowledge. Matter and meaning, and the ways in which these are entwined, thus take centre stage.

Chapter 2

Eating at home: Kinned, shared and acquired bodies

Introduction

This chapter examines the ways in which bodies are socially and corporeally kinned through the sharing of the substances of food in the context of family relations. Drawing upon and rereading classic ethnographic studies of kinship and commensality, such as those by Carsten (1995, 2004) and Weismantel (1988, 1995), I interrogate how eating draws bodies together into networks of relatedness. These intimacies and proximities, I argue, are fostered through the symbolic meaning and materiality of the food being shared, which is further entangled with emotion and affect. Individuals are thus made – both socially and corporeally – as kin, even though they may not share the other substance more commonly associated with kinship, blood. Drawing upon my reading of these texts, I then turn to analyse my experience of eating roast guinea pig (cuy) in an Ecuadorian household located in the village of Jima. Cuy is a dish laden with social efficacy, and its role in making and deepening social relations has been widely acknowledged (Abbots 2011; Archetti 1997; Bourque 2001; Weismantel 1988). In this chapter, I move beyond this argument and attend to the material substance of cuy and how it is understood to act upon the body to make Jimeños. As such, I look to explore the ways in which matter and meaning interplay and highlight how a focus on eating can bring new understandings to this relationship. I hence consider how agency is distributed across an assemblage that includes the non-human mediators of cuy meat and the substances that the animal had ingested before slaughter, the means and objects of preparation and cooking, cultural knowledge and, of course, the bodies of the cook and the eater. Consequently, I suggest that the cook can be seen as a bio-authority who permeates the boundaries of the eating body.

The embodied experience of eating cuy is central to my discussion in this chapter and I draw attention, in part through autoethnography, to the feelings and visceral responses to which the meat can give rise. This leads me to consider how taste is socially and corporeally acquired and how foods are evaluated through embodied encounters, a discussion thread that, in turn, leads to my suggestion that we can conceptualize food acquiring our bodies just as much as our bodies acquire food. Agency here, while present in the substance of food, is also situated in the body of the eater, and I assess the ways in which an eater's desire, acceptance, or rejection of a food can be interpreted as an expression of their embodied agency. Eating can be as conflict-ridden and fuelled by tension as it can be cohesive and unifying, and the process of kinning may not be as smooth as suggested by classic texts on commensality, such as those by Carsten and Weismantel. Questions of bio-authority hence come to the fore once again, and I close the chapter by returning to the notion that cooking and eating are political practices through which, often gendered, authority can be enacted and contained.

Sharing substance and the social production of kinship

The argument that commensality produces and defines social relations and contributes to the creation of personhood has been long established (Holtzman 2009), and scholarship has drawn attention to the vital substance of food and the ways in which it establishes links between bodies, especially in the context of kinship relations and family life. Carsten's (1995, 2004) discussions of eating and relatedness among Malays is one such example. Preferring to use the term 'relatedness', to allow for the fluid and processual nature of relation-making and to move beyond anthropological notions of kinship, she draws attention to how food is a shared substance that establishes embodied, social and affective ties. Carsten explains that, for the Malays with whom she worked, food, particularly rice and milk, is mutable and understood as being transformed into blood once ingested and incorporated into the body. The boundaries between rice, milk and blood are hence blurred. These seemingly discrete categories of substance are located on a continuum in which each slides seamlessly into the other. As a consequence, those who continually eat together – or in Malay terms share food prepared on the same hearth – are regarded as having the same blood in common, as being related. Food, in this context, is therefore blood. As such, and resonating with Mol (2008), Carsten presents the boundaries of bodies as porous; they become united through the flow of shared substances of food and blood. As she notes, 'It seems hard to say where one person stops and another begins' (1995: 235).

Carsten's (1995, 2004) ethnography shows how, for Malays, one is not simply born with blood, but instead continually makes it by eating. It is these conceptualizations and the mutability of rice, milk and blood that enable fostered children to effectively become kin and be fully incorporated into the household, to the extent they are understood to physically resemble its other members. It is perhaps not surprising, then, that eating away from the house and hearth is strongly discouraged, as it disturbs the long process of becoming and 'implies a dispersal of intimate substance' (Carsten 1995: 234). It also implies a dispersal of emotion, as Carsten further points to how the sharing of food's substance is not only entangled with affective relations, but also gives those relations a vitality and efficacy. A child's love for a mother, for example, stems from being fed breast milk. The bonds between children and mothers are seen to be particularly robust because it is the mothers who perform food labour within Malay households and are 'the source of shared substance' (ibid.: 228). As food becomes gradually and continually transformed into blood within the body of an individual, emotional closeness is concomitantly forged.

Carsten's studies illuminate how eating makes persons, both biologically and socially, and situates them within a network of relatedness and kinship ties. In short, eating constitutes kinship, with food being one of the primary unifying substances. This argument is echoed in other ethnographic contexts, such as Weismantel's (1988, 1995) account of eating and feeding in Zumbagua, Ecuador. Focusing on the process of adoption, Weismantel explains how people become parents by eating with and feeding their adoptive children, instead of through a jural process. She (1995) elucidates this through the example of Iza, who wished to become a father to a young boy. Iza expressed his intention of fatherhood by feeding the boy soup from the same bowl from which he had eaten. This act, while seemingly symbolic and ritualized, is also, Weismantel argues, inherently material as, similar to Carsten's Malay participants, the sharing of substance creates a material connection between human bodies. She explains that adults 'by taking a child into their family and nurturing its physical needs through the same substance as those eaten by the rest of the social group can make of that child a son or a daughter who is physically as well as jurally their own' (1995: 695) and concludes that 'those who eat together in the same household share the same flesh in a quite literal sense: they are made of the same stuff' (1995: 695).

Weismantel, like Carsten, further emphasizes that this is a gradual process, with bodies being made as kin through continuous layers of feeding and eating. They acquire substance through time: one shared meal does not make a kinship relation but, instead, kinned bodies are produced by an accumulation of many shared meals (see also Holtzman 2009). Weismantel is keen to stress, however, that, while this process is material and corporeal, it is not exclusively so – it is also social and symbolic. Kinship is not solely produced by eating. Rather, eating forms part of a wider series of social activities, such as sleeping in close proximity, providing clothing, linguistically articulating the relationship and generally sharing experiences. In drawing attention to these interplays, Weismantel implies an entwining between matter and meaning and the ways, albeit not in her terms, that food and eating are situated within a wider assemblage of practices, knowledges, affects and relations. It is this wider assemblage and the dynamic between matter and meaning that I now look to interrogate by turning to my own research in the Ecuadorian Andes on the eating of cuy.

Matter made to matter: Embodied interactions with cuy in the Ecuadorian household

Cuy is a particular dish in the villages and towns of Southern Ecuadorian High-lands, as in other parts of the Andes (Archetti 1997; Bourque 2001; DeFrance 2006; Weismantel 1988). Eaten only on festive and ritual occasions, its preparation is carefully orchestrated and its shared consumption within a household context limited to those who have, or wish to have, intense social connections. As such, it helps define and intensify a social network, as well as incorporating new members. As Weismantel concludes, 'To kill a cuy for someone … is an open declaration that you would like to deepen and formalize the relationship between your household and theirs' (1988: 131). The symbolic efficacy of cuy and its specific role in Andean social and ritual life, together with its class connotations and characteristics of being a 'traditional' food, has been discussed at length elsewhere (Abbots 2011; Archetti 1997; Bourque 2001; Weismantel 1988), and I wish to move beyond these accounts here by interrogating embodied and affective interactions with the substance of cuy, the interplays between matter and meaning, and the ways that agency is distributed across cuy's assemblage. In so doing, I bring eating into the analytical foreground.

The majority of cuy eaten within the Jimeño households with whom I conducted research had been raised within that household, with additional animals being acquired, in moments of shortage, from others within a household's primary social network. The circulation of cuyes thus forms a sphere of restricted exchange (cf Bohannan and Bohannan 1968) that reflects and helps maintain a defined set of social relations between households (see Abbots 2011). To my knowledge, any additionally acquired animals were always obtained live and were slaughtered, butchered and prepared at home alongside those from the household; I give a possible explanation for this below. My research participants, who were primarily women, all consistently drew my attention to the importance of using local animals from known and socially connected households, and often framed this through the rubric of taste. I was told that it was crucial that the cuyes were fed on local grass as they would 'taste better' than those obtained from 'other' places, and my participants indicated that they could taste the localness of the meat upon eating it. This extends to a household's own cuyes, which are preferably fed on grass cut down from a household's own land, although when supply is limited grasses are purchased from members of a household's social network or cut from common land. The cutting of grasses, often by scythe, is laborious work, but it is deemed a worthwhile task due to the resulting enhancement of the flavour of the meat. The only acceptable exception to the grass is the leaves of locally grown corn, although this is not a common foodstuff and the cuy only receive the surplus leaves when the household is preparing corn-based snacks such as *humitas*.

In stressing the importance of the feed of cuyes and expressing how this is materially manifested in the eating of the final cooked dish, my participants point to the vitality, not just of the flesh of the cuy, but also of the substance that helped constitute it – local grass. In this context, what the cuy eats is a key component of its assemblage; that which gets incorporated into the cuy's body ultimately gets incorporated into the human eater's body. A thread of relatedness hence emerges between the human eating body, the animal's eating body and the matter of grass, with the boundaries between these, being stretched and rendered semipermeable as each arguably gets incorporated into, and transformed by, the other (cf Mol 2008). The grass is transformed into animal flesh, which is turned into raw meat upon slaughter and, in turn, cooked into an edible substance that is consequently ingested, digested and incorporated into the bodies of my research participants. The micro-matter of the meat, then, has to be considered a vital agentic substance that lodges itself into the eating bodies of both cuyes and humans. Taste here plays a critical role, as it is through the final tasting, feeling and sensing of the meat in the mouth of the human eater that the vitalism of the grass is experienced.

But it is not just the grass, the cuy's body and the human eating body that are entangled and blended together through eating. So too are the bodies of those who have prepared the meat. Preparing cuy is an intricate, time-consuming, labour-intensive and embodied process, which is generally led by the senior woman of the household. First, the cuyes are killed in the intimate spaces behind a house or in the kitchen area. The common and preferred method is to take the creature's neck in one hand and smother its nose and mouth with the other, while pushing downwards in a twisting motion until the neck bones crack. It is then immediately pulled downwards by its hind legs to disjoint the spine and one eye is popped in order for the meat 'to bleed'. The carcass is then immersed briefly in hot water and dissolved ash before the fur is plucked off in handfuls. This process of immersing and plucking is repeated several times and the carcasses are inspected thoroughly to ensure no fur remains. Following the washing of the carcasses, the cuyes are manually disembowelled by a delicate and meticulous operation. First, the innards are located and a tiny vertical incision made along the length of the body with a sharp knife. The stomach cavity is then gently torn open with hands and the carcass is held horizontally in the air, shaking it gently until the innards become visible. The intestinal tracts and stomach are then painstakingly removed by pulling each thread away from the membrane to which it is attached; the stomach and other lower organs are removed by a sharp twisting pull. It is at this stage that the acrid smell of blood and intestines becomes almost overpowering, and yet it is also at this time that the cook will be intimately engaged with the cuy's body, taking great care to ensure that the bladder is not ruptured, for fear that urine will seep into the meat. This is a critical part of the process and caution is required, as the smallest of errors will make the final cooked meat 'taste bitter'.

Following the removal of the intestinal organs and the bladder, the cuy's body is turned inside out and the sexual organs gently pulled out and the anus pushed through with a forefinger and cut off. The carcass is then turned back and the heart and lungs removed by punching firmly though the ribcage, grabbing the organs in the hand and giving them a strong tug. Finally, the teeth and any remaining claws are pulled out by hand and the jaw is cut open almost to the point where the head joins the neck. The body is then washed thoroughly both inside and out, with the cook massaging the cuy's skin until she is satisfied that all blood has been removed, before a marinade is rubbed over the inside and outside of the carcass. The meat is then left to rest before being inserted onto its own long pole and roasted slowly over a bonfire with the meat of other cuyes. It is at this roasting stage that other members of the household become involved, as they each take an individual cuy and pole and sit around the bonfire slowly turning the meat until it is cooked and the skin burnished and crispy. This practice is deemed an essential component to the resulting flavour and overall eating experience, as well as being enjoyed for the inherent sociality that takes place. The flames do not just produce crackling skin, but also imbue the meat with the flavour of smoke, which is another material substance, like grass and blood, that eaters use as a marker of 'good cuy'.

The purpose of this rich description is to illustrate the extent to which the cook's body becomes physically entangled in that of the cuyes she is slaughtering and preparing, and I wish to suggest that through this visceral process of merging bodies, the essence of the cook is imbued into the substance of the meat. This accords with the arguments posited by Holtzman in reference to Samburu social relations, which he states are constituted 'through the stomach' (2009: 72). Stressing the materiality of shared substance, he explains that food is understood to create a 'supernatural tie' between individuals due to the manner in which it serves an 'exchange of *vital* substances' (ibid.: 73, my emphasis). In particular, the eater is understood to be consuming the bodily fluids of the producer, and Holtzman suggests that it is this which gives, at least in part, food its efficacy. He concludes, 'In eating someone's food, you have partaken of and benefited from their sweat (*latakuny*), creating a tangible bond that is strengthened through repetition' (ibid.: 73). Returning to Jima, waged domestic servants did not cook or eat cuy with their employers' families and, when viewed through the lens of Holtzman's argument, the reason for this prohibition comes into view: their bodily engagement with the meat would draw them too closely into the household and create intimacy in a context where distance is required and is often difficult to be established (see Abbots 2012b). Likewise, the cultural implausibility of purchasing ready-butchered cuy can be, at least in part, explained from this perspective.

Recognizing the ways in which the cook's body is infused with that of the cuy, and in turn the eater of the cuy, extends Carsten's (1995, 2004) Malay conclusions about how shared substance creates connectedness. It is not just the hearth – the place of cooking – that is of symbolic and material import in Ecuador, but also the body of the cook that produces the food to be shared. Moreover, sharing takes a different form here. Carsten's argument, similar to other established discussions of commensality and connectedness, suggests that it is the sharing of substance through eating, the mutual ingestion of the same matter that is broken up and incorporated into individual bodies, that produces relatedness. But I wish to argue that my Ecuadorian ethnography shows this is not as mutual a process as initially appears. Instead, by extending the logic of how the cook becomes fused into the matter ingested, the notion that the eater is ingesting the cook can also be entertained. This suggestion builds on the framing of socialized eating laid out by myself and Anna Lavis in *Why We Eat, How We Eat* (2013). We posited that eating bodies are entangled across multiple scales as they 'become coterminous with other bodies over geographic, affective and social distances' (Abbots and Lavis 2013: 3). In the same volume, Coles (2013a) takes up this argument in his account of how the production and ingestion of coffee in London's Borough Market is mediated by multiple bodies – including those of producers, roasters, tasters and retailers – who all 'imprint' themselves into the final drink (see Chapter 5). Concluding that 'coffee is mediated by a constellation of bodies, to drink coffee is to drink a lot of bodies' (ibid.: 268), Coles elucidates how multiple bodies bump up against and fold into each other through their leaky, semipermeable boundaries (cf Haraway 1990; Mol 2008).

Building from this literature brings to light a different power dynamic, in which the cook traverses the semipermeable boundaries of the eater's body to effectively be *inside*, rather than just being externally connected to it. This efficacy of operating within the subjective depths of an eater's body indicates a dynamic of bio-authority. The cook is an influential and intentional mediator in the assemblage of cuy; she not only makes the eating of the meat possible, but also brings together the meat and the eater in a manner that shapes the flavour of the substance being eaten and, through the rituals of butchery and cookery, informs its cultural and social significance. She also draws into the assemblage other mediating bodies, such as the local grass on which the cuyes are fed, the bonfire which the cuy is roasted over, the poles on which they are cooked that shape the embodied experience of those participating, and the marinade that imparts a unique flavour. Following Latour (2005), then, the cook is a mediator in the sense that she makes other mediators do things. In essence she gives the matter of the meat vitality: she makes it matter by working to engineer affect in the eater. And in so doing, she plays a key role in bounding the vitalism of cuy's assemblage. She is not, of course, the only mediator in this process, as all the mediating bodies discussed thus far encounter one another and interact to create affect and effects in the eater's body. All therefore can be seen to have an agentic capacity (cf Bennett 2010). In this context, however, the agency of the cook differs somewhat in that it is arguably intentional as well as affective. As I wrote in the previous chapter, not all mediators are created equal, and this has, in turn, as I discuss further below, consequences on the way we understand the bio-authorial influence of the cook.

The vitality of the meat then comes not just from its inherent substance but in the method this substance is *made* to matter through cultural practices and social relations, particularly those orchestrated by the cook. It is in the feeding of local grass to the cuyes – the restricted methods of exchange and distribution, and the slow, skilled and engaged method of slaughter and butchery that (in)fuses the cuy's body with that of its cook – that the matter of the meat becomes symbolically charged and affect created.

The taste a/effect

'But it would taste horrible, bad. Urgh! The skin would be all flabby and soft. That's not cuy'.

This quotation was exclaimed by Zoila during a group discussion, who was aghast at the revelation that her friend Sonia had once tried to cook cuy in the microwave. The experiment had not been a success and Sonia avowed never to attempt it again on the basis that the resulting dish was unpalatable and, echoing Zoila, produced something that 'was not cuy'. These comments interest me because they point to how altering the substance of the meat through different cooking methods changes not just its meaning, but also its material essence. The two women imply that cuy is simply not cuy if cooked by any other means than that detailed above. Their observations also draw attention to the importance of taste and 'mouthfeel'. Cuy can be slaughtered, butchered and prepared, it seems, following the usual rituals and practices, but if the final cooking stage is not completed correctly and the skin is flabby instead of crispy, and the meat tough instead of tender and juicy, it is just not cuy. Similarly, if the meat is not butchered correctly and if blood seeps into the meat, taste is understood to be adversely affected. It is in the final eating, then, that the assemblage of cuy is culminated and the multiple mediators drawn together to produce a very specific eating experience.

This experience is, of course, embodied, with the substance of cuy being assessed and evaluated through the process of taking the meat into the mouth and chewing it, biting into the skin and sucking the fat from the flesh and bones. As the cuy is ingested, the extent to which it can be deemed cuy becomes evident: it is in its disassembling by eating that the assemblage of cuy becomes evident. The eating body thus mediates and places value on the experience, determining through taste and mouthfeel whether it is good or bad cuy, or even whether the meat *is* cuy. I was taught this process of evaluation through my initial and subsequent eating encounters with cuy.

My first taste of cuy was somewhat unpleasant. Contrary to the common misconception, the meat did not taste like chicken but was instead rather rich, gamey and fatty, with a slightly acrid aftertaste. It was unlike anything I had eaten before, despite having (what I like to think of as) an adventurous palate. Being the polite anthropologist, I tried to disguise my distaste by nodding enthusiastically and affirmatively to my participants' gentle probing assertions that I was eating 'good cuy' that was '*riquisimo* [very tasty and delicious]' and expressing delight every time they placed another piece on my plate. Yet my participants were clearly not deceived with Felicia reassuring me:

> Don't worry if you don't like it. It has a strange taste, but keep eating it. You will learn to like it; the more you eat it, the more you will like it. You *have to* like it; you will be more like us then. (Abbots 2011: 214, my emphasis)

Familiarity, then, would breed not contempt but pleasure. My participants commonly reiterated this point upon every subsequent cuy meal by enquiring whether I liked the meat more now that I was becoming accustomed to its taste and texture. Following notions of shared substance, belonging and the sociality of cuy, clearly the only correct answer to this question was a firm yes: not partaking in eating the meat would have distanced me from the intimacies of the social group. But this affirmation was not without verity, as I was learning to acquire a taste for cuy. My personal notes in my field diary chart this trajectory from pain to pleasure. I noted that it was easier to digest the meat and that eating it was making me less queasy than on previous occasions, and commented that I was looking forward to a cuy meal and had even enjoyed meat that was 'well cooked, fresh-tasting and *rica*'. Indeed, my enjoyment in cuy reached a point that I started to crave and dream about eating the meat – pangs that continued long after I left the field. In Jima, my palate also became more discerning as my participants guided me towards identifying good cuy from bad. This came to the fore particularly during a community event where cuy was distributed among all those gathered to celebrate two villages being united by a new road. While unusual to see cuy served so publicly, it made cultural sense in this context as it symbolically connected the two communities through shared substance. Yet, according to my participants, and my own palate, the cuy was 'not good', primarily because it tasted too acrid, too bitter and too gamey. Paraphrasing Sonia, the taste of the grass was absent and the meat didn't taste sufficiently fresh or clean – the cuy was just too strong and flavourful.

Assessing the extent to which there are significant objective differences in the taste of Sonia's home-cooked cuy and that of the 'road-opening cuy' is not my concern here. What I wish to draw attention to instead is that both myself and my participants subjectively noticed a distinction and made a value judgement through our own embodied eating experience. As such, our bodies mediated our encounter with the road-opening cuy and compared it to the memories of previous, more intimate, encounters, evaluating and determining what cuy should taste like, or more accurately what cuy is, in the process. But our taste buds are not the only factor here. The affective background or 'condition' (Anderson 2011) – cuy being shared across a number of strangers, being publicly cooked, and the overall social environment of its eating – also mediated the way we judged the flavour of the meat. Arguably, it could objectively taste exactly the same as Sonia's home-cooked cuy, but it could never subjectively taste the same to us because of the context in which it was served. The substance of the meat, while potentially the same, was symbolically different. And this difference manifested in taste.

The affective background through which cuy is eaten and assessed extends beyond the immediate context in which it is prepared and served, as other mediators, for example knowledge of its social import, are drawn into its assemblage. This informs, and is co-produced by, the embodied experience of the eater. To elucidate, my visceral reactions to cuy, whether distaste or pleasure, stems in part – and only in part – from the material substance of the meat and my body's biological reaction to it. But that reaction, while not fully governable (Mol 2008), is also informed by the cultural knowledge that I was taught by my participants – that cuy is a socially and symbolically important dish and that sharing it with my social group would help incorporate and root me to place and kin. These lessons were taught through everyday conversation and the way the dish was presented to me, for example the valorization of grass as fodder, as well as the ritualized practices of slaughter, butchery and cookery that accompanied it. The cook, therefore, materially shaped the taste of the meat by her preparation methods, but these preparation methods, coupled with the attendant oral discourses, also socially shaped the material taste of the meat. As such, they informed not only how the meat tasted, but also the eater's expectations – the affective background – of how they expected it to taste. In short, the eating body was socially primed to corporeally experience the meat in a particular way (see Chapter 4).

These observations and suggestions further draw attention to the ways in which the embodied experience of tasting food is both individually subjective and culturally informed, a point that has also been made by Probyn (2000) and Hayes-Conroy (2014), among others (see Chapters 3 and 5). What I wish to initially stress here is that it is not just the individual eating body that mediates the encounter between food and eater, but also the cook, as argued above, and society and its discourses more widely. This builds from Carolan's (2011) argument that tastes for particular 'global foods' are 'tuned' by the food industry (see Chapter 5), in the sense that literal and metaphorical tastes are shaped by influential bio-authorities. Carolan's focus is on the public sphere of the food industry and the ways in which consumers' palates and bellies are tuned towards processed food, but the ethnography from Jima suggests that this process of tuning can also be applied to the domestic realm and home cooks.

To surmise, the ethnography from Jima shows that the food practices and knowledge surrounding cuy imbued its substance with vitality. This is not to state, contra Bennett (2007, 2010), that the substance of the meat is inherently vital but rather to argue, following Jessica Hayes-Conroy (2014), that matter and meaning collide. Thus far I have looked to elucidate this argument by further interrogating the practices, people and processes of how matter is made to matter and drawn attention to the bio-authorial role of the cook in bounding the vitality of cuy within a certain assemblage. I unpack what this dynamic means in terms of (often gendered) power relations within the family below, but first I turn to the ways in which eating bodies potentially uphold and contest such bio-authorial lessons of the home and family through the lens of desire.

The agency of the eater?: Desire, acceptance and refusal

Felicia's comment to me above, that I would 'have to like' cuy to be 'more like' my participants, not only reiterates the importance of sharing substance in the making of relatedness, but also indicates the role of enjoyment, pleasure and desire. For Felicia, it was not sufficient that I just ate cuy with my adopted kin group, I had to 'learn to like' the meat and express my pleasure and enjoyment at eating it. It is in this pleasure, her comment suggests, that my incorporation into the social group was performed: I had to *want* to eat cuy just as much as I could and did eat cuy. And it is not too much of a stretch to argue that expressing this desire for the meat is tantamount to expressing a desire to be part of the social group, insofar that a refusal of the meat is a rejection of social relatedness (cf Abbots 2011; Bourque 2001; Weismantel 1988). This points to the import of the emotional and affective sensations that an eating body experiences, which have received little overt attention in accounts of commensality and kinship but are evidently salient here. In a similar vein, Sonia professed pride in her son's greedy passion for cuy:

Look at him eat, how many pieces is that, three, four? Pablito always eats so much cuy. When he was a little, you know, very young, one or two years old, he would always want cuy. 'Mami' he would say, 'when can we have cuy?; are we having cuy today Mami?' he would say. He loves it! It is because he is a son of Jima; he is a good Jimeño; that is why he loves his cuy! (Abbots 2011: 214–15)

In stating that Pablito is a 'good Jimeño', Sonia is clearly extending the terms of her son's relatedness beyond her immediate kinship group to the broader community, a theme of social proximity I develop in Chapters 3 and 4. What interests me here, however, is not only the way that Pablito's belonging is inscribed and enacted by his eating and 'incorporation' (cf Fischler 1988) of cuy, but in the manner this belonging is expressed. Pablito is a 'good Jimeño' because he loves his cuy, not just because he eats it. Moreover, his desire appears to be naturally imbued, almost innate, as it has been in evidence since he was a small child. The implication being that his love of cuy stems from his community of birth and is as an inevitable part of Pablito's essential being, as well as a character trait that is to be noted and celebrated.

Desiring, seeking and taking pleasure from shared substance thus emerge as core principles in this context, and this further draws attention to the agency of the individual eater. Pablito's passion for cuy reflects and actively works to construct his being and belongingness, and his greed can be interpreted as an eater's desire to be socially made in a certain mould. His desire for cuy is a desire to be continually (re)made Jimeño much in the same way that my learning to like cuy expressed my desire to be incorporated into my kin group and be 'like us'. The slight distinction here is that, unlike Pablito, I was not born in Jima and my liking for cuy was therefore not constructed as innate, but instead had to be nurtured through repeated eating. This raises a subtle distinction in mine and Pablito's agentic capacities. Pablito's hunger is constructed as inherently vital, as naturalized, thereby implying that he has had little choice about his passionate greed, whereas mine is understood as having to be cultured.[1] Notwithstanding this difference, our desire, or more accurately our eating bodies' desire, for the meat can be regarded as an expression of our own agency.

Or can it? For when the vitality of food's matter is taken into account, a question emerges regarding the extent that requesting, enjoying, hungering for, or even craving a food can be seen as an expression of individual agency. As I have previously explained, it is not my intent to measure the agency of each mediating body or assess which actors have the most bio-authorial influence. Instead I draw attention to the who, how and why particular mediators have arguably more influence in particular assemblages and eating encounters, as well as raising the possibility that other, oft-overlooked, human and non-human mediating bodies have the agentic capacity to create affect in the eating body.

To explain this further I return to Felicia's statement that 'the more you eat it [cuy], the more you will like it'. Felicia seems to be suggesting here, in line with Bennett (2007, 2010), that the substance of cuy has an inherent vitalism that has the agency to create changes in the eating body. Resonating with

Carolan's (2011) notion of tuning tastes to create increasing wants through repeated eating, the implication is that the more substance of cuy I ingest, the more my body will want to ingest – and I will take pleasure in doing so. These continued engagements with foods over time further echo how personhood and relatedness are made through repetitive eating (cf Carsten 1995, 2004; Holtzman 2009; Weismantel 1988, 1995). As such, I am, or more specifically my body is, acquiring the taste for cuy through every eating encounter. Yet it is not just the cells of my body that are acting here upon the cuy, but also the cells of cuy acting upon my body. A vital encounter thus takes place between food and the eating body in which both are mediators combining to create an affect – my increasing desire for cuy. Cuy, then, is acquiring my body as much as my body is acquiring cuy.

Desire can therefore be understood as a product created by the encounter between body and food. Whereas Bennett (2010) stops at this point, I argue, and hopes to have demonstrated, that each eating encounter is, in itself, framed by the background of affect that is co-produced from bio-authorial practices and the interplays between multiple mediators that form a food's assemblage. Queries thus emerge as to who is performing the labour of encouraging desire in bodies for certain foods, even when those bodies are corporeally absent – or, in other words, who is performing the primary bio-authorial role? Carsten (1995, 2004) and Weismental (1988) stress the gendered dimensions of this process and my ethnography too shows women are central figures. I discuss the implications of this vis-à-vis gendered power dynamics below, but first I want to draw attention to the agentic capacity of the body being fed. Thus far, I have represented eating bodies as somewhat acquiescent of the bio-authorial lessons they are receiving through food, as they seem to be absorbing, upholding and even encouraging such knowledges and lessons by desiring the food towards which their bodies are being tuned (cf Carolan 2011). But eating bodies can also reject or refuse that which is being offered, and questions arise as to whether this refusal is tantamount to the rejection of the dominant cultural discourses and those who propound them.

DuPuis' (2000) account of the 'Not-in-my-Body' tactics used in relation to the organic milk industry provides a springboard for thinking through these questions, as she indicates ways in which the embodied politics of refusing to eat particular foods co-produce networks of relatedness in which eating bodies are embedded. DuPuis locates political action in consumption by showing how eaters evaluate claims by the food industry, scientists and government 'every time they reach for a milk carton or bottle at the store' (ibid.: 293), as they negotiate the potential risks to their body of ingesting the substance contained within. Drawing on ANT, she further demonstrates how such everyday actions co-produce the very networks in which consumers, milk and farmers, among others, are embedded. Political activity does not, therefore, have to take the form of social activism or even be politically conscious but can, instead, be identified in eaters' participation in 'reflexive consumption'. This account, then, provides a way of conceptualizing how refusing to eat a substance is not only a political act, but also a productive one that can create and shape new social networks and knowledges and make the bio-authorities contained within them. Thus the eating body acts as a mechanism through which power dynamics are contested and reformed.

In concert, Bell and Valentine (1997) highlight the aversion that some individuals have to being fed by others, and Giard (1998 in Probyn 2000) argues that children's refusal to eat is a 'trump card' through which they can 'resist' their mothers and hold them in their power. Similarly, Wilk (2010) demonstrates that family meals can be fraught with tensions and difficult memories, and Probyn (2000) calls for a deeper consideration of what lies beneath the veneer of commensal relations, writing that

> the claustrophobia of being cooked for and being fed is an important undertow
> beneath the bucolic images of eating together. As a flip-side to comfort food,
> the power-plays that structure familial eating and the ideology that the family-
> that-eats-together have been largely under-theorized. (ibid.: 38)

Moreover, as Holtzman (2013) explains in his commentary of how comfort foods can become 'dis-comfort foods', a meatloaf may invoke either a mother who lovingly prepared it or one who forced their family to eat it (see also Batsell et al. 2002). He concludes, 'Food can construct and conjure a fantastic range of intimacies, yet closeness is not always good' (ibid.: 145). In their different ways, all these authors thus indicate the power struggles that come with intimate food relations and the attendant attempts to mould bodies in certain ways: a political dynamic that is oft disguised through softer notions of 'care' and 'commensality' (see Abbots, Lavis and Attala 2015).

But an eating body does not have to refuse food so explicitly to reject the bio-authority of the cook or feeder. As I have argued thus far, eating takes place against a 'background of affect', which a bio-authority works to effect and arguably manipulate alongside other mediators. Yet the recognition that there are multiple mediating bodies in the assemblage of each eating encounter and these all dynamically interact to continuously co-produce affect also suggests that not all elements are within the control of the cook. In essence, there are too many bodies at play here – the embodied experience of eating cannot be fully controlled by one, however influential. Relating this back to cuy, we can recall that the cook as bio-authority may attempt to encourage my consumption of the meat and my desire to do so though both material and discursive measures. And the meat itself, as well as what the animal has eaten, may also act upon my body and tune its tastes. But, following Mol (2008), my body is itself an agent that cannot be fully governed and which brings its own memories, emotions, sensual feelings and workings to every eating encounter. Agency does not act as mechanical causality but is emergent, creating different effects and affects in different bodies at different times (cf Bennett 2010: 41–2). My body could have therefore just as readily rejected cuy as much as it accepted and desired it, albeit not so easily considering the measures taken to sway the outcome towards acceptance. It is this swaying of the outcome, I argue, that bounds the vitalism of food. Thus, while the cook may work to discipline my body towards cuy, the outcome – the extent of her authority – cannot be fully predicted. The odds, however, can be stacked through bio-authorial practices that imbue the matter of food with meaning and vice versa.

Gendered food labour and the bio-authority of the cook

Throughout my discussion thus far, I have situated the cook in a position of relative power within the domestic household, as she, notwithstanding the agency of the eater, materially and socially sculpts the bodies of her eating family and inscribes cultural knowledge into those bodies. My use of 'she' here is intentional, not least because my own ethnographic findings show that food labour is feminized, but also because this observation accords with those of other commentators in varied cultural settings (see, for example, Cairns and Johnston 2015; Counihan 1988; DeVault 1991; Murcott 1983; Weismantel 1988). I therefore close this chapter with a brief reflection on the political dynamics within the household through the lens of gender.

While cooking and preparing food in Jima is not the exclusive domain of women and my few male participants informed me they too could cook cuy, in practice, it is the women of the household who dominates both everyday and exceptional cooking activities. The kitchen is generally a female preserve, as is the case in other Andean households (cf Bourque 2001; Harris 2000; Weismantel 1988). Moreover, women are not regarded as 'proper women' unless they can cook to the acceptable standard of 'rico', (tasty, delicious) and men in the kitchen are seen as a humorous anomaly. These attitudes were evident during my fieldwork when I was constantly referred to as a novice housewife when I demonstrated my lack of ability to peel and chop an apple in the correct manner, made untidy misshaped *humitas* and could not crimp the edges of *empanadas* quickly. In contrast, my then-husband, who accompanied me for a time and quickly learnt the *truco* (knack) of cooking *empanadas* and *humitas*, was a constant source of amusement for local men and women who all tried to reason with him that the kitchen was not his proper place, and made jokes about his perceived lack of masculinity. As Carlo, another 'anomaly', surmised:

> Men don't cook in Ecuador. It is a woman's job. I cook, but I'm different. I like it, and all the great chefs are men. But cooking is a job for women; in most houses it is the women who cook. It is their job, since they were girls. They learn to cook because they have to feed their families.

My female participants held a similar view, and our conversations frequently referred to a woman's correct role, learnt from childhood, as the feeder of the family and the centrality of cooking prowess to their own sense of womanhood. Through this frame, food work was valued as being a crucial aspect of becoming and being Jimeña.

As Carlos's commentary indicates, this does not mean that boys and men are excluded from the kitchen, as they do occasionally participate in cooking 'traditional' foods, such as cuy, *humitas* and *empanadas* as part of a larger cooking collective.[2] On such occasions, which are treated as exceptional leisure activities in contrast to the 'work' of cooking for the family on a quotidian basis, male participation is not taken seriously. Many of my female participants told me that men did not have the skills or attention required to make, for instance, good *empanadas* or *humitas*, and my experience in a number of mixed-gender cooking collectives partially bore out this assertion. The men involved appeared not to want to learn the skills required and had a tendency to deviate from the prescribed, often time-consuming and careful, methods that my female participants laboured to teach me as part of my journey towards Jimeña womanhood. Such 'short-cuts' included using a fork rather than manually crimping and the edges of *empanadas*, making the pastries larger or misshapen, or experimenting with different fillings. These were firmly censured by the women around the table and the men were not infrequently reprimanded, albeit in a joking yet firm manner.

So what can this tell us about gendered bio-authority? And the extent that the kitchen is a site of (female) bio-authority? There has been much discussion regarding the extent that food work can be a source of female empowerment, and scholarship has highlighted myriad nuances between responsibility and control (cf McIntosh and Zey 1998), the division of labour (cf Ray 2004; Strathern 1988), gifting and reciprocal relations (cf Counihan 1988), the ways food preferences are taken into account (cf Murcott 1983), and how food served by women is valued and by whom (cf Weismantel 1988) – to name but a few factors that can enable and limit the agentic capacity of women. It is not my intention to discuss all of these variants here or to assess the value and limitations of each perspective and argument. Instead, I merely wish to signal the subtle ways that food *can* provide a mechanism through which agency can be enacted – and curtailed – by both the feeder and eater and the ways in which this interplays with gender dynamics.

It is clear that the provisioning and withholding of food is a considerable source of power, although it has to be remembered that if one is the primary preparer of food, it does not automatically follow that one has economic control over food provisioning. That being said, there are examples where women have contested inequitable gender relations through their food work: Weismantel (1988) observes how women can punish husbands who drink too much by feeding them large quantities of rich food, which entrenched values of reciprocity compel them to eat (often to a detrimental effect on their short-term bodily health), while Holtzman (2009) more radically writes of young Samburu women starving their older husbands. He explains that men's lack of knowledge and practical access to food makes them vulnerable to the culinary power of their wives, and writes that 'food is both beyond the view and purview of men' (ibid.: 87). He surmises:

> In contrast to women – whose status appears low but whose agency is high in regard to food – men are regarded as deserving a privileged position in regard to food distribution, but are highly limited in their means of exercising this privilege both for practical reasons and for reasons related to contradictions in the construction of Samburu masculinity. (ibid.: 88)

Holtzman thereby draws attention to the distinction between discursive values and lived reality, and highlights how such values paradoxically legitimize female agency.

Women, then, are sometimes able to exert considerable influence through their food work but, as Counihan (1988) notes, this only reaches as far as the boundaries of the household, an argument partially disputed by Harbottle (2000) who comments that, in being responsible for the caring of guests and for hospitality, women play a critical role in maintaining the reputation of their husbands and families. What the family eats, however, can by shaped by men, as women put their husbands preferences and needs above their own (Murcott 1983). In short:

> Men can exert power over women by refusing to provide food or by refusing to eat or disparaging the food they have cooked. Women can also exert power over men by refusing to cook, controlling their food, or manipulating the status and meaning systems embodied in foods. (Counihan 1998: 7)

Through my frame of reference, this argument suggests that food can enable women to reach into the bodies of others and is a potential source of female authority. Yet, the extent of this reach is dependent on cultural context and is by no means clear-cut. Highlighting such cross-cultural complexities maybe a somewhat typical anthropological motif, but this does not diminish the veracity of such a statement, and it is in teasing out these nuances that the bidirectional flows of power between eater and feeder, with each informing the other, can be better understood. Such is the value of an ethnographic approach. Taken together, these studies also show how agency is dispersed and variably performed across a household, as well as indicating how bio-authority may coalesce around one particular social actor. The extent of this coalescence and the forms it takes, in short how the scales of power are weighted, is further dependent on social norms and how expected gender roles relate to individual household dynamics and personal aspirations and circumstances. Another factor to consider is the ways in which personal affective relations and intimacies interlace with wider cultural values about the gendered division of labour, in addition to how such intimacies can 'disguise' and enable social asymmetry (Abbots 2012b).

It is also evident that bodies remain somewhat in the background in many accounts on the gendered division of food labour. Bodies are implied but rarely overtly considered as an analytical frame through which to consider gendered power dynamics, which is perhaps surprising given the presence of the body in discussions of the social construction of sex and gender (cf Butler 1993). Thinking through these questions through the lens of bio-authority can, perhaps, bring another layer of comprehension and shed light on a power dynamic that is oft-obscured. To what extent the expressions of gendered agency performed through food, whatever form they may take, translate to shifts in gender relations in society at large is, of course, another question that takes us back to Goodman's (2016) distinction between ontological and political agency. I do not wish to make any sweeping claims here by arguing that, by feeding families and possibly guests, women have political and economic parity or that agency in the domestic realm equates to political power in the public domain (or vice versa). I am, however, suggesting that unearthing the biopolitical dynamics that take place at the level of the household can deepen our insights and add another dimension to the study of gender relations.

It is important to note that, while I have focused on gender, it is not solely gender relations that matter here; class relations are also salient. And, just as there is a distinction between provisioning and preparing food, so is there a difference between managing and doing food work, as studies into waged domestic labour portray (Abbots 2012b; Frøystad 2003; Gill 1990). Indeed, the extent to which petty battles are waged between mistress and servant over the food that is served to a household and the wrestling that takes place about who ultimately has control of the kitchen, as I have expounded elsewhere in relation to Jima (Abbots 2012b), indicates the efficacy of food as a site of empowerment and authority. Moreover, as I indicate in Chapter 4, a further distinction needs to be made between those who do the work of upholding culture through feeding and the bio-authorities who politically shape which food practices are valued as 'our culture'. In the next chapter, I return to this discussion thread by considering the ways in which women, through their food labour, can act as gatekeepers and upholders of culture in a migratory context.

Concluding remarks

In this chapter I have explored, initially through a rereading of classic ethnographic texts on kinship and relatedness, how bodies are socially and corporeally kinned through the sharing of food in the domestic realm, and I have attempted to demonstrate the value an analytical focus on eating can bring to such discussions. Applying this approach to my experience of eating cuy, I have interrogated the meat's vital essence to make individuals as Jimeño, showing how its matter is understood to act in a certain way once ingested into the body, shaping, in turn, that body into a particular local form. Eating cuy draws multiple human and non-human bodies into a bounded assemblage, which includes cultural knowledges about the dish. Matter and meaning are consequently enmeshed. Knowledge about cuy – that it is 'traditional' and 'special', and that eating it (and desiring it) makes you Jimeño and defines your place within a household – is critical, I have argued, in shaping the meat's affect and effect. Without this knowledge, the meat's vitalism is diminished. In short, the matter of cuy is charged through its cultural meaning, and this cultural meaning is made manifest and viscerally experienced through its matter, which is realized through eating. The vitalism of cuy is thus bounded by the form of its assemblage; an assemblage that is shaped by its symbolic efficacy and its material form and the ways in which these two elements are entangled. While agency is distributed across cuy's assemblage – and I have indicated a number of mediators including the substances the animal had ingested and the objects of its preparation – as a source of cultural knowledge and as a key actor is drawing cuy's assemblage together, the cook can be seen as a bio-authority that permeates the boundaries of the eating body. Agency thus coalesces around her.

The visceral experience of eating has been a key theme in this chapter and I have considered how taste is socially and corporeally sculpted, and how food is evaluated through embodied encounters. I have thereby suggested that we can conceptualize food as acquiring our bodies just as much as we can see that our bodies acquire food. This does not mean, however, that agency is solely situated in food. It also resides and is expressed in the eating human body, and I have explored how desire and rejection can be understood as an enactment of an eater's agency. Showing that eating can be as conflict-ridden as it can be cohesive and unifying, I have further raised questions of how the bio-authority of the cook is contested and upheld through the politics of embodied rejection, and briefly reflected upon how these household dynamics interplay with gender relations. Gender roles emerge also in the next chapter as I turn to the ways in which bodies are kinned through the sharing of substances in a migratory context, a discussion that develops the theme of the interplay between place, food and bodies implied thus far, and further examines how sameness and otherness are produced through food's matter and meaning becoming entangled in a migrant's eating body.

Chapter 3

Eating away from home: Displaced and (re)rooted bodies

Introduction

In this chapter, I explore the multiple ways in which migrants construct their personhood, senses of belonging and social relations by eating both food 'from home' and the unfamiliar, and sometimes risky, foods they encounter in their new environments. Developing the themes of sameness and difference, and proximity and distance, I continue to consider the redrawing and blurring of gustatory boundaries and the production of coterminous bodies that occurs through eating. Yet, rather than focusing on the same locale, as in Chapter 2, here I attend to the practice of eating together across geographical distances, thereby extending my discussion towards the enactment of bodily and social relations across space – a theme I pick up again in Chapter 5. Place, then, plays a significant role in what follows, in terms of how people imagine, belong and anchor themselves to place, as well as how the material assemblages of the places through which food is acquired and eaten interplay with its symbolic meanings. Thus, sensory experience comes to the fore once more, as I interrogate the ways in which migrants' interactions with food are framed and mediated, and how eating can transport a migrant 'home' through recourse to their affective background and previous gustatory encounters.

My primary aim in this chapter is to show how eating matters by drawing attention to the embodied experience of eating in migratory environments and by demonstrating how these visceral encounters with the matter of food inform food's social role and cultural meaning. As I have noted elsewhere (Abbots 2016b), corporeality has not been at the forefront of scholarship on food and migration, which has tended to privilege, with some notable exceptions, meaning over matter. Yet, bodies are critical to comprehending migrants' everyday lived experiences. Indeed, migration can exacerbate bodily differences and responses. Migrant bodies are subject to multiple risks – for instance, pollution from exogenous foods and the foreign bodies of 'the other', being weakened and lost, and being made ill. Social, cultural and corporeal boundaries are transgressed, constructed and reaffirmed in ways that can bring a migrant's body closer to 'other' bodies, while withdrawing it and creating boundaries from others. Physical, gustatory and social boundaries are thus blurred, new hybridized identities forged and new spaces of belonging opened up. This can, however, give rise to tensions, conflict and closing down, just as much as it can produce social cohesiveness, cosmopolitanism and openness.

The relationship between commensality and shared identities, whatever form it takes, emerges strongly in accounts of food and migration. Scholarship on this subject, however, while hinting at the vitality of the matter of food, has been somewhat blind to the material interactions between migrants' bodies and the substances they are eating, and the ways in which those substances are framed and given meaning by sensorial encounters with broader material assemblages. My argument in this chapter is that a closer examination to this oft-overlooked materiality and embodied experience can deepen our understanding of the ways migrants' affective relations are maintained and reinforced (and sometimes broken) to places and people who are physically distant, as well as being forged and disturbed by those in proximity. This perspective, I hope to show, can provide deeper insight into how eating is a critical mediating practice through which notions of sameness and otherness are produced, agency is expressed, and bio-authority is bestowed.

Here and there: Drawing gustatory boundaries

The argument that migrants' eating practices reassert their communal identities and relationships with their home communities, as well as provide a route through which previous, commonly ethnic and class, boundaries become challenged and merged into new forms of belonging, is well established. As I expound below, much scholarship on food among diasporas examines how, in myriad ways, eating food from home – or that which is defined as such – helps root migrants to home places and people, as well as exploring the ways that notions of 'our food' are articulated through the food of others. This literature, not surprisingly, resonates strongly with accounts of the role eating plays in the construction of local, ethnic and national identities and not uncommonly indicates how 'our food' is a fluid and hybridized category (Caplan 1997; see also Chapter 4). Ray's (2004) study of first- and second-generation middle-class Bengali-Americans is one such example. Treating food as a 'place-making practice' (ibid.: 5), he examines how and why certain meals and eating practices are upheld and asserted as Bengali, whereas some 'traditions' are creolized inventions, and on other occasions 'exogenous' food influences are readily incorporated. He presents a dynamic and relational picture of Bengali cuisine though which broader questions of 'assimilation and accommodation' (ibid.: 4) can be explored. Bengali food, he argues, is constructed in opposition to 'American', although this process is not unidirectional as the influence of Bengali food filters into 'American' cuisine also. Culinary identities, or in his terms 'gustatory boundaries', are thus made and remade not in isolation, but instead through engagement with other cuisines, meals and foods.

Reasserting boundaries and rooting migrants to home is enacted in Jima by the sending of packages of cuy and *zhima* corn from the village to migrant kin in the United States; a process that helps maintain the cohesiveness of a distributed, transnational household. The majority of my Jimeño participants' husbands and male kin are living in the United States, many for a decade or more, while their wives and younger children remain in Jima. Relatedness across these dispersed households remains, in most cases, robust and the sending of food parcels is one of the mechanisms through which kinship is performed and maintained. These parcels are most frequently sent on ritual occasions and family life cycle events, although migrants, at times, also request them. These requests, as I have demonstrated elsewhere (Abbots 2011), reflect a migrant's desire to not only maintain affective connections to his Ecuadorian home, but also to be corporeally (re)made as kin and rooted to his home through shared substance. As in the previous chapter, the agency of the eater and the matter being eaten in the production of desire comes to the fore here, together with the central mediating role that the cook plays in the process, however geographically distant she may be.

This is illustrated by Sonia and her husband Don Pepe. Don Pepe had been living in New York for over ten years when I first started working with Sonia, and she placed great importance on telling me that he often requested the 'cuy of home' – which she would duly prepare in the same manner as she would for her Jima-based household – because he was still 'of here'. As with her son Pablito discussed in the previous chapter, Don Pepe's continuing enthusiasm for cuy was interpreted as being demonstrative of his constant 'home' personhood and belonging. Intimacy was thus formed across space and transnational divides, with cuy providing a vital material bond between the couple. This connection did not always happen equitably, however, and there were moments when Sonia would find a reason to 'push' cuy onto Don Pepe, especially on the occasions her remittance receipts dwindled. Such 'gifts' served to remind her husband of his obligations and prompt a return 'gift' (see Abbots 2011). There were also moments when Don Pepe attempted to source cuy himself, as well as requesting it from his wife. He explained to me that he had, on occasion, 'craved' the meat and that these cravings had led him to acquire cuyes from somewhat dubious sources, such as pet shops, and cook them himself, although these did not 'taste as good' as the ones he had received from his Jimeño home.

Cuy then, it appears, had acquired and was acting upon Don Pepe's eating body, while his own body mediated his ingestion of cuy meat through the rubric of taste, allowing him to make a value judgement on 'proper' cuy. Following my arguments on shared substance outlined in the previous chapter, he was continually symbolically *and* materially remade as Jimeño and re-rooted to both his kin group and his Jimeño home as the substance of that home became physically incorporated into his own body. This stretching of his bodily boundaries kins Don Pepe's body across space with those members of his family eating the same meat from home – a process that draws dispersed individuals together while creating a distinction between proximate bodies not consuming the meat.

Eating particular foods, then, that are embedded, both materially and symbolically, to a home locale can help reaffirm a migrant's identity and affinity to a place and people by socially sharing the same food, albeit across space. Through shared substances – sometimes literally in the context of Don Pepe's and Sonia's cuy and on other occasions by ideologically associating a food as traditionally from home as in the case of Ray's Bengali-Americans – relationships of social proximity are enacted across geographical distances. This process, as Ray shows, can concomitantly create social distance between those who are geographically proximate. Boundaries are thus dynamically formed.

But boundaries can also be dissolved and reformed in different ways, as illustrated by Saber and Posner's (2013) discussion of Eritrean and Sudanese asylum seekers' restaurants in Tel Aviv. They argue that such restaurants become 'culinary safe heavens' (ibid.: 198), which provide migrants not just with the familiar foods from home, but also an emotionally secure environment through which they can articulate their emergent 'diaspora identity' (ibid.: 216). Underneath the traditionally Sudanese or Eritrean 'national' exterior is a process of hybridization that is both transnational and multicultural, as different ethnic groups and communities merge through the shared and familiar experiences of eating together in a foreign land. Similarly, Tuomainen (2009) elucidates how ethnic boundaries that are entrenched in Ghana become blurred in London as

Ghanaian individuals start to eat foods associated with other ethnic groups in their attempts to establish a new form of Ghanaian or African subjectivity. Her account further highlights the ways in which class boundaries are blurred as, in contrast to their kin in Ghana, migrants in London are able to easily access the British foods that forms part of 'high cuisine' back home. A different form of belonging that is constructed and articulated in relation to a new 'other' is thus enacted, with food playing a pivotal role in diminishing differences with some groups while creating distance from others.

In their different ways, then, Ray, Toumainen and Saber and Posner all point to how previously entrenched values around food – and the people who eat them – can shift when eaters are situated in a different geographical context that encourages them to form new social relations and communities. Gustatory boundaries, and the 'other' with whom they are associated, are consequently crossed, merged and (re)created. This dynamism warns us against the tendency to essentialize the 'food from here' and the 'food from there', as so easily occurs when attempting to account for migrants' eating preferences. A clear line cannot, and should not, be drawn between 'traditional' foods from home and hybrid foods in migrants' host contexts (Collins 2008; Saber and Posner 2013). As I demonstrate in the following chapter, food traditions and heritage are likely to be re-invented in any geographical context and the framing of a food as specific to a locale, while often based on its materiality, is also founded upon a political process of selection and valorization: 'We have to remember that just as people and food (and their narratives) travel and circulate, so do the meanings attached to them' (Abbots 2016b: 120).

Chapman and Beagan's (2011) study of the culinary practices within two Punjabi-Canadian families lends further support to this argument. They stress the multiple subjectivities of migrants by demonstrating how eating can create and reflect social connections in sometimes contradictory ways, as individuals navigate between local and global attachments. The authors thereby challenge the notion of 'dietary acculturation' and the idea that migrants gradually lose, retain or reassert the eating behaviours of a reified 'home'. In so doing they present a far more dynamic and fluid process through which eating makes and reflects migrant identities and sense of belonging, concluding that

> individual subjects have discontinuous, divided, possibly conflicting identities, reflecting, among other things, their ethnicity, gender, class, age and intersections of these with transnational attachments. Food, as a symbolic representation of identity, is both influenced by and constitutive of these multiple identities. (ibid.: 369)

In summary, what these illustrative examples show is that the established literature on eating among migrants and diasporas commonly focuses on the manners in which new hybridized identities are forged through foods and the extent that eating can both reassert and dissolve social boundaries. The tendency here is to centre on the symbolic meaning of foods, in the sense that they continuously shift in reality while simultaneously being culturally reified and (re)invented as tradition. These approaches have offered numerous insights and I do not wish to diminish their contribution, but I also want to consider an aspect of this process that is often overlooked – the ways in which eating connects bodies to places through food's vital substance and the assemblages that frame its materiality and imbue it with meaning.

'Culinary safe havens': Memory, materialities and affect

Sonia's sending of cuy and Don Pepe's requests and attempts to acquire it indicate the importance of vital substances in the context of migration and the continuing performance of transnational kinship. I wish now to build upon these conceptual foundations by exploring ethnographic accounts of how food's materiality invokes the senses to transport an eating to body to a different place to that in which it is corporeally located. In short, I examine how 'culinary safe havens', to borrow from Saber and Posner (2013), are created and subjectively experienced through visceral encounters with food.

An anthropological interest in the senses can be read as a response to the dominance of narrative and a 'visualist bias' (Sutton 2001: 13), and a desire to move away from reading the body semiotically, as exemplified by Douglas (2002), to a more embodied, experiential perspective that more fully accounts for phenomenological interactions between humans and their material worlds (Csordas 1990, 1994). With the underlying premise that sensory perception is both cultural and corporeal, engagements with the material world are understood to be shaped by cultural context and, hence, can be understood as expressions of cultural values (Classen 1997). This is not to deny symbolic meanings, but rather to treat textuality and embodiment as a dialectic (Csordas 1994), much in the same way as I approach food as both matter and meaning. This anthropology of the senses, or sensory anthropology as Pink (2010) defines it,[1] thus invokes a methodological and conceptual approach through which the subjective embodied experience of feeling, smelling, hearing and tasting the world is more deeply considered (see also Howes 1995, 2003; Jackson 1989; Stoller 1989).

While arguably underdeveloped in the anthropology of food, cross-disciplinary dialogues have highlighted how a greater emphasis on the senses, and the ways they interplay with symbolic and political economic understandings of food, can bring a deeper comprehension to the way eating situates an individual in the world (see, for example, Korsmeyer 2005). This approach has been particularly productive in discussions of food and memory, as indicated by Serematakis' (1994) account of disappearing Greek peaches and her cutting of wild greens. She notes how her embodied knowing of food 'emerged in exile' (ibid.: 16), as the absence of the foods of which she had memories invoked a 'stillness' that lifts the food from everyday banality. Thus it is through the 'forced experience of crisis, separation and cross cultural contact' that 'hidden substances of the past' are released (ibid.: 17). Disjuncture is also present in Johnston and Longhurst's study of migrant women in Hamilton, New Zealand, which further stresses the importance of the visceral. Writing that 'taste and smell were the senses that prompted feelings, memories and new connections' (2012: 330), they draw attention to the affective relations that circulate and the emotions that surface through cooking and eating, in addition to demonstrating the insights that a more sensory approach can bring to our understanding of how belonging and not-belonging are *felt* (see also Longhurst, Johnston and Ho 2009).

Sutton's (2001) monograph of eating in Kalymnos, Greece, builds upon the foundations laid by Seramatakis and it is still, perhaps, the most substantial and influential ethnography exemplifying this approach. He demonstrates how eating is a particularly intense practice of memory provocation because of the manner in which it invokes the senses. Food here does not just stand for something – a nation, a place or a community – but is experienced affectively and viscerally. Its materiality matters as it is food's very substance that gives it the tastes and smells that trigger memories and emotions. But a foodstuff is not eaten in a vacuum of the present moment. Instead, Sutton shows us how eating involves looking backwards to past meals and forward to those in the future, as a food in the present is situated in a broader frame of previous food encounters and local knowledge. Embodied experience and meaning are thus entwined, and time and space collapsed.

This is illustrated by a taste for Greek feta cheese that, for one of Sutton's participants, represented Greek national identity (especially following challenges by other nations to produce cows' milk feta), local connections, and personal recollections of how, when buying feta as a child, the shopkeeper had a special way of spearing the cheese in cans on brine and cutting it (ibid.: 85). Echoing the fluid model of food discussed above, Sutton thereby highlights how eating works at multiple levels of national, regional and local belonging, but extends our understanding by interrogating the cognitive and affective processes through which such relations between food, place and belonging are formed. This further shows how eating can transport migrants across place and time, and Sutton concludes 'there is an imagined community implied in the act of eating food "from home" while in exile, in the embodied knowledge that others are eating the same food' (ibid.: 84). Eating is, then, an intensely emotional experience, especially for the geographically distant who have an embodied 'burning desire' for food from their homeland that can be only satiated with a sensory experience of consuming it (ibid.: 81).

Although Sutton does not refer to it in such terms, his arguments accord with my notion of affective background indicated in the previous chapter (see also Chapter 4) in that he demonstrates how eaters bring embodied memories of previous eating experiences and cultural understandings of a food's meaning to an eating encounter in the present. Thus, in my language, we can start to see how Sutton's participants' experiences of food are framed through an assemblage that stretches across space and time and both incorporates sensory recollections of food and socially produced knowledge. Through this lens, we can start to conceive of memories as mediators in that they create affect and effect within the eating body and shape the way an eating encounter is experienced. Considering how the substances of food produce the tastes and smells that provoke memories takes us back to the import of food's matter and its interplays with symbolic meaning. This is further elucidated by Ben Ze'ev's (2004) account of the return visits of Palestinian refugees to lands appropriated by the State of Israel, which expounds how embodied experiences of foods are entwined with abstracted political and social discourses.

Like Sutton, Ben Ze'ev draws on notions of Proustian recall in exploring how rituals of picking and eating the plants from refugees' homelands facilitated their (re)construction and continuation of *their* Palestine. She writes that 'these rites of return are sensual experiences, whereby taste and smell play a major role, assisting in the retrieval of memories through embodiment' (ibid.: 155). This visceral encounter does not, however, remain a personal moment, but is instead abstracted through conversation and the circulation of images. Personal recollection is thus shifted into and forms part of collective memory as subjective embodied experience is translated into social narrative. Although the point is not expanded, Ben Ze'ev hints that these wider discourses inform individual encounters, a dynamic that ethnographically illustrates Csordas' (1994) and Jackson's (1989) arguments that textuality and embodiment should be treated as a dialectic. What we see here, therefore, is a process in which a material encounter between an eating body and food contributes, through wider discursive practices, to the food becoming a culturally important symbol. In addition, embodied interactions with that food acquire their significance because of the social assemblage in which that food is situated. Matter thus helps produce meaning and the meaning, in turn, bestows the matter with its cultural efficacy. The plants to which Ben Ze'ev refers are not inherently vital, as a reading of Bennett (2007, 2010) would suggest, but rather acquire their agentic capacity through a potent mix of locale, narrative and substance.

Human action thereby plays a pivotal role in provoking an emotive experience that evokes all of the senses. Returning to Saber and Posner (2013), they argue, in line with Sutton (2001), that asylum seekers' restaurants can be understood as a 'full-intensity sensorium' (2013: 113) that draws together visuals – such as customers eating together and African television channels – olfactory cues of familiar smells, auditory experiences of familiar languages and dialect, and the taste of the food being eaten. Restaurateurs therefore create an environment that simulates, and transports a migrant, 'home' through a fully immersive embodied encounter. Although not framed in such terms, Saber and Posner's ethnography gives an indication of the embodied processes that make food such a powerful site for the construction of migrant identity, as well as pointing to a key orchestrating social actor – the restaurateur. A similar thread is found in Mankekar's (2002) account of shopping in Indian grocery stores in the San Francisco Bay Area, although here the retailer emerges as the critical mediator.

Mankekar explores the affect produced by the stores frequented by Indian migrants and, like Saber and Posner, draws attention to the multifaceted sensory experiences invoked. Indian grocery stores, she tells us, are 'spaces of familiarity' (ibid.: 90) through which migrants encounter the powerful smells, sounds and sights of home. They provide consumers 'not just with the spices, lentils and other ingredients deemed crucial to Indian cooking, they also make available a range of objects, artefacts, images, and discourses for consumption' (ibid.: 81). Mankekar thus represents the stores as an assemblage in which the foods from home are situated among the loud music and shouts from customers, posters and advertisements, and glares from shop assistants with a particular style of 'customer service'. Even the way the goods being sold are laid out in a disordered fashion, with 'lentils, icons of Hindu gods, and posters of Sikh gurus' (ibid.: 89) placed in disarray on a shelf, signals the store's Indianness. As such, there are multiple visual cues and discourses. But this is only a fragment of the experience; the distinctive smell is also a critical element. This goes beyond the aroma of the spices and cooked foods extending to the bodies of consumers themselves, with one of Mankekar's participants highlighting 'the smell of the press of the people, of Indian bodies' (ibid.: 90). This encounter continues outside of the store, with another participant explaining how, when she was a child, she hated going somewhere after a visit 'smelling of spices, smelling of India' (ibid.: 90). Smelling, and smelling like, an Indian grocery store consequently becomes a mechanism for emoting a feeling of sameness and familiarity. Nevertheless, it can just as readily be a marker of (embodied) difference. Familiarity is not always pleasant and Mankekar writes that the stores can also invoke strong emotions of claustrophobia and a feeling of being surveyed. While being spaces for forging identity and community, migrant 'safe havens' can also be sites of ambivalence, resentment and dislocation.

In highlighting the multisensory experience of food, Mankekar's observations, much like those of Sutton, Ben Ze'ev and Saber and Posner, encourage us to reflect on what constitutes eating. Is it merely the putting of food into the mouth, chewing and tasting? Or is it, as Mol (2008) defines, the process of ingestion and digestion? Or is it more, perhaps, than any of these, with eating extending beyond the mouth and biological functions to incorporate the full sensory encounter of smelling, feeling, hearing, seeing and absorbing food through multiple mechanisms, including its material context and the bodies of others? In short, this literature points to eating as a 'synesthetic' experience (cf Sutton 2001) – a co-joining of the senses. I attend more fully to these questions of what eating is and draw these multiple threads together in following chapters, but for now I wish to briefly note how a scholarly understanding of food as a multisensory encounter can engage with and extend discussions of food's inherent vitalism and agency (cf Bennett 2010).

For this, I return to my notion of 'bounded vitalism'. Mankekar's grocery store, I suggest, can be seen as a framed assemblage that creates a broad multisensory material experience situating and positioning specific foods and stimulating affect in the consumer. The store's objects, sights, smells, tastes and sounds – and the knowledges that accompany them – charge the matter of the food being consumed with a certain Indianness that derives from its material substance *and* the ways in which it is culturally framed. This framing thus bounds the possibilities of both the matter and the meaning.

The extent to which this is deliberate, with affect being the 'object-target' (Anderson 2011) of grocery store owners, is perhaps impossible to fully measure, but it does indicate the mediating role such actors play, either incidentally or intentionally. The frame of Mankekar's store includes multiple and distributed mediating agents – the bodies of shoppers, advertisements, smells of spices, the arrangement of goods, and the stares of the shopkeeper among others. All of these mediators interdependently inform the shape of the assemblage and the social and material vitality of each other. To elucidate: taken in isolation a food, such as a dhal, may have a certain *material* vitality in that it will act upon the body and provoke bodily responses. It also carries a symbolic meaning that stems from the cultural discourse and social relations in which it is embedded. But situate that food in a broader material assemblage, like a grocery store, and it becomes imbued with a *social* as well as a material vitality. Matter and meaning are thus drawn together through the food's situatedness and its interactions with other objects in its assemblage. It also invigorates the vitality of other objects in this assemblage – they work dialectically in combination with each other to produce, in Mankekar's context, the Indianness of the Indian grocery store. This framing, I argue, is limited and bound not only through the practical actions of key bio-authorities, such as restaurateurs and storekeepers, and the knowledges they produce, but also the affective background and previous experiences of the eater. These experiences are carried and felt, as the examples above show, in and through the body. I now turn to explore this in more depth by considering what it feels like to be living and eating in a migrant's body.

Being in a migrant body: Eating away from home

'When migrants move to a new place their bodies are disciplined in new ways, including through food and eating' (Johnston and Longhurst 2012: 328), yet bodies, both in terms of subjective embodied experience and in the more abstracted social constructionist sense (cf Butler 1993) have, with the notable exceptions above, been commonly overlooked in accounts of food and migration. The body is often implied in the literature, but rarely has it been developed as a specific line of enquiry (Abbots 2016b: 116). So, as I have previously (Abbots 2011, 2016b), I turn again here to Strathern's (1988) *The Gender of the Gift* as a starting point. I do so because this work indicates how ingesting the vital substance of food from home can also help stem the loss of the body that comes from eating exogenous food.

In her discussion of Jolly's (1981 in Strathern 1988) ethnography of a *kastom* village in the Vanuatu peninsula, Strathern shows that bodies of men who labour away from home are locally understood as subject to being lost, as they are primarily ingesting the 'foreign' foods of rice, tinned fish and corned beef. These foods are understood as threats that weaken male bodies, and to fully comprehend this, the role that food plays in constructing masculinity 'at home' has to be taken into account. Stathern tells us that Jolly reports that yams are strongly associated with men to the extent that the growing of yams is 'part of a male cult' (Strathern 1988: 80). While the other main crop of taro is grown cooperatively between men and women, men dominate the production of yams, which is subject to a distinct gendered division of labour likened to sexual relations. Men control yam distribution and production and the food is regarded as a sacred male food, for example boys eat yams at circumcision to symbolize their masculinity whereas taro is fed to newborn babies, as it has female associations (ibid.: 81). Consequently, the weakening of men's bodies that occurs through migration and the subsequent eating of foreign food can be counteracted by the consumption of yams. Yams replenish the male body and reinforce its masculinity. Moreover, they also re-root those bodies to home and, while neither Strathern nor Jolly fully expand upon this point, the implied argument is that yams have this capacity because of their symbolic resonance *and* the facticity that they are materially derived from home soil. This is especially salient, given the ways that Vanuatuans consider land as 'part of one's human substance' (Jolly 1981: 269 in Strathern 1988). As Strathern concludes, 'There is thus an intimate equation between the food one eats and one's bodily and social state' (1988: 81).

Strathern conceptualizes the body in this ethnographic context in a manner that echoes both Mol (2008) and Haraway (1990) – it is 'leaky' with semipermeable boundaries that interface with, and absorb, the material and symbolic properties of other active agents, in this case yams and exogenous foods. There is a risk that the bodies of migrants can be absorbed too much into 'other' worlds, as their boundaries become too open and stretched too far by the foods of others. Countermeasures are therefore required against such threats. We can see this process unfolding in Jima and the sending of cuy to migrant kin. A sense of potential loss was ever present in this context, and while there was an expressed confidence that men would return and remain connected to their Jimeño family, there was also an undercurrent of practices that helped ensure this would be the case. The sending of food packages is one such practice. Drawing together Strathern and my discussions of cuy as shared substance above and in Chapter 2, we can start to interpret such packages as a way of corporeally and culturally remaking and re-rooting a migrant to his or her home territory and kin (see also Abbots 2011, 2016b). The food selected to send to migrants is not incidental; it is the most socially and materially vital foods that have the strongest capacity to minimize loss and remake bodily connections to people and place.

Cuy packages, like yams, of course, do not just come to migrants through happenstance. There is a process of labour involved and a human agent, or more, behind the process of preparing, cooking, packaging and sending the meal. This role cannot and should not be overlooked, and there is often a gendered dimension here. In Jima, as I have discussed in Chapter 2, women take on the primary responsibility of food work including the sending of food packages to migrants, and Strathern argues also that it is women, although actively prohibited from engaging with the outside world, who ensure that male migrants remain rooted to home in Vanuatu. Women, then, 'become visible reminders of enduring norms of social conduct' (ibid.: 76–7). There is little work on food and migration that addresses this theme through the lens of bodies, although a number of writers have drawn attention to the labour women perform in (re)asserting gustatory boundaries (see, for example, Flowers and Swan 2015b; Frost 2008; Harbottle 2000; Vallianatos and Raine 2008). As Harbottle (2000) explains, everyday domestic food work was highly valued by the British Shi'ite Iranian women with whom she conducted her research *and* their families, not least because of its 'symbolic significance in the maintenance of ethnic identity' (ibid.: 41). A similar argument is also made by Vallianatos and Raine who state that Arabic and South Asian female immigrants in Canada act as 'gatekeepers' who uphold 'family and community values via traditional foods and cuisines' while brokering 'outside' influences (2008: 357). In accord with Strathern, then, women, in these contexts, become the primary upholders of custom and cultural values.[2]

While those, predominantly women, who labour to provide food clearly perform a critical role in rooting migrants' and migrated bodies to kin, communities and culture – and can thereby be regarded as bio-authorities in this context – we also have to consider the other side of the equation and ask how migrants themselves relate to the foods they are eating, as they ingest foods 'from home' in addition to that which may have been previously unknown. The work discussed above provides some indication of this; for instance, Toumainen (2009) shows us how Ghanians in the UK redefine previously entrenched relations through food, and Saber and Posner (2013) elucidate the dynamic processes of hybridization and the production of a diaspora identity. Moreover, as my own ethnography shows, migrants are not without agency and take their own measures to maintain their bodily integrity – Sonia was the instrumental actor in sending packages of cuy, but Don Pepe also requested the meat and attempted to procure it himself while in New York (Abbots 2011). But what this work does not provide is a full sense of the subjective embodied experience of eating away from home. We are able to conceptualize how ingesting a food (re)makes a body in an abstract sense, but what does it feel like to be eating in that body? To help answer this, we need to turn to rich ethnographic description.

One of the most striking themes that emerged from my fieldwork with privileged migrants (more commonly referred to as expats[3]) in Ecuador was the extent to which they avoided local food and food spaces because of issues of trust, risk and food safety. These concerns were not merely abstracted, but were instead viscerally experienced through the body, often in uncomfortable ways. This is exemplified by one of my participants, Josie, who was originally from the United States and was following a restrictive body ecology diet when I met her in Ecuador. Josie's diet relied heavily on imported supplements and foodstuffs that could not be obtained in-country, and resulted in her avoiding all local foods to the extent she would bring her own foods when dining in restaurants. The reason for such restrictions, she explained, was that her body 'could not cope' with local foods, even fruits and vegetables that had been peeled and thoroughly cleaned. These foods had sent her body 'into a tailspin':

> When I arrived, I ate loads of fruit – I mean I concentrated on the fruit you could peel, or I washed it – but my body just went into a tailspin; I guess it's just that there are so many germs here and my body isn't used to it. So now, the only way I can get by is by being on this diet. I need to sort out my intestines, y'know, the balance of them – they've been put completely out of whack here. (Abbots 2013: 130)

Josie's experience points to the material vitality of the fruits she ate on arrival and the ways, following Mol (2008), in which she has limited agency over her own bodily functions. Her new diet can be interpreted as an attempt to reassert control over her intestines and readjust the balance between her will and the internal workings of her body. What interests me here in particular is that she does so, not by consuming other local foods or continuing to eat local fruits in an attempt to accustom her body, but by reverting to the foods from home – foods that have to be brought into the country at great expense and inconvenience. Josie's attempt at reasserting her agency involves effectively withdrawing her body from the space in which it is corporeally located. She is clearly still physically occupying that space and has chosen to remain in it, but she does so by reinforcing her bodily boundaries with the food from home (cf Douglas 2002). Much like the male migrants from Vanuatu replenishing their bodies with yams, Josie is replenishing it with foods that serve to not only give her greater control over her body, but also re-anchor that body to her home territory. In short, following its exposure to 'foreign foods' and its subsequent weakening, Josie is attempting to take her intestines back to familiar territory even while they are corporeally located in an alien space.

Josie's behaviour may seem extreme, but she was not alone in her experience of local foods, and many of the privileged migrants with whom I conducted research commonly expressed similar visceral encounters, many of which had led to them avoiding local foods to some degree. Experiences of food poisoning, both mild and severe, were commonplace and attributed, nearly without exception, to unfamiliar foods obtained from unfamiliar places and people. Toni, for example, told me that she 'would never eat anything sold in those places again' after being ill, and I was privy to many a discussion about the most effective antibacterial measures that could be taken and the safest places to eat. Such concerns may not, at first glance, seem surprising. But the readiness to blame specific local foods for undesirable bodily responses may seem a little disproportionate when privileged migrants acquire the majority of their foods from supermarkets, higher-end restaurants, or Western-style, higher-end private stores, such as 'The German Bakery' or 'European Deli'. In contrast, my Ecuadorian friends were sceptical of the quality and safety of the food from such 'modern' establishments, preferring instead the 'unsafe' local markets, which the majority of migrants avoid. I am not stating here that one source of food is any less safe than the other, but merely observing that both groups – privileged migrants and Ecuadorians – readily located risk in the foods of the 'other' and took measures to eat more familiar foods from familiar places. These risks, moreover, while discussed, rarely remained purely discursive, but were instead seen to be made manifest through, often unpleasant and unwanted, embodied experiences.

Privileged migrants, then, despite wanting a 'simple life and simple food' (Abbots 2013), tended to remove themselves from local 'simple' food spaces and retreated to those that were deemed as less harmful to their bodies – such as restaurants run by other migrants, the sterile 'modern' and familiar spaces of supermarkets and Western-style grocery stores, and those places that served familiar food or became communal by hosting events such as Gringo Night. These spaces were all 'higher-end', which further served to remove migrant bodies from the majority of local bodies that do not have the economic or social capital to frequent such establishments. Or, at worse, migrant bodies would be situated next to 'higher-class' – read white(r), cultured and more urban – Ecuadorian bodies; in other words, those that were less 'other'. As a result, a particular migrant foodscape emerges, with migrants occupying and engaging with different food spaces in different ways to many of the local population, which further exacerbates difference and segregation. A not dissimilar process has been observed in Frost's (2008) account of Indonesian migrant women in Sydney, which shows how they know the city differently to Sydney-siders, as they find innovative and strategic ways to source 'their' food. This knowledge not only enables them to engage, to a limited extent, with their host country and its participants, but also to 'mildly subvert' (ibid.: 181) Australian hegemony as they forge their own paths through the city. There are thus points of intersection as well as boundaries and distinction.

Frost's participants are far less privileged than the privileged migrants with whom I conducted research, but her findings, in many ways, are in accord. Her account raises the question of food knowledges and how foods, and the places in which they are sourced, become known, and she highlights how not knowing food of their host country can be alienating and a marker of difference for migrants. Food knowledges were circulated freely among my privileged migrant participants, and what to eat and where to obtain it was a common conversation topic, but they often also looked to specific bio-authorities. In this ethnographic context, these authorities were established members of the community, 'safe' restaurant owners, and hired domestic help – even an incumbent anthropologist. Not knowing – the food, what to do with it, and whether it was safe – was a common trope among migrants for not participating in local food spaces, and this lack of knowledge presents those with some knowledge the opportunity to mediate migrants' eating experiences. In directing them to specific locales, restaurants and stores these bio-authorities have a political and economic effect on the local foodscape, as well as on migrant bodies, and I observed interactions that suggested migrants' favour was explicitly sought by some traders, who quickly seized the commercial opportunity such as absence of knowledge presented. Migrants' experience of eating, while not dictated by such bio-authorities, was very evidently shaped by these transactions that defined the assemblage of what they 'chose' to eat and where they did so. Moreover, the lack of food knowledge facilitated migrants' willing bestowal of food authority onto others, and they sometimes actively sought guidance about what they should put into their bodies from 'trusted' local sources. As Abi told me, 'I don't know what all these strange fruits and vegetables are; I've got no idea how to cook them or eat them, what I should pay for them – or even if they're safe! We need someone to show us – we don't know this food' (Abbots 2013: 127).

Unpleasant embodied responses to local foods, the desire to eat risk-free food, the lack of knowledge of what and where to eat, and the subsequent bestowal of bio-authority on specific mediating actors all combined, in this context, to result in the creation of distinct privileged migrant food spaces that established distance between migrant bodies and that of the majority of local people, primarily those that belong to the lower classes. This can be seen as the antithesis of the sharing of substance and commensality discussed in the previous chapter, and is what I have framed elsewhere, drawing on DuPuis' (2000) notion of Not-in-my-Body, as 'not alongside my body' (Abbots 2013: 124). What we see here, then, is a process through which body, food and place are entwined. The reassertion of bodily boundaries, as exemplified by Josie's stringent measures to control what she eats, is a production of gustatory boundaries that are enacted through, and produce, spatial boundaries. Privileged migrants literally become isolated sites: their bodies are enclaves of their food, and this facilitates, and perhaps reflects, a broader social withdrawal from the bodies of others. Clear boundaries are created through the embodied politics of refusal.

There are, as always, ethnographic exceptions to this rule, and some privileged migrants, in exemplary cases of mind over matter, continued to eat and attempted to enjoy local foods, despite its previous ill effects on their bodies. The strategy for doing so was twofold. First, they looked to 'domesticate' (cf Caldwell 2004) local food spaces by building long-term relations of trust with a select number of vendors and by asserting control over those relations – and by extension those foods and food spaces – by determining the price to be paid, handpicking produce, and repeating interactions to the extent that encounters with 'foreign' foods were slowly familiarized. This tactic was adopted by Bryan who told me that he goes to 'the same two or three stalls [in the market], and have been for some time' and that, while standard practice dictates that the vendor bags the produce, they 'even let me fill the bag now' and 'I select which ones [avocados] I want … I choose each individual strawberry too'. Others invested in a process of training their body to accept the local foods they were eating by repeatedly affirming to themselves that the foods were tasty, good for them, healthy and pesticide and pathogen free. Thus, although grass-fed beef was commonly not to their palate and was often found to be 'chewy', they would continue to eat it on the basis that they would start to like it, much like I was encouraged to with cuy in Chapter 2. Similarly, Steve explained that, while he knew in his heart that the strawberries he was eating were not organic because of their size and tastelessness – an assessment he based on previous encounters with trusted organic strawberries eaten in the United States – he did not want to believe it and so kept telling himself they were organic, concluding 'I keep trying to believe 'em! [the vendors]'.

In part, Steve was reverting to his will, the power of positive thinking, and a Cartesian model of the body that disaggregates the mind from phenomenological experience. But there is also a sense here of food's vital matter and its agentic capacity to acquire eating bodies. It is very much implied, and far less explicit than in the case of cuy discussed in the previous chapter, but in different ways the subjective eating experience of privileged migrants points to the capacity of the food being eaten to work upon their bodies. This can take the form, if migrants continue eating local foods, of their eating body becoming domesticated by such foods to the extent that the foods are no longer seen as foreign, but are instead familiar. In short, migrant bodies can be seen as being subjected to being colonized by the foods being eaten, as their intestines become accustomed to the new bacteria being ingested. Much like cuy acquiring my body (as discussed in Chapter 2), we can start to think, then, of food starting to take over the migrant body, and by extension, in the case of exogenous foods, of foreign cultures and peoples acquiring that body in a manner that subjects it to becoming socially weakened and potentially lost (cf Strathern 1988). I now turn to explore this process, and the tensions to which it gives rise, in more depth by exploring what takes place when migrants eat the food of 'the other'.

Eating otherness: Incorporation and appropriation

Eating and incorporating the food associated with 'an other' can provide a mechanism, as discussed above, through which previously entrenched boundaries are dissolved in the construction of new hybridized identities and notions of social belonging. This process is not uncommonly presented as somewhat tension-free, especially in the contexts where multiple dislocated groups engage underneath a broader sense of community, as can be found for instance in accounts by Saber and Posner (2013) and Toumainen (2009). Yet, as my Ecuadorian ethnography shows, engagement with 'the other' may be less desirable and they may be too different. Hence corporeal and social distancing is required. This distancing is not always possible, however, and even in the most extreme scenarios, when 'the other' is constructed as 'the enemy', it can give rise to processes of incorporation.

Campbell's (2014) discussion of eating Iraqi food, while being a serving member of the US military during post-Operation Iraqi Freedom, sensitively explores the tensions that emerge when eating the food of 'the other'. She writes of a voracious appetite for Iraqi food that had to be satiated, often at great personal danger. In contrast to privileged migrants in Ecuador, falling ill did not quell US soldiers' enthusiasm for dishes such as the chicken and flatbread or *kofta* sold at the 'unauthorized food stands', to the extent that some risked their lives by leaving their protected base to eat the food sold by Iraqis in 'back alleys' (ibid.: 149). Campbell reflects on the motivating factors for such desires, especially as the soldiers' nutritional needs were being fully met by official rations. She finds the answer in a desire to connect to humanity in the most inhumane of circumstances, stating 'cultural needs, the needs of humanity dwelling within our disciplined civilized bodies, drove us across enemy lines in order to be satisfied' (ibid.: 149). This form of 'rebellious consumption', as she defines it, was not without tensions, and she documents the inner struggles veterans experienced when trying to deal with their cravings for Middle Eastern food upon their return to the United States. The struggles, Campbell explains, are a step towards humanizing the enemy and coming to personal terms with the conflict and horrors of war by framing 'the other' as familiar and integrating them into new post-conflict identities.

Campbell frames such 'rebellious consumption' as an expression of personal agency that subverted and renegotiated the super-nationalistic discourse of the US military, which constructed Iraqis as faceless 'bad guys' (ibid.: 150) who were ultimately to be destroyed. Eating Iraqi food produced by 'the people we were taught to be disgusted by' (ibid.: 149) enabled soldiers to break out of this ideology by putting a face onto a previously faceless enemy. In short, the more the soldiers ate Iraqi food, the more human Iraqis became. Campbell concludes:

> Disgust for the other and his food is a mechanism that mentally aids in the execution of the unnatural acts of war, thus, the adoption of enemy cuisine signifies much more than a change in palate, it signifies a defiant act of agency and the first step in the difficult process of shifting from soldiers fighting faceless enemies to men and women engaging with other men and women. (ibid.: 146)

Eating the food of 'the other', then, draws 'the other' into closer proximity and starts to enable, if not a social connection in Campbell's context, at least a recognition of the other's humanity. The process of incorporating the food of the other into the self is expressed through a somewhat positive frame by Campbell, in which there is an openness of both bodily and social boundaries that can defy previously entrenched values. A similar tone is found in Van Otterloo's (1987) account of 'other cuisines' in the Netherlands, in which she demonstrates that relations 'at the table' were less confrontational and fraught than in other contexts. Commensality paves the way for, if not integration, then at least social understanding.

Eating otherness can, however, be regarded as a form of appropriation and control, rather than integration and incorporation. Viewed from this perspective, Campbell's ethnography, if not her argument, is reminiscent of work on the power dynamics of metaphorical (and literal) cannibalism (hooks 1992), as 'the other' gets materially and figuratively consumed. By critically unpacking assumptions about gustatory openness, especially under the guise of multiculturalism, a number of writers have elucidated how structural inequalities and stereotypes can be reiterated, and they have variably drawn attention to the politics of appropriation that are at play (cf Hage 1997; Heldke 2003; Molz 2007). bell hooks refers to this practice as 'consumer cannibalism' (ibid.: 31), with the white mainstream metaphorically eating racialized black bodies that are decontextualized and fetished. 'Eating the other' is thus enacted from a dominant subject position and motivated by self-serving interests through which otherness can be explored and used to spice up the mainstream without disrupting core positionality (see also Heldke 2003).

In accord with this, Hage (1997) shows us that white Australians' desire for Vietnamese cuisine is based on a caricature of Vietnameseness that prevents any real interactions between the two groups and has little impact overall on Anglo-Australian identity, thereby creating 'multiculturalism without migrants' (ibid.: 118; see also Flowers and Swan 2015b). There is a danger in these accounts of appropriation, however, that the agency of the other is overlooked and migrant groups are represented as rather passive producers of ethnic food (Cook, Crang and Thorpe 1999) or colluders in the reproduction of stereotypes (Hage 1997). Cook et al. stress the importance of recognizing the differentiations taking place at the point of consumption, as individuals relate to 'others' in myriad ways and through multiple social imaginaries that blur the oft-assumed dichotomies between us and them. A similar point of variation and dynamism is also found in Heldke (2003), who reflects on how 'adventurous eating' has the potential to be an anti-colonial project of social interaction and understanding despite the preponderance of narcissism found in gastro-tourism (see also Hage 1997). As Molz concludes, 'Culinary tourists are eating the Other ... but they are also eating the differences between various Others' (2007: 79).

So, how do these discussions of multiculturalism and eating the other illuminate the ways in which matter and meaning are drawn together and mediated through the body? Molz interrogates the embodied experiences of travellers and demonstrates how they are 'playing with cultural and bodily boundaries' (2007: 85) by eating unfamiliar food and taking corporeal risks. It is in these very embodied encounters, which are more focused on exploring the boundaries of the self than experiencing the culture of others, that differences are produced, contested and upheld. Notions of otherness, then, are not only experienced, but are also created through the body as alien foods are viscerally tested, tasted and ingested – a process that, dialectically, enables an embodied performance of the self as cosmopolitan. Molz thereby shows us the ways in which the material properties of food are experienced through the body and indicates how this embodied encounter mediates the relationship between self and other: as in the examples of Campbell's Iraq and my Ecuadorian ethnography, among others, the eating body literally becomes the site through which other peoples, through their food, are defined, distanced, brought closer, incorporated, and appropriated into the self. Eating, then, becomes a critical encounter through which the self in relation to others is materially and symbolically made. To disregard the embodied practice of eating is to disregard the moment when such relations are made manifest.

Concluding remarks

Eating in unfamiliar and exogenous environments and encountering new foods opens up possibilities and risks, produces and blurs differences, creates proximities and distances, and reasserts, erodes and redraws culinary boundaries. Eating as a migrant is a deeply ambivalent experience; connections to home can be re-established through the sharing of substances across geographical distance, but a threat of potential loss persists that can, in part, be countered by food. Eating away from home can incorporate and appropriate 'the other', but the dynamic is not unidirectional and the self can just as easily be absorbed into 'the other's' world. A dynamic and relational picture of eating thus emerges, in which bodily and gustatory boundaries are in a constant process of being made and remade through encounters with familiar and foreign foods and the bodies of others. A further factor in this process is place, both real and imagined, as migrants look to anchor themselves amid the flux and flow. This anchoring is not, however, as Mankekar (2002) shows, always harmonious and tensions can emerge as migrants work to negotiate and carve out their eating identities and spaces.

The material encounters among migrants' bodies, food, place, and the bodies of 'others' produce and are informed by social relationships, political dynamics and cultural meanings. Throughout this chapter I have looked to stress the import of the embodied and sensory experience of eating in a migrant context, and interrogate the ways that eating is mediated through visceral encounters and bio-authorial engagements. This focus on eating, I hope to have shown, offers a deeper insight into the ways that materialities and meanings are drawn together and interplay in and through bodies, and I call for greater attention to be paid to the body, affects and feelings in discussions of migrant eating practices. Doing so would help us better understand the very real lived experience of being and eating as a migrant from their own subject position, which can only enhance and extend more established arguments and approaches that tend to lean towards the symbolic meanings of food. Bodies, I contend, are critical to understanding migrants' food lives. Moreover, migratory contexts number some of the most productive sites through which to explore questions of bodily experience, as such experiences are, following Serematakis (1994), heightened when bodies are dislocated and subjected to greater transgressions than they would be 'at home'. The eating body, then, is a critical mediating site through which sameness and otherness are produced, and agency is enacted and distributed, across networks of relatedness that both coalesce around place and stretch across space.

Chapter 4

Eating heritage foods: Proximate and distanced bodies

Introduction

In the previous chapters, I have introduced the argument that eating enacts relations between bodies, which are both embedded in place (Chapter 2) and distributed across space (Chapter 3). I have drawn attention, moreover, to the ways in which eating can disrupt and rupture relations, and create otherness and distinction, just as much as it can blur boundaries and produce cohesion and sameness. In this chapter, I extend these discussions by interrogating the nexus of bodies, food and knowledge in the context of local food festivals, food heritage and nationalized food. I thus continue to explore the ways in which eating can root bodies to places and construct both real and imagined relations by creating affinities between bodies.

These processes, however, are not entirely enacted by the self, but are also shaped by local and national agents and institutions, which work to form associations between particular foods and places. Events such as food fairs and festivals, as well as engagements with food valued as heritage or labelled as local, regional or national, can be seen as bio-authorial encounters, and in what follows I examine how the cultural lessons imbued in such encounters are both upheld and challenged. As such, I tease out how matter, bodies and knowledge intersect to elucidate how seemingly mutual and politically benign celebrations of eating 'our food' work to establish social proximity and distance, enable bio-authority to be both exercised and contested, and provide a mechanism through which individual eaters can politically align and connect to places and the bodies within them. I thereby wish to argue, drawing on the arguments of shared substance laid out in the previous chapters, that celebrating local foods acts as a bio-authorial mechanism through which local, regional or national citizenship is enacted through the making of coterminous bodies.

Some of the ethnographic contexts I discuss, such as the Jima Health Fair, are politically designed to be pedagogical, whereas others have 'lessons' that are far more implicit and subtle. Nonetheless, while aims and intentions may differ considerably and events and discourses vary dramatically, similar dynamics can be discerned. The shared material ingestion of 'our food' and the mutual co-production of kinned bodies can also obfuscate the construction of otherness, and I consider the ways in which 'our food' can alienate as much as it can include and cohere. This valorization of particular foods further constructs particular social actors as bio-authorities and I draw attention to the implicit, sometimes incidental, ways in which specific social actors, for example food festival organizers, create their authority about a food, as well as illuminating the politics that lie behind, and often motivate, seemingly benign encounters such as festivals and cookbooks.

I further explore how such encounters simultaneously charge and bound the vitalism of foods by situating them within a broader assemblage of cultural meaning. These attempts to produce sameness – and difference – not only encourages the local community to ingest certain foods, but does so by objectifying and reifying such foods to the extent that they start to stand for or 'flag' (Cusack 2000) the community. In this sense the vitalism of the foods being iconized is bound by the culturally accepted meanings laid out by key bio-authorities, such as festival organizers and state actors. Food festivals and nationalized artefacts, then, discursively (re)charge the matter of selected foods with meaning and seek 'buy-in' to that meaning from the community – a process that enables the forging of the seeming hegemonic symbolism of a foodstuff as 'our heritage' or 'our food'. I further stress the dialectic role affect and bodily interactions play in producing meaning, both in terms of the 'buzz' (cf Coles 2013b) created at events, such as food festivals, and the 'affective background' that each eating body brings to each food encounter. This helps illuminate the agency of individual eaters in mediating the meaning and matter being consumed, as well as broadening our understanding of what eating is and does.

Local food festivals: Producing sameness and difference

It was the Health Fair in the village of Jima. While ostensibly organized as a public health initiative, the event also afforded the opportunity to celebrate the region's local food heritage: Villagers were encouraged to set up impromptu stalls selling *comida típica* (defined as local typical food)[1] and the organizers hosted a cookery competition that centred on the local delicacies of cuy and *chicha* (maize beer). As the community members congregated around the primary school playground for the judging of the contest, the head teacher of the secondary school, who was also the chair of the Tourist Foundation that organized the fair, gave a brief history lesson:[2]

> These are our traditional foods. The Incas were here, but not for very long. Before the area – all of Sígsig canton – was Cañari, and it is our Cañari traditions and Cañari foods that live on today. The *mestizo* [mixed race] town of Jima has Cañari origins and traditions, and this gives us our culture. (Abbots 2014a: 91)

He then continued to explain that it was crucial that Jimeños continue to prepare and eat 'our traditional foods', especially as 'they' were under 'threat' from exogenous forces, such as fast food chains and '(North) American culture'. Measures to counteract such 'threats' included the Tourist Foundation banning foods such as hamburgers, beer and fries at the fair.[3] The reason for this prohibition, according to one of my participants, was that they 'not good for you, for your body'. She also pointed out, however, that they were also 'foods that aren't from here – they're from the USA' (Abbots 2015a: 78). In contrast, the foods celebrated, while not necessarily being normatively healthier by nutritional measures, were 'from here'. They were also foods, as I have elucidated in reference to cuy in previous chapters, which are socially and culturally potent. It is not just the foods that are under threat, then, but also Jimeño bodies, culture and community – the erosion of 'traditional' food practices is a metaphor here for the wider societal effects of globalization and social change.

As this brief vignette suggests, the valorization and representation of certain foods as cultural heritage are political acts. As with any representation of a community's past, traditions or cultural practices – culinary or otherwise – a process of arbitrary selection, imagination and (re)invention occurs in which some aspects are brought to the fore and others receded (Bond and Gillam 1994; Hobsbawn and Ranger 1983; Lowenthal 1985). As Lowenthal (ibid.) writes, this is not a benign process but one rife with power dynamics as the past is shaped according to motives in the present. Labelled as 'heritage', selected aspects of the past are consequently imbued with economic, social and cultural value. In arguing that 'interaction with heritage continually alters its nature and context' (1985: 263), Lowenthal presents us with a mutable and socially constructed model of history, which we see illustrated in Jima by the celebration of cuy and *chicha*. On one hand, these seem rather obvious and, dare I say, natural choices, given the historical and social import of the dishes (Abbots 2011; Archetti 1997; Bourque 2001; Morales 1995; Weismantel 1988). But they are not the only foods produced in the region nor are they as commonly ingested as others, many of which were introduced by Spanish colonialism. Cuy and maize-based comestibles are, nevertheless, the core indigenous, pre-Hispanic foods in Jima: Cuy is valued for its particular social meaning and peasant connotations, and corn celebrated in oral history that refers to the village taking its name from the corn variety, *zhima*. Yet an alternative oral history circulates that emphasizes how zhima derives from Shuar people (a neighbouring Amazonian group) and is a term for chilli peppers. It is almost inconceivable, however, to imagine chilli peppers being celebrated in the same way as cuy or chicha in this context, in part because they are rarely eaten (except as the condiment, *aji*), but also because the Shuar origins of the village are highly disputed, and highland Jimeños have a tendency 'to other' and derogate lowland Shuar people as less cultured and more animalistic 'Indians'.

This selective interpretation of the past is highlighted in the lesson given at the Jima Health Fair. Cuy is Cañari and it is 'Cañari foods that live on today'; not Shuar, which arguably predates Cañari (Aguilar Vásquez 1944), not Incan, which colonized the Cañari population (Fock 1981; Garcilaso de la Vega 1966), and not Spanish despite the village being mixed-race. We thus see a somewhat discriminatory, and temporally contingent, representation of 'traditional foods' at the Jima Health Fair that can be partly explained by recognizing the political agenda of promoting the region's precolonized highland origins.[4] As Cusack states 'cuisines, whether national, regional or "ethnic," should not be considered as neutral, innocent concoctions' but are instead 'clearly products of dominant ideologies and related power structures' (2000: 207).

The relationship between eating particular foods and the (re)production of regional belonging has been long established, particularly through the lens of ethnicity and migrant eating practices, as I discussed in the previous chapter. Yet the cultural performances that celebrate, and help define, foods as particularly salient to a locale, and the bio-authorial relations embedded within such events, have received significantly less attention. An exception to this is an emergent body of literature that attends to the reification of foods as heritage, although the dominant themes in this field coalesce around the institutionalized elements of heritagization, such as inventories of culinary heritage (cf. Bessiere 1998) and legislative demarcations, such as AOC, PDO and Geographical Indication (GI) (cf Barham 2003; Bowen and Zapata 2009, Gade 2004, Parasecoli and Tasaki 2011; see also West 2013 and 2016 for an overview). This work, in line with broader debates on the 'heritage industry' (cf. Hewison 1987; Lowenthal 1985), does nevertheless point to the myriad, often conflicting, actors and viewpoints involved in such politicized processes. Despite this, detailed ethnographic accounts of the food festivals that form part of 'food patrimony' (West 2016: 417) and discussions of the ways they are subjectively experienced and constructed remain rather scant, with the literature tending to frame festival accounts through the rubric of gastro-tourism and the development of the rural economy (West 2016; see, for example, Boniface 2003; Hall et al. 2003; Long 2004). Consequently, while commentators have explored how particular groups self-identify and relate (or not) to others through the establishment and maintenance of 'gustatory boundaries' (Ray 2004) and, in some contexts, have interrogated the political relations that result in specific foods being identified as 'our food', the role that food festivals, as affective bio-authorial encounters, play in creating such dynamics and forging belongings has often been glossed over.

Events that can be loosely defined under the umbrella of food festivals vary significantly in form and ideological background, from the small informal affairs like the Jima Health Fair to large-scale enterprises, such as the Gilroy Garlic Festival in California, which attracted some 132,000 visitors in 2003 (Adema 2009: 30). Some festivals develop from an already cultural salient food, often relating to particular ethnic group, whereas others are 'rationally constructed' (Lewis 1997: 73), in that they attempt to link a particular foodstuff to a locale, often for commercial benefit. Events in this latter category include Stockton's (California, USA) annual celebration of asparagus (see Lewis 1997) and Gilroy's Garlic Festival (see Adema 2009). Although varied in form, what links the differences in motivation, background, size, and scale of festivals is the extent to which they involve an element of extraction and/or invention of an aspect of a foodscape, in either the past or present, and seek to value it as community heritage with the intention, however implied, to create a sense of cohesion between people, place and food. As Adema states,

> Community festivals continue to be a metaphor for and an articulation of the host-locale's collective identity, or, rather, the identity that image makers and festival organizers hope to affirm among residents and have associated with the locale for visitors. (2009: 32)

This process of community-making is ethnographically explored in Lewis' (1997) essay on Stockton's asparagus festival in which he demonstrates that, in selecting an 'ethnically and culturally neutral food' (ibid.: 75), the promoters could include all the groups living in a socially diverse community in a bid to foster social cohesion and a spirit of collectivity. Asparagus, according to Lewis, provided an 'excuse' (ibid.: 76) to rationally construct a new tradition that helped put Stockton 'on the map' and reap the consequent economic rewards. The choice of food – and even the fact that the object selected is a food – appears somewhat incidental, defined by its neutrality more than its cultural significance. In Gilroy, garlic is more embedded in the local economy, but, as Adema (2009) argues, this makes its selection no less political. Instead, she points out that its iconization is rooted in the locale's agrarian past, or more accurately the romanticization of this past. As such, the cultural celebration of garlic facilitates the construction of a communal identity; it acts as an 'affirmative event' that can 'embody a hyper-awareness of communal life or of an idealized cohesion' (ibid.: 32–3). Food festivals, then, can 'transcend social, religious, and cultural differences that might otherwise be divisive within a locality' (Adema ibid.: 147).

To present food festivals as inherently inclusive would, however, be misleading. Although scholars stress the cohesive capacity of food festivals, there are sufficient pointers in the ethnographic data to suggest some groups and individuals are alienated from the process, whether they are the Filipino asparagus pickers noted in Lewis' footnote, Gilroy's migrant garlic pickers, or the Bergamo salami aficionados discussed by Cavanagh (2007). Cavanagh explores consumers' ambivalence as a salami that was once deeply embedded in small-scale production and the domestic sphere, and hence laden with sociality, is extracted and valued as heritage, commodified, and potentially regulated under GI protections. As the sausage becomes increasingly celebrated as a community icon, as typified in an annual 'Festival of Our Salami', Cavanagh points out that the product becomes less 'our salami' (salame nostrano), as it is appropriated by local political actors and larger-scale producers. This perspective is echoed in West and Domingos (2013), who in their account of Serpa cheese in Portugal elucidate the ways in which Serpa producers, many of whom have shifted to a less risky and more modern form of production, were effectively excluded from a Slow Food Presidia that values 'traditional' production processes. Social and historical inequities are thus glossed over as an elite group of actors sought to reify the cheese in a historical moment that ironically rendered the product and its producers ahistorical.

The politics of heritage are not, however, solely a top-down dynamic. As Samuel (2012) argues, heritage, and the emergence of a heritage industry, can make the past more democratic and open up spaces for social change. This theme is picked up by Avieli (2005) in his analysis of the feasts that are a defining feature of Chinese community festivals in Hoi An, Vietnam. He stresses that the dishes consumed transcended regionalism and ethnic identities, and were identified as pan-Chinese – similarity was thus emphasized over difference. This is all the more surprising as each festival commemorates the founding of individual communities and therefore appears, at first glance, to be steeped in regionalism and celebratory of ties to specific Chinese locales. Yet Avieli shows us that festive food in this context helps facilitate the forging of new Chinese-Hoianese identities and spaces of belonging, and, although he stresses that such culinary encounters should not be regarded as a form of conscious counter-hegemonic conspiracy, he does indicate that the freedom afforded to the feasts in an otherwise monitored environment enables a 'culinary subversiveness' (ibid.: 291).

Avieli tells us that food, in part due to its seeming mundane nature, can open up spaces for contestation just as much as Adema and Lewis show it can provide an insidious mechanism for the affirmations of dominant political ideologies. As the ethnography demonstrates, the selection of a particular food to be reified and valued as a marker of cultural identity is not a politically benign process, but one that is motivated by multiple factors including community building, economic development, regionalism and a desire to protect and preserve the past. Some elements of a culinary past and present are deemed worthy of protection more than others and, as such, there is a need to critically question why some foods are chosen over other possibilities, which social groups are included in these celebratory processes and which are alienated, and who has the cultural authority to make such valorizations and distinctions. The extent to which food festivals enable cohesion and encourage difference seems to be as variable as the festivals themselves, but what does emerge from this literature is the prevailing argument that festivals imbue certain foods with a cultural significance. They also point, moreover, to the ways this process is socially mediated.

Mediating affect: The materialities of festivals

Food festivals are not solely about the presentation of a chosen food's cultural heritage through the educational medium of history lessons, like those that took place in Jima's Health Fair. Even the smallest of events incorporate a number of food performances, such as cooking competitions and demonstrations, while the larger ones may include eating contests and musical interludes. All of these activities arguably not only help embed the food being celebrated in cultural traditions – both established and newly invented – but also contribute to an affective background that helps 'charge' the foodstuff with a vitality and enhance the bio-authorial effect of the festival. I argue that the wider material environment of a food festival, especially the embodied interactions that take place, therefore need to be taken into account. In short, we need to think about the materialities of a food festival as subjectively experienced by a participant – or eater – and not just its political economy, although these macro-dynamics remain a critical consideration through which to better understand the experiential. In turn, this opens up definitions of what it means to 'eat' food.

The wider sensorial experiences of food festivals have tended to be overlooked in analysis, despite the tantalizing ethnographic hints contained in some accounts. Cavanagh, for example, tells us of the costumes, dancing and strolling musicians that accompany the taste tests, salami-making competitions and food stalls in Bergamo, and she evocatively presents an energetic encounter in which 'hundreds of local people of all types filled the piazza and jostled for places along the long tables set up for the occasion, eating, drinking and socializing' (2007: 157). Similarly, Adema writes of the 'positive energy' and 'hive of activity' (2009: 24–5) generated by Gilroy's Garlic Festival that has grown over the years to include on-site stores for festival merchandise, arts and crafts areas, a children's area and multiple stages, as well as strolling musicians, bands and other performers. This is in addition to beauty queen and baby pageants and parade floats. At the centre of Gilroy's festivities is 'Gourmet Alley', where chefs, noted for their dramatic cookery displays, produce an array of garlic-infused foods over flaming propane burners and grills. The resulting carnivalesque effect, Adema suggests, creates a full sensory experience laden with the heavy odour of garlic.

Festivals are thereby lived embodied experiences in which festivalgoers not only cerebrally learn about a foodstuff, but also physically interact with it or view others doing so. They ingest the food through a variety of different dishes, feel it, transform it, hear songs about it, and watch it being performed – all within a material environment that unquestionably celebrates it. These materialities are not benign, but can instead be understood as a mediating process through which the foodstuff is iconized and imbued with symbolic meaning. Much like Mankekar's (2002) Indian grocery store discussed in the previous chapter, festivals can be regarded as an assemblage of multiple objects, symbols and bodies. Adema refers to this assemblage as the 'festival frame' that serves to direct participants' experience and conveys the message that is to be taken from the event. The medium thus shapes the meaning. Compounding this is the positive and playful affective energy found within the festival, which, she argues, helps affirm the mediated message the celebrated foodstuff carries. Festivalgoers at Gilroy, then, 'not only partake in the festive fun, they literally and ideologically consume the Gilroy-garlic association' (ibid.: 33). This theme is also found in Coles's (2013b) discussion of the 'buzz' of Borough Market in London.

While not a festival in its strictest term – but rather an artisan food market – Coles indicates the ways in which a fully sensory experience is produced 'materially, socially, discursively and affectively' (ibid.: 520) through the use of semiotic devices, such as stall displays, signs and images that key the consumer into experiencing both the market and its foods in a certain manner. He writes:

> As people, things and ideas come together in place, Borough Market buzzes, and its buzz is addictive. Its buzz attracts more and more of these elements and reaches a self-sustaining critical mass. It becomes something to participate in, an affective experience. (ibid.: 517)

Coles's account, alongside Adema's observations, highlights how the intangible feeling of a festival, while subjective, is orchestrated by the tangible environment and symbolic messages they convey. Within my framing, these 'buzzy' materialities and embodied interactions, which dialectically reproduce and sustain each other, charge the food being celebrated and marketed with a vitality that appears to give it an agentic capacity. But it also can be seen to limit – or bind – a food's vitalism by situating it within a specific cultural, ideological and material assemblage that frames and works to direct a festivalgoer's visceral experience. Matter, meaning and affect are thus drawn together to produce a powerful engagement within the participant's body.

Affect, then, comes to the fore and I wish to suggest that it is through affect that biopolitics and vitalism meet in the subjective depths of the eating body and charge a food with a cultural efficacy. In short, affect primes the body to accept (or not) the lessons and meanings conveyed in the bio-authorial encounters of food festivals, and those lessons are all the more powerful because they are experienced in and through the body, often insidiously. Affect, as Thrift (2004) charts, has multiple interpretations and definitions (see also Gregg and Seigworth 2010), and it is not my intention here to explore the myriad ways in which affect can be defined. There are, however, two key and interrelated aspects of affect, as identified by Thrift, that dovetail into the ways I approach processes of mediation and knowledge making – affect as embodied practices that express the ways individuals experience and respond to the world, and the Spinozist and Deleuzian attention to networks and interactions. Both elements challenge Cartesian dualism in that thinking and doing are understood to occur simultaneously. Knowing, therefore, emerges from and concomitantly with embodied encounters, although the forms this takes are shaped by the social and affective backdrop through which individuals respond to the encounter. Affects may be indefinite and unpredictable, but an individual is also disposed to be affected by an encounter in a certain manner. In turn, affect 'structures encounters so that bodies are disposed for action in a particular way' (Thrift 2004: 62). Thus affects 'occur in an encounter between manifold beings, and the outcome of each encounter depends upon what forms of composition these beings are able to enter into' (Thrift 2004: 62). While hypothetically infinite, in the reality of lived experience there are only so many possibilities. Translated to a food festival context, this means that bodies are orientated to *feel* the food and the festival in a certain way through its framing.

The point of 'manifold beings' is of import here as it emphasizes that, in the Spinozist tradition, any human and non-human entity can cause affect. As Bennett confirms, 'Organic and inorganic bodies, natural and cultural objects ... are all affective' (2010: xii). She is particularly interested in the agentic capacity of the non-human – of matter – to cause affect, contending that it emerges not just from transformative interactions, but from the matter itself. For Bennett, then, affect is materiality (ibid.: xiii), which she demonstrates by referring to the moods and emotions affected by omega-3 fatty acids. Yet she, as I discussed in Chapter 1, treats this vitality – the capacity to cause affect – as somehow inherent in matter instead of being made to matter, and thereby bypasses the political dynamics that inform the creation of affect. This point is addressed by Rose (2001, 2007), who considers biopolitical enmeshments with affect by pointing to the ways in which pastoral power is enacted by mobilizing affect, concluding that such 'encounters entail intense bidirectional affective entanglements between all parties to the encounter, and indeed generate multiple "virtual" entanglements with parties not present' (2010: 10). Put somewhat crudely, for Bennett materiality is affect whereas for Rose, biopolitics is affect. Biopolitics and materiality are thereby drawn into concert through affect.

Rose brings the political aspect of affect to the fore, as does Thrift (2004) who points to the propensity for affect to be engineered and manipulated for political purposes, as we can see by the 'buzz' (cf Coles 2013b) created at food festivals and markets to promote consumption of a selected foodstuff. As such, politics is practised through affect. This line of thinking is extended by Anderson who emphasizes the intensification and new forms of biopower that 'work though affect' and traces the ways affective relations become the 'object-targets' for discipline (2011: 28). Of particular interest here is his notion of 'affective condition', meaning the emotive backdrop that informs the ways individuals encounter the actors and agencies that look to manipulate affect: a concept that relates to my use of 'affective background' introduced in earlier chapters. Applying and developing this to food festivals indicates how existing engagements with, knowledges of and feelings around the iconized food inform the ways that such bio-authorial encounters are received. Festivalgoers thus arrive with their own 'affective background', based on their previous subjective experiences of a food among other memories, and this interplays with the affective framing that festival organizers create to co-produce new meanings and experiences. Following Foucault's (1980) model of productive power, possibilities for contestation and spaces for life to escape are thus opened up (cf Anderson 2011; Caldwell 2007; Sedgewick 2003). Agency is thereby distributed across the organizers, participants and the material environment of festivals, although the organizers can be seen to be orchestrating the vitality of matter to 'object-target' (Anderson 2011) the embodied experience, and thereby the knowledge experience (cf Thrift 2004), of participants.

In essence, building from Anderson points to the politicized ways in which affective backgrounds are both mediated by and mediate food-body knowledges and how, consequently, food assemblages are made and unmade through embodied bio-authorial encounters. Layering Bennett's argument and critiques onto this, together with a recognition of distributed agency, further stresses the import of matter and the non-human mediating bodies that sit within these assemblages. But this does not mean that matter is inherently vital, as Bennett argues. Or even that they are drawn together organically. As, however, fluid and fleeting assemblages are (cf Anderson et al. 2012), ethnographies of food festivals show us that the material and sensorial assemblages of the food being celebrated are constructed as a 'frame' (Adema 2009) that looks to direct the festivalgoer's experience. Multiple things – whether they are strolling musicians, flaming grills and history lessons – are brought together by certain people with the aim of achieving a certain objective. These are not incidental 'coming-togethers' but are instead politically constructed framings that work to charge the foods and objects presented, through their mutual association, with symbolic and political meaning. These orchestrated framings further look to powerfully convey the cultural and social lesson of the iconized food by attempting to create a desired affective experience in the festivalgoer. The wild card here, of course, is that a festivalgoer's experience cannot be fully predicted, as each arrives at a festival with their own 'affective condition' (cf Anderson 2011) through which they engage with the frame presented by the organizers. In sum, the vitality of the festival food is bounded by, and takes meaning from, a mediated assemblage laden with political dynamics.

Nonetheless, the dynamic is not unidirectional, and the bio-authorial encounter of a food festival opens up possible spaces to disrupt and contest the discourses of cultural authorities, as not only does life escape (cf Foucault 1980; Sedgewick 2003) in the form of the unpredictable nature of the interplays between a festivalgoer's affective backdrop and the organizer's framing, but the meaning of the framing itself can be usurped through changes in its matter. To illustrate this, I return to the Jima Health Fair.

Sonia was one of the villagers who opened a 'pop-up' food stall during the fair and she decided to sell cuy with all the trimmings. At first glance, her stall appeared to uphold the normative message of the Tourist Foundation; she promoted it with a banner that stated '*Comida Típica*: Come and Taste Delicious CUY From The Area' and her sister Felicia's sales pitch drew attention to how the localness of the meat could be identified in its taste. Felicia proclaimed: 'We have delicious local cuy here, fed on local grass. Our cuy is the healthiest, most natural and the tastiest. It's fed on local grass for a delicious flavour' (Abbots 2014a: 92). Yet Sonia also subtly shifted the representation of cuy as traditional by bringing new elements into the food's assemblage. The day before the fair, her kitchen and backyard were hives of activity, as approximately fifteen cuyes were slaughtered and plucked following the same time-consuming process as when the meat is eaten at home (as detailed in Chapter 2). A significant difference, however, was that she made use of hired domestic helpers who are normally, due to the notions of intimacy inherent in the meat, kept at a distance. As the morning of the Health Fair dawned, tarpaulins and tents, table and chairs, a freestanding four-ring gas hob and canister, plates, cups and cutlery, kitchen knives and chopping boards, and saucepans and cooking pots were all piled into the back of a *caminoneta* (truck), alongside the raw meat and uncooked potatoes and vegetables. During this activity, a mechanical spit-roasting machine, which I had never seen before despite living with Sonia and enjoying many a home-cooked cuy dinner with her household, was 'unearthed'. This subsequently took pride of place at the front of Sonia's stall, which was sandwiched between those of two other villagers, Anita and Susana, both of whom were selling the corn-based 'traditional' snacks of *humitas* and *quimbolitos*. And like Sonia's, these stalls – which in their totality physically dominated one side of the fair – boasted an array of gleaming kitchen equipment and waged domestic workers.

Throughout our discussions, Sonia and her friends classified both their kitchenalia and domestics as symbols of their modernity, economic capital and social mobility, and further associated them with 'foreign' locations such as the urban centre (Abbots 2012b). Their ready display suggests the women appropriated the Health Fair for their own political purposes; by importing modern objects, they communicated their own message that ran counter to that of the Tourist Foundation. Instead of the perpetual reproduction of the cultural continuities and timelessness conveyed by the public history lesson, there was change, disruption and progression. And while the foodstuffs themselves appeared, at first glance, not be materially different from those Cañari dishes valued in the official discourse, the assemblages through which they were produced and performed – domestic labourers, mechanical spit-roasts, gas hobs and gleaming saucepans – were very different to the timeless food practices the fair was attempting to celebrate. 'Not from here' foods such as hamburgers and fries may have been banned, but other objects 'not from here' were stealthily introduced.

I wish to contend that this changing of the assemblage shifted the meaning of the food. Sonia's cuy, while seemingly made of the same matter as traditional cuy, was framed as a hybrid of tradition and modernity, localness and exogenous influences, and continuity and change. The stalls set up by the women are not establishing and reinforcing boundaries between 'our food' and that of 'others'. On the contrary, the women drew 'the other', into the space of local tradition, and in so doing not only created an alternative narrative for the dish, but also, in changing its meaning, changed its substance. They thus offered festivalgoers the potential to ingest a type of substance other than that promoted by the Tourist Foundation, one which was constituted from otherness and modernity as well as sameness and continuity. New forms of food knowledges were thereby produced that potentially disturbed the cultural authority of the fair's organizers.

This shift in meaning was further compounded by the manner in which Sonia distanced her body from the intimacies of the meat by introducing waged labour into its production. The introduction of monied relations, both in commodifying the meat and using waged labour to produce it can, drawing on Marx (1995), be regarded as a process of alienation in which Sonia is purposefully taking measures to distance her own bodily engagements from the fruits of her labour – a practice that enables her to minimize intimacy and create a fetishized product that can be sold to those with whom she does not have established social relations. The meat is constructed as a less intimate food than that discussed in Chapter 2. This is not to argue that, in being a commoditized, marketable object, the dish is no longer embedded in social relations – to do so would counter well-established substantivist conclusions about the moral economy (Carsten 1989; Parry and Bloch 1989) – but instead highlight that it is constructed as such by Sonia's actions. The introduction of distancing mechanisms – the modern assemblage, waged labour and monetary exchange – helps the producer and eater mutually produce social distance from the other. This is not to state, of course, that these two bodies are not drawn into networks of relatedness, together with those of the other human and non-human bodies involved in the meat's production. Instead, I am suggesting they are constructed as less social from the perspectives of those involved. In so doing, I stress the subtle yet critical distinction between an analytical understanding of the para-social relations made and unmade through eating, and individual affective experiences and understandings.

Inscribing citizenship: Coterminous bodies and shared substance

I have thus far indicated how important bodies are to understanding food festivals through my discussion of affect and the senses and, in framing food festivals as bio-authorial encounters, have sought to demonstrate how cultural lessons about food are transmitted by, in and through bodies. I have also pointed to the ways food festivals can construct social cohesion and community spirit. I now want to draw these two threads together and consider how sameness and difference are constructed through eating and the body, as well as introduce ways in which eating can enmesh bodies to those of others and root them to place. I therefore return to questions of shared substance and relatedness.

Eating is curiously absent in the food festival literature. Ethnographies detail which foods are cooked, how they are transformed into various dishes and how much food is consumed, in addition to giving accounts of the smells, noises and sights. These multiple embodied and affective moments can all be seen as aspects of eating but, despite representations of these multisensory encounters, we rarely get a sense of festivalgoers' experiences of tasting, swallowing, ingesting and digesting the food being celebrated. Echoing much work in interdisciplinary food studies, so much attention – with good reason – has been centred on which foods are valued and why, and the political and economic processes and consequences of these selections. Scholarship has tended to stop at the festival stall instead of following the food into the eating body. The critical role that eating plays is nonetheless implied. In reference to Bergamo salami, Cavanagh states that 'consuming this salami would equate with consuming a little bit of that culture and history' (2007: 159), and Adema writes that 'the production and consumption of communal identities come together in the symbolic consumption and the literal consumption of iconic foods' (2009: 19). It is on these foundational hints that I look to build and, in order to do so, I turn to work on citizenship and belonging in a national context.

Earle (2012) explores the relationship between food, bodies and colonialism in the Americas in the period 1492–1700, and demonstrates that diet was underpinned by and produced sameness and difference between Spaniards and Amerindians. European foods were essential, she argues, for keeping the colonizers Spanish and also for drawing the indigenous population into the colonial centre by making them more civilized. This civilizing process was, in part, performed through cultural practices, such as dress and language, but was also enacted through a corporeal transformation. Earle explains that Spaniards understood that Amerindian bodies would become European if they were to ingest European foods. Hispanicization and the associated notions of civilization and humanness were thereby to be produced by changes in diet. She states: 'Amerindians would not merely becomes more civilized but would actually become more like the Spanish were they to eat their foods' (ibid.: 165). The converse is also the case, and there was a concurrent 'danger' that the colonizers would become less Spanish should they eat the foods of the New World.

Corporeal transformation thus became entangled with cultural and spiritual acculturation. Earle also points out, however, that while Spanish colonialism had the objective of Hispanicizing the indigenous populations in order to encourage their acquiescence to colonial hierarchies, this created tension as Amerindian bodies could not be too close to Spanish bodies: corporeal and social distance had to be maintained. The eating of particular foods, then, became a route for establishing both proximity and distance because it produced bodies that were both same and different. Earle concludes, 'Food helped make them who they were in terms of both their character and their very corporeality' (ibid.: 2); it 'helped *create* the bodily differences that underpinned the European categories of Spaniard and Indian. Spanish bodies differed from indigenous bodies because the Spanish diet differed from the Amerindian diet' (ibid.: 5, original emphasis).

Earle demonstrates how bodies and eating practices became sites in which colonial power relations were played out, and in so doing also highlights that bodies, in this context, were understood to be mutable. The model of humoral bodies invoked by the Spanish is, on one hand, culturally and historically contingent, but it is also not that far removed in essence from the model of the eating body I am working with here (as detailed in Chapter 1). Moreover, while she does not frame her analysis in terms of vitalism and shared substance, her work can be read through this lens. Spanish food in this context had the vitality of matter to transform Amerindian bodies into Spanish bodies, and the sharing of Spanish substance produced corporeal and cultural sameness between the colonizers and the indigenous population to such an extent that other measures had to be taken to re-establish distance. As Earle states, 'The adoption of a European diet and European practices of bodily maintenance would transform the indigenous body itself' (ibid.: 165).

Through this lens, we can see the import of promoting cuy over hamburgers in Jima. In order for regional belonging to be inscribed, for bodies to be made

Jimeño, Jimeño foods must be eaten. Encouraging the eating of cuy at the Health Fair can be seen as an attempt not only to make local bodies in a particular mould, but also to do so in a way that creates sameness through the production of coterminous bodies united through shared substance. In providing specific knowledges about foods 'from here', the fair's organizers worked to construct, reinforce and maintain the boundaries of the community by repelling the 'dangerous' food 'from there'. Following Douglas' (2002) body as a metaphor for society model, repelling polluting exogenous foods from individual bodies maintains the purity of the social body. The boundaries of the individual and social body are thus concomitantly reasserted, and done so in a manner that creates distinctions between a cohesive 'us' – with the same bodies made from the same local substance – and an 'other' who resides on the other side of the 'gustatory boundary' (Ray 2004). The extent to which this 'us', in lived experience, is as cohesive as it appears is subject to question, especially once we acknowledge that the seemingly same food can continually shift in matter and meaning, as Sonia's reformulation of cuy at the fair indicates.

Further distinctions emerge when we consider that it is not uncommon for those promoting the consumption of a certain dish to refrain from consuming it themselves, as has been shown in the case of cuy and the middle classes in Ecuador (Abbots 2011, 2012a; Bourque 2001; Weismantel 1988). This social distancing from 'our food' by key bio-authorities can, as discussed briefly in previous chapters, place the burden of upholding food traditions and of creating the matter of food in a particular form onto specific social actors – often those from the lower rural classes, women, and those from specific ethnic groups. Taking the semipermeability of both the individual and social body into consideration (Douglas 2002), a picture emerges in which particular groups within a community are required to perform the labour of policing the boundaries. There is a subtle difference here in the labour of biopedagogy (Harwood 2009; Wright 2009; see also Flowers and Swan 2015a). Teaching others what to eat by giving history lessons, compiling a cookbook or organizing a food festival is arguably valued differently from the growing, preparing and feeding of iconized foods. Nevertheless, both types of labour charge matter with vitalism as well as limiting it by defining the boundaries of a food's assemblage, although the social value placed on these different forms of labour and the extent to which it equates to political agency and authority differ.

The sameness implied by 'our food', and those who produce and define it, can therefore be illusory and warrants critical unpacking in each specific ethnographic context. In sum, questions need to be asked as to which members of a community are made as 'kinned bodies' by eating the same matter and which remove themselves, or are removed, from the process by not eating it. Answers to such questions could bring fresh insights into the ways in which food festivals include and alienate specific social actors. This gives rise to further questions about the politics lying behind which group or individual identifies and selects 'our food' and frames its assemblages, and who plays the role of upholding and performing 'our food'. It cannot be assumed that these are the same individuals or groups, and identifying the political dynamic between them can give further insight into the making of bio-authority. This further highlights the import of distinguishing discourse and practice by examining the subjective and multiple forms eating an iconized food can take.

Returning to and extending the making of coterminous bodies in Jima, it also becomes apparent that eating cuy produces a network of relatedness between multiple bodies and place. I have indicated in Chapter 2, which is further supported by Felicia's sales pitch, that this process occurs, in part, because the meat has material qualities that come from the soil and climate in which it is produced; the meat is Jimeño because the grass the cuy has eaten comes from Jima. Eating the meat is therefore ingesting the food the animal has consumed. The notion of kinned bodies, then, does not exclusively relate to human bodies, but also those of animals and microorganisms. This interplay between matter and meaning is further elucidated by Yotova's (2013) account of Bulgarian yogurt. Yotova asks what are people eating when they ingest a yogurt that is classified as 'typically Bulgarian' and 'loaded with strong patriotic sentiments' as it is prepared with the unique bacterium *Lactobacillus bulgaricus* (ibid.: 170). This yogurt nourishes both individual bodies and 'the national soul' (ibid.: 181) due to the 'bio-national' qualities of the bacterium, which, Yotova explains, 'is in the soil, on the leaves of plants and trees, or in the morning dew' (ibid.: 178). She poetically argues, then, that the yogurt, due to its unique micro-component, is embedded into its material landscape, and thus it follows that ingesting the yogurt symbolically and materially roots an individual to the bacterium's homeland. The bacterium does not keep within national borders, however, but extends beyond, and Yotova interrogates how the value of the bacterium, and in turn the yogurt, is crystallized through internationalized discourses and consumption, which serve to bodily, socially and culturally connect those who eat it.

We see a similar process institutionalized through the concept of *terroir*, which draws attention to the distinct ecological properties in which a food is produced and gives rise to its unique characteristics. *Terroir* implies a vitalism of matter grounded in place. As West (2016) writes in relation to artisan cheese-making, makers value the multiple ever-changing factors of the environment, such as the types of grasses and flowers on which animals graze, because they produce and are reflected in a foodstuff that is inherently variable in composition, in contrast to industrial food that favours consistency. Much like Yotova's bacterium and Sonia's cuy, West's cheeses are shaped by ecological matter that can be traced to a particular locale – a locale that is made manifest upon eating and tasting the food.

However, as Demossier (2011) points out, *terroir* becomes abstracted as it is commodified and valued in circuits of exchange, and solidified through institutional regimes of origin (see also Barham 2003; Gade 2004; Trubek, Guy and Bowen 2010). Thus, while the designation of a product as PDO, AOC or GI, for example, reflects the distinct constitution of its ecology as it is subjectively experienced in the eating body, it also arguably becomes disassociated from the matter of its production, with its status as protected acting as a mere symbolic referent to its place (see Cavanagh 2007). It is not just matter, then, which is of import here, but instead the way it interplays with meaning, specifically the way that meaning is constructed through recourse to matter to establish a connection between food and place. We see this in the food festival literature: Garlic becomes associated with Gilroy not just because it happens to be grown there, but also because of the multiple discursive and embodied practices that dynamically construct the knowledge that Gilroy is garlic and garlic is Gilroy. The materiality provides the foundations upon which meaning is overlaid and the meaning makes the material matter.

This begs the question about whether matter really matters at all. I have already drawn attention to the arbitrary and constructed nature of iconizing food as heritage, and supporting this claim is a convincing body of literature that has attended to the discursive invention of regional and national cuisines and asserted the relationship between food and territorial identity (see for example Cusack 2000; Guy 2001; Harbottle 2000; Klein 2007; Ohnuki-Tierney 1994; Pilcher 1998). As Bell and Valentine conclude, iconic dishes represent regions 'even if – as it is so often the case – regional traditions are exposed as mere inventions' (1997: 147). Appadurai (1988) elucidates this in relation to printed recipes in India, and argues that regional dishes become codified as ethnic and representative of the region. These codifications are drawn into national cookbooks and while this facilitates interethnic foodways and cosmopolitanism, it also, he contends, creates 'ethnoethnicity' and a culinary other (ibid.: 14–18). The process also creates a culinary self, as exemplified by Ayora-Diaz and Vargas-Cetina's (2005) account of Yucatan foodways that are defined and articulated in opposition to the Mexico core. Consumption of local dishes, then, 'is turned into a defining marker of local identity' (ibid.: 172), although, as Avieli (2005) shows, it can blur boundaries just as much as it can create them.

This relationship between eaters, foods and locale is not, however, static, but instead has to be continually remade and recreated, especially as new foods and ways of preparing and eating them are integrated into regional and national foodscapes (see Abbots 2012a, 2014a; Wilk 2002, 2006). Bio-authorial encounters, such as food festivals, can play a significant role in either repelling those foods, as in the case of Jima's Health Fair, or rebranding them as local. But these are not the only forms. Appadurai (1988) and Cusack (2000) both draw attention to the role cookery books play in promoting particular ways of cooking and eating, with the latter writing that 'a national cuisine is often built by appropriating and assembling a variety of regional or ethnic recipes' (ibid.: 207) and demonstrating the ways this process is mediated by a number of actors and reflects both dominant ideologies and power dynamics. A critical point that we can take from these accounts is that meanings about food travel and become abstracted from their material origins as they become appropriated and refracted through an ideological lens. In so doing, their meanings can shift and the food can symbolically stand for another entity entirely.

This shifting is evident in Avieli's (2016) account of the 'Hummus Wars' and the record-breaking attempt to produce the largest hummus dish in a Palestinian-Israeli village. He demonstrates the ways in which food metaphors can travel and be given new local, regional and national meanings as they traverse different ethnographic contexts in this politically charged area of the Middle East. This symbolic pliability goes in tandem with, and is facilitated by, mutable material characteristics. Hummus, Avieli tells us, can take on multiple different forms across the region and, as such, has a 'metaphoric multivocality' that interplays with its adaptable material substance. Developing the concept of 'gastromediation', he shows us that hummus can be used to arbitrate difference and conflict, and he elucidates how the food's myriad and flexible meanings are entangled to hummus' material elasticity. Hummus is a paste, then, that can be socially and materially shaped and reshaped into multiple forms.

Avieli thereby indicates the ways that, in the process of preparing and eating, discourses can be disaggregated from a food and travel, only to then become reattached, sometimes in a different guise, to matter. Intangible knowledges about foods and the ways individuals should regard and value them are thus made tangible, and are experienced, as they shape a material substance that is then felt and absorbed into the body. Abstracted discourses about foods are made materially manifest once again, as they are affectively ingested by eating and the sensorial embodied encounters between foods and bodies.

My argument here is that matter does matter, even in contexts when knowledges about food become disassociated from their original ecology. It is in the occurrences that food is materially experienced that the constructed knowledge about it is inscribed onto, and acts upon, the eating body. Matter and meaning are thus drawn, and affectively felt, together at this moment. Interrogating the discursive formations and mechanisms through which knowledges about food are made and circulated, such as cookbooks and food festivals, and elucidating the political and constructed process through which this occurs, as much work has done thus far, remains an important topic of investigation. But this can only provide us with one side of the story. It is only when we take eating seriously by following knowledges into the body, and seek to understand ways in which they are subjectively encountered and made materially manifest in a food that, in turn, is eaten and shapes and becomes part of a body, that we can start to more fully comprehend the political power of food knowledges and those that create them.

Concluding remarks

In this chapter I have looked to highlight the significant role that key bio-authorities, for instance festival organizers, can play in iconizing a food and embedding it to place. Framing food festivals as bio-authorial encounters, I have illuminated the ways such events can provide a space for a select number of mediators to create a knowledge-power dynamic (cf Foucault 1980) that helps establish their authority as a 'competent teller of the truth' (Rabinow and 2006: 197) about a food. Moreover, paying attention to affect and the sensory 'buzziness' (cf Coles 2013b) of such occasions, as well as the ways these are orchestrated, indicates how such lessons can be received by festivalgoers. Yet these lessons do not go uncontested by others, as exemplified by Sonia's reframing of cuy, and while this points to the agency of individuals to shift meanings of food by changing its material assemblages, among other practices, questions still remain as to whose 'truth' has greater social resonance. I have sought to indicate ways in which multiple values, understandings and emotional experiences – the affective background an eater brings – interplay with the stuff of food. Foods shift across contexts, in the case of cuy from the domestic sphere discussed in the previous chapters to the more public spaces discussed here, and each encounter produces different knowledges and embodied experiences. Food festivals can consequently be interpreted as providing another layer of knowledge and meaning to a foodstuff that, in turn, potentially enhances and limits the vitalism of its matter by drawing it into a wider assemblage of meaning, affective background, social relations and political dynamics. Publicly valuing a particular food as heritage imbues another layer of symbolic efficacy onto its matter. These knowledges do not always neatly align, of course, but are instead dynamically remade through a process of negotiation in which some voices and meanings have greater authority than others.

Taking Yotova's (2013) lead, we therefore have to ask what are people really eating when they are eating at a food festival. And what are they eating when they are eating a food iconized as heritage or 'our food', or as regional or national. I have looked to indicate possible answers to this question, including cultural belonging and place. But most importantly, I have worked to draw attention to the agency of the eating body in this process, and the ways in which thinking more about bodies – how they feel, experience, smell, hear and taste the food presented to them as local or national heritage – not only provides us with a greater insight into the political dynamics at play, but can also help elucidate the ways in which sameness and difference are inscribed and maintained as bodily boundaries are established and transgressed. In so doing, I have further indicated how definitions of eating can be opened up to include multiple sensory encounters and have stressed the import of treating eating and the body as key sites through which abstracted meanings about food are made (in)to matter.

Chapter 5

Eating 'Global Food' and its alternatives: Anxious, obscured and active bodies

Introduction

This chapter continues the interrogation of how relations of distance and proximity, and sameness and otherness, are enacted through networks of relatedness between bodies, foods and discourse, and extends the discussion to consider how these processes take place, even in the context of globalized and seemingly place-less foods. As such, it continues to explore a theme introduced in Chapter 3 – how food relations are performed and how bodies are brought together across geographical distances. In this chapter, I extend this earlier discussion by focusing not on the context of individuals knowing each other or being part of the same community, but instead attending to relations among strangers or individuals who may never actually meet or 'know' each other. I thereby consider how intimacies are fostered over distances by eating and, conversely, how corporeal proximity can produce social distance. As in previous chapters, my interest here is in examining how both matter and meaning are entangled and mediate each other through the practice of eating, how agency is distributed across assemblages of eating, and how bio-authority can coalesce around particular actors, in addition to elucidating how such processes bind the vitalism of matter and shape the form of a food's assemblage.

The chapter opens with globalized food and the ways in which disconnections, both real and imagined, between eaters and 'complex' foods can lead to increased anxieties. It thereby picks up the thread of safety and risk introduced in Chapter 3. Drawing attention to how eaters' fears are produced through obscured, unseen and unknown networks of production and the ways in which this is experienced through the body, I examine the, sometimes radical measures taken by eaters to reassert control over the substances they ingest and, in turn, reinforce their bodily boundaries. This question of eater agency and food's vitality extends to Carolan's (2011) concept of bodies being 'tuned' by the bio-authority of 'Global Food', and I investigate how bodies are trained by the matter of food and the abstracted symbols and knowledges with which matter travels. In so doing, I attend to the ways in which food's language and semiotic markers, such as fair trade and Slow Food, act as mediating symbols that bind a food's vitality and shape its assemblage. I suggest, however, that such symbols invoke shared embodied experiences and through 'alternatives' that which is disconnected becomes reconnected – in a fashion. I consequently call for more attention to be paid to the oft-overlooked theme of embodied experience in accounts of fair trade, which have leaned heavily towards political economy and have tended to gloss over eating and the body. This leads me to reflect upon the recent turn to 'visceral geographies' (Hayes-Conroy and Hayes-Conroy 2010b) that has worked to illuminate the sensory experience of alternative foods and the ways in which they are subjectively experienced and known through the eating body, in addition to expounding the ways such experiences can (re)produce and potentially counter political dynamics and social categories.

Obscured and unknown bodies: Safety, anxiety and risk

While it can be argued that the contemporary food system is more connected than ever – due to the vertical and horizontal integration of production, processing, distributing and retailing, not to mention contract farming – Kneafsey et al. (2008) write that consumers are increasingly disconnected from their food, in both their lived reality and their perception. Indeed, they observe, it is the very connections of agri-industry that contribute to the sense of consumer disconnection (ibid.: 6–7). This, in turn, leads to heightened consumer anxieties about food: as food becomes more 'distanced' and its production more 'opaque' and 'placeless', eaters' concerns about the safety of food grow. Jackson (2015) goes beyond this headline and looks to explain the paradox as to why there are such anxieties about food at a time when it has arguably never been more abundant, safe and affordable. He draws attention to the disparity between the high level of anxiety reported in surveys and the ways in which consumers have negotiated these at an everyday practical level to the extent that food anxieties are 'routine and relatively unconsidered' (ibid.: 4). He is therefore careful to ensure that the root of anxieties are attributed exclusively neither to consumers, especially their perceived lack of knowledge, nor to the agri-industrial complex and the overextension of supply networks.

One of Jackson's objectives is to trace the nuanced ways in which consumer anxieties about food are transmitted through multiple connections and traverse myriad issues that intersect with class, gender and location. Nevertheless, in accord with Kneafsey et al., he writes that the geographical and social distance between consumers and the sites of their food production can result in issues of trust and confidence. Or, as Coles (2015) puts it, the sites of food production are discursively rendered as 'placeless' giving rise to concerns over safety and security (see also Abbots and Coles 2013; Blay-Palmer 2008). The relations and processes of production, then, become increasingly invisible and obscured as they become more complex. The individually wrapped chicken breast purchased from the supermarket shelf, for instance, is a fetishized commodity that comes to the consumer through multiple transactions and labour relations, all of which are congealed, yet hidden, in the chicken's materiality (Coles 2015, 2016). As food becomes increasingly dislocated from its production context, eaters become, or feel they become, disconnected from both their food and those workers who have grown, raised, procured, slaughtered, prepared, packaged or transported it.

There are a number of human and non-human bodies in even the shortest of supply networks, as I have illustrated in relation to cuy (see Chapter 2), and when these networks reach out more widely to produce a more complex and industrial food, the amount of bodies increases exponentially. This is illustrated by Ormond's (2013) account of the actors involved in contemporary low carbon milk production, which encompasses cows, farmers, scientists, retailers, the taste buds of consumers, pasture- and concentrate-feed, additives and supplements, regulators, and genes and genetic engineers – to name but a small selection. In short, it takes a lot of bodies to produce a foodstuff (cf Coles 2013a). These invisible unknown bodies, in both their human and non-human form, can give rise to a feeling of distrust and unease about food that can result in eaters attempting to reconnect to and 'know' their food. This can take varying forms, from buying into trusted brands, eating fair trade goods, advocating Slow Food, shifting to organic produce, buying from farmers' markets, and/or participating in community-supported agriculture and grow-your-own schemes, and I discuss some of these 'alternative' practices below. But first I turn to a more radical attempt to know, and assert control over, the bodies of food and, in turn, the eating body.

In the city of Cuenca, one of the most striking changes was the visible emergence of the privileged migrant community. In Chapter 3, I have discussed this group's unease with local food and the ways in which they navigate this, and I now want to focus upon their reasons for moving to Cuenca and the desired food practices they hope to enact upon arrival. Within this group it became immediately apparent that a desire to reconnect to food and assert control over their bodily health was a critical motivating factor in shaping the decision to migrate. 'Wanting a simple life and simple food' was a common refrain among my participants, who all drew my attention to their desire to escape industrial food chains and obtain pesticide- and pathogen-free food from small-scale local producers. The reality in which they found themselves differed significantly from this 'dream' (Abbots 2013, see also Chapter 3), and here I wish to unpack the anxieties about invisible bodies that helped produce that dream and encouraged such dramatic changes in lifestyle and eating practices.

While I define my North American participants as 'privileged', in that they are in a far more comfortable position than many others who, like the kin of my Ecuadorian participants, migrate out of political or economic necessity, their move is no less emotionally fraught and practically difficult, especially as many are in the later stages of their life and are not in a position to return to the United States. For many, Ecuador is expected to be their final home. This level of emotional and financial investment in 'a new life' gives some indication as to the depth of feeling about agri-industry and complex food, and their yearning for simple food it produces. This is illustrated by Steve, who had survived a serious health scare while living in Minnesota and explained his recent arrival in Cuenca as wanting 'to get away from this complexity of the food-chain in the US, you know, with all its pathogens, salmonella and mad cow disease' (Abbots 2013: 121). He continued to explain that he now 'wanted to live a more simple way of life', which for him meant 'eating in a more simplified and less complex manner, you know, cutting out some of the links of the food chain, and eating clean food that hasn't been produced on these great big industrial farms' (ibid.: 121). Likewise, Kiki told me that she was looking for a plot of land where she could grow her own food, one that would preferably have its own water source so she would 'be able to be in control' of her food, with the ultimate goal of knowing the provenance of everything she ingested and 'living quietly away' from political and capitalist 'forces'. In essence, Kiki was looking to live 'off-grid' as a way of empowering her life and asserting her agency over what she regarded as corrupt and powerful corporate interests. Indeed, what emerged from our discussions, as typified by Steve and Kiki, was a strong wish to move away from industrially produced food in order to establish control over the substances being ingested.

A familiar motif in discussions with many privileged migrants was a concern over their political agency to know their food. This has little to do with food education – many were extremely knowledgeable about food systems and actively sought information about what they were eating (and thought they should be eating). Rather, the issue centred on what was unknowable, unseen or purposely obscured. Anxieties hence surfaced and coalesced around issues of transparency – or more accurately a lack thereof. In my participants' narratives, the complexities of industrial food give rise to disconnections that, in turn, create obscurity. And it is in this very obscurity that the 'dangers' of industrial food were seen to lurk. For some, this encouraged a care-less attitude in producers that, as far as my participants were concerned, characterized agri-business, while for others, especially those who leant more generally towards conspiracy theories, the hidden spaces of industrial food facilitated adulteration and economic manipulation. Thus, privileged migrants echo the participants of Jackson's (2015) study in that their anxieties over what they are eating have been bound up with other political concerns and subject positions relating to, in this context, Big Pharma, corporate greed, a police state, waste and environmental relations. What interests me here though is that these anxieties and fears are played out and experienced in my participants' bodies. Or, more accurately, they felt as if their own bodies were being damaged by the hidden human and non-human bodies that, to their minds, are an intrinsic part of the industrial food complex. My participants' answer was to make the complex simple by placing their own bodies in an eating environment in which they assumed there would be minimal hidden entities. This would provide greater transparency and consequently more control over what they ingested.

The unfortunate irony here, as I discussed in Chapter 3, is that such a radical shift in location affected many privileged migrants' bodies in unwanted ways, and the reality in which they found themselves presented greater risks and more hidden dangers than they had imagined, as they were exposed to unfamiliar 'foreign bodies'. Nonetheless, many still enjoyed the idea – if not the reality – that they could connect directly to a grower and eat food obtained through seemingly short supply networks.[1] A number of migrants would have preferred to do this back in the United States but believed that, in order to do so, the food of farmers' markets, which was price-prohibitive, would have had to have been the mainstay of their diet. Cuenca, they assumed, would offer such personal connections to a food producer in a more economically feasible manner. Corporeality is important here, as it is not enough to know intellectually the producer of the food they are eating. Instead, migrants eased their anxieties by physically engaging with the (assumed) producer; knowing the source of food and forming a social connection became akin to corporeally inhabiting the same physical space as the grower. The closer the body of the grower the more privileged migrants believed they could trust the food they offered. Here a tension arises, however, between ideology and practice, with many finding, in their everyday lived experience, local growers and sellers and local food spaces, such as markets, distrustful and damaging to their bodies (see Chapter 3).

Privileged migrants' move to Ecuador was, then, strongly informed by a need to change the terms of their food relationships by having a deeper connection with producers; a connection that was to be made by embodying the same physical space. What underpins this is a desire to reassert control over their own bodies and bodily boundaries by (re)gaining control over what they ingest. This control was seen to be impossible to attain back in the United States, at least not without considerable financial cost, because of the obscured relations of production of agri-business that, for my participants, opened up the possibility for various unknown bodies to enter the food system and, in turn, permeate their own bodies. Closing the distance between eater and food source can thus be understood as an attempt by privileged migrants to assert their own agency over their own corporeality, and renegotiate the terms of engagement between what they eat and who produces it.

These conclusions seem, at first glance, to be in accord with DuPuis (2000) and the politics of rejection she illuminates in the context of organic milk consumption (see Chapter 2). Privileged migrants are, after all, rejecting an offering from agri-business and choosing another product/producer. Yet their actions are less about renegotiating and coproducing networks of relatedness with industrial food producers, and more inclined towards opting out completely. They are thus less of a mediator in the assemblages of globalized food and, in turn, the mediating impact of 'Global Food' (cf Carolan 2011) and agri-industry on their eating practices is arguably lessened. Privileged migrants are no longer members of the Global Food's network of relatedness. Or are they? In opting out of such assemblages, they are still, I suggest, shaping the form it takes. Their absence can be seen to be as just as important as their presence, as producers and agri-industry adapt accordingly – a process illustrated by the mainstreaming of alternative food and the rebranding and repositioning of global foods (Carrier and Luetchford 2012; Guthman 2004; Lewis and Potter 2011; see also Chapter 6). Moreover, the political might of agri-industry is evident in privileged migrants' 'choice' to move to Ecuador in the first instance, as it encouraged them to make a radical change in the way they live their lives. In attempting to escape and reconfigure the relationship, migrants paradoxically thereby reinforce the bio-authority of agri-industry over their lives and bodies in the most pronounced and life-changing manner.

Bodies of production: Tuning, tasting and training

The bio-authority of agri-industry is further evident in Carolan's (2011) account of *Embodied Food Politics*. Adopting a somewhat normative stance to subjective notions of good and sustainable food, he examines the ways in which consumers' bodies have become 'tuned' to, and by, 'Global Food' – 'Global Food' being his term for the industrialized, complex, conventional, globalized, large-scale food system. He writes that '"Global Food" … through the embodiments it creates, helps foster particular knowledges, tastes, and feelings about food' (ibid.: 7) in consumers that, in turn, encourages them to enact preferences for such foods. The system is thereby upheld and reproduced as consumers' bodies are effectively trained, through repeated visceral experience, to prefer 'Global Food' over alternatives. What is more, these embodied preferences do not occur incidentally, but are instead the result of considerable labour, capital and political intervention. Carolan illustrates this through the history of the US adoption of the soybean, which was adapted to incumbent tastes and subject to extensive lobbying to ensure its place on school meal programmes, as well as later being adopted as a low-cost meat extender and a nutritional addition to a healthy diet. As a result, the population gradually became 'tuned' to the value of eating soybeans from a position of previously regarding it as inedible item only fit for livestock.

We consequently get a sense from Carolan of bodies and bodily experience being situated within a broader political economy, as tastes (literal and metaphorical) are shaped by 'Global Food'. Or, in other words, Carolan elucidates how particular embodied engagements with food and eating preferences are politically nurtured over others (LeHeron 2014). To counter these processes, Carolan, echoing Guthman's (2008b, 2011) argument that consumers do not need more knowledge to make different (and what Carolan regards as more sustainable) food choices, points to the need for a different type of food knowledge. This knowledge, he writes, should be borne from embodied practices and visceral experiences with food, such as growing, raising livestock, and cooking. Just as bodies have been detuned and tuned, so they can be retuned towards new relationships with food. He explores this through three alternative spaces – community-supported agriculture, heritage seed banks and backyard chicken coops – which 'quite literally, help to make 'Global Food' out of tune to bodies that come into repeated contact with them' (ibid.: 8). The argument being, then, that lived experiences with alternative food spaces shape the body and its preferences, and that it is through these embodied knowledges and relations that change can occur.

Rather than thinking solely about the structural constraints of food's political economy and the ways these are external to the individual eating subject, as he argues much work on agri-food focuses, Carolan radically locates political agency in the relational body. He concludes, 'If we hope to understand social change, and perhaps even play a part in shaping its trajectory, we will need to expand our understanding of "constraints" to include assemblages of the body' (ibid.: 144).

Carolan's perspective accords with my own in emphasizing how bodily experiences with food are inherently political. This recognition, as others have also noted (cf DuPuis 2000; Hayes-Conroy 2014), opens up the possibility for a new politics of food that is anchored in, and flows from, the subjective body. From this vantage point, the eating body becomes a space of contestation and resistance, as much as it is shaped and governed. Yet a lingering sense remains in Carolan's work that consuming bodies are somewhat passive. Despite their theoretical agentic capacity to create political change, they still have to be taught new ways of experiencing food and their current experience has, without being overly deterministic, been shaped by key food authorities. I am largely sympathetic to Carolan's central argument that eating is a fine balancing act between the individual subject and the societal and political dynamics to which an individual is party – and one of my key aims is not dissimilar to Carolan's own objectives, as I explore the multiple bio-authorities that inform an individual's embodied experience of eating and examine how those power dynamics are enacted relationally upon and through bodies. Likewise, I parallel his ambition to focus on embodiment and echo his concerns that much scholarship that centres on the body, even that which stresses viscerality and affect, can paradoxically render the lived experience of food from view.

My critique of Carolan is that he does not go far enough. Despite its potential, the eating body does not emerge as a strong mediator in his discussion. First, he depicts embodied knowledges as being shaped by 'Global Food' rather than being mutually produced, and then for the body to be retuned, it needs to engage with alternative spaces, which again can have multiple authorities and discourses. I am not denying that the eating body is always subjected to bio-authorities and political dynamics (quite the contrary), but am instead contending that, despite its relational foundations, Carolan's argument leans more heavily towards the agency of food authorities than that of the individual embodied subject. The balance of power maybe relational, but it is heavily weighted in one direction. To put it crudely, at first glance, his argument seems to locate agency in the eating body – or at least to allow for its agentic capacity – but his discussion still presents these bodies as having things done to them rather than doing things themselves. Hence, while Carolan's overarching argument is relational in ethos, the active processes of mediation – between eating bodies, the matter of food, knowledges about food, and food's political authorities – are still in danger of being glossed over, as hard political structures are brought to the fore.

Moreover, although Carolan states that 'living bodies populate our food system' (ibid.: 4) and has a nuanced awareness of the unproductive false disjuncture between producers and consumers (see Goodman and DuPuis 2002; Goodman, DuPuis and Goodman 2011), the bodies of producers are somewhat lost under the seemingly faceless monolith of 'Global Food'. Yet, as Roseberry's (1996) now-classic study of coffee marketing reminds us, we have to be careful that, in our desire to critique the political economic might of agri-business and the industrial food complex, we do not neglect the fact that it is composed of myriad individuals all going about their business in different ways for varying objectives. This gives rise to broader questions about the mediating power of the bodies of food producers, distributors and retailers, among others, which constitute the complex networks of relatedness through which foods are materially and discursively produced, and through which they travel to their final destination of the eating body. As I have indicated above in my account of privileged migrants, these, often unseen, bodies can have a significant impact on the way eaters interact with particular foods. Likewise, in the previous chapters, I have also demonstrated how multiple bio-authorities can imprint their body into the individual eater's body, as well as indicating ways in which this process can occur across spatial distances.

Coles's (2013a) account of the bodies involved in coffee production details this process. As I briefly noted earlier, Coles observes that 'to drink coffee is to drink a lot of bodies' (ibid: 268). I now want to examine this argument, and the ethnography on which it is premised, in more depth, in order to interrogate how multiple embodied interactions with a food are abstracted and made manifest in its symbolism. Coles explains that particular tastes, for example 'earthy' and 'peaty', become attached to a specific coffee to signify its place of origin and its material properties, properties that, *in part*, are informed by the physical materiality of the place in which the coffee beans are grown. To drink a coffee is therefore to go on a journey to a different locale, albeit one that is mediated by a 'tour guide'. The guide in this specific ethnographic context is the Monmouth Coffee Company's promotional literature and branding that, while partially based on factual information including the region, estate and grower of the beans, also draws on the abstraction of multiple and subjective embodied encounters that have resulted in a particular coffee's defined taste profile. It is this process – of abstracting the embodied drinking experience of coffee experts into signifiers such as 'earthy' and 'peaty' that are then imprinted onto the coffee and, in turn, inform the ways consumers' corporeal interaction with the drink – that I wish to unpack here, and it is worth reproducing Coles's description at length:

> Producing a taste profile entails a series of tasting rituals where members of the industry gather to 'cup' – meaning to taste through proscribed procedures – coffees from a particular region. Whilst tasting, individual tasters detail the aromas and flavours of a coffee and enter them on a proforma. Afterwards proformas are compared and a profile is compiled from the collective palate of the group. Regional taste profiling is an iterative process where numerous coffees from the same region are tasted and over time generic characteristics are ascertained and documented. As a result, specific regions have taste profiles that dictate a set of flavours and textures associated with them. Indonesian coffees, for instance, are said to be 'smoky', 'peaty' and 'earthy', with a 'heavy body' mouth feel. Coffees from individual producers in a region are therefore evaluated based on how their coffee matches up to the regional profile as well as to each other. The tastes of places are ultimately 'stored' in the collective body of expert tasters who collaborate to produce socially and affectively imagined geographical knowledges about coffee origins. (ibid: 261)

One of the most striking themes in this description is the way in which the corporeal encounters of many are co-joined and flattened into a defining characteristic, one which can be communicated to both expert tasters and consumers alike. Coles further shows us how expert tasters come to each coffee encounter with an affective background that is premised on their expectations of the flavour, which is founded on their previous subjective experiences of coffees from that place and how they should taste. This is further informed by their knowledge of the material properties of that place and how they have infused the coffee with specific characteristics. These characteristics are socially and corporeally produced as the bodies of expert tasters are 'trained' (ibid: 262) through a process not dissimilar to that described by Latour (2004) in his account of how those in the perfume industry acquire a 'nose' through their embodied and affective engagements with the objects and knowledges of their world. Hence symbols, in the forms of defining terms, material substance and bodies are drawn together in an assemblage to produce and mediate knowledges (see also Domingos 2016) – knowledge that is crystallized through the embodied experience of eating (or drinking).

Taste profilers, industry experts and roasters are not the only bodies present. Consumers' bodies are also found in coffee's assemblage, and Coles writes that AJ, who sources beans for Monmouth, always thinks about what the customer would like to drink when tasting a coffee. The end drinker is not just present, however, in terms of abstract preferences and sales results, but also lurks in the imagination of the expert taster who has to speculate how the coffee drinker will corporeally encounter, or expect to encounter, the coffee he or she is currently drinking. As AJ explains, she is always buying with the flavours the customer would like in mind (2013a: 261), and Coles surmises, 'The ingesting body of the consumer is present, albeit mediated by proxy' (ibid: 261). One could take this further and state that, as AJ is always mindful of the customer's taste preferences, the drinker's body also mediates expert tasters' embodied encounters with coffee.

As a geographer, Coles's primary interest is in how place is materialized through the multiple bodies that jostle against and unfold into each other in the networks of coffee. This perspective can be productively reversed and enhanced by the recognition that this is a dialectic process through which bodies are also brought together and constituted by place (both real and imagined) and the substances associated with that place. His ethnographic description shows that myriad human and non-human bodies mediate and act upon each other in assemblages of matter and meaning. Being socially informed by 'trained' bodies, these assemblages are further bound by, both real and imagined, previous material encounters and the knowledges produced though them – in short, the affective background – of those expert bodies that are contained wherein. Moreover, by applying Bennett (2010) to Coles's ethnography, we can see that, through continuous ingestion, coffee has a vitality that trains drinkers' palates and how this, in turn, informs drinkers' expectations. But this is not an inherent, infinite vitality, I argue. Rather, what Coles's example demonstrates is that vitality is somewhat limited by the socially produced meanings attributed to the substance being tasted and ingested.

Whether it is in the language of being trained or tuned, and regardless of where they locate mediating agency, both Carolan and Coles show that matter acts upon the eating body to orientate it towards specific experiences, while also demonstrating that the ways matter is encountered is informed, to a greater or lesser extent, by the social actions and discourses that accompany it – discourses that themselves are limited by the symbolic possibilities matter presents. Both matter and meaning are thus assembled and bound together through the eating body.

Mediating symbols: Fair trade and Slow Food

Coles's ethnography elucidates how embodied encounters can become abstracted and made manifest in food's visual and textual language, and the ways in which this language can then evoke imagined eating experiences in the future. I want to now attend to this mediating capacity of food's language, which is perhaps most explicitly depicted in logos and brands, in the context of two 'brands' – fair trade and Slow Food. I focus on these for three key reasons. First, they are significant and visible dynamics in both the food system and social science research on food, and hence have a certain political vitality. Second, as commodified signifiers of caring, ethical food relations, as well as quality, good tasting food, fair trade and Slow Food have a considerable capacity to evoke affective relations, especially as they play out in the construction of the self (Barnett et al 2005a). And, finally, bodies and embodied encounters are absolutely implied in the language of fair trade and Slow Food but have, to date, been largely unacknowledged in the vast and ever-growing body of research. Bodies – of growers, consumers and eaters – remain rather ghostly entities that are rarely brought to the fore, and eating has, to be blunt, been widely disregarded. In many ways, studies of fair trade and Slow Food, then, typify Carolan's (2011) critique of agri-food research in that they absent the living, feeling and sensate body. My argument here is that eating matters and that making bodies more analytically visible gives us greater insight into political dynamics and the very foundations on which such dynamics rest.

It is not my intention here to rehash and retread the ground that numerous writers have covered, or even to summarize the debates and discussions to which fair trade and Slow Food give rise. To do so in a way that does this scholarship justice would take considerably more space than I have here, and there are numerous carefully considered works that offer nuanced and detailed analysis of: the cultural politics of fair trade (cf Goodman, DuPuis and Goodman 2011); alternative food as collective and individualized political action (cf Barnett et al. 2005a,b); fair trade and Slow Food in the context of ethical consumption and its mainstream appropriation (Carrier and Luetchford 2012; Lewis and Potter 2011; Guthman 2004); the class, race and ethnic ideologies permeating such movements (Guthman 2008c; Slocum 2007; Slocum and Saldhana 2013; West and Domingos 2012); and the economic and political consequences on producers (Lyon 2011) – to name but a few. What I do here, instead, is to read between the lines and raise oft-neglected questions that suggest possible future analytical directions. As such, I glean existing accounts for clues about bodily connections and how multiple bodies get drawn together and potentially produced, although the conceptual direction and overarching arguments of these works may differ significantly from my own approach.

Goodman et al. give us a route into thinking about bodies by framing fair trade as 'a social-material thing' (2011: 196) enmeshed in a dynamic and ever-shifting network of relations, discourses and practices. They indicate the ways in which fair trade, as a symbol, is both mediated by and mediates a wider assemblage of matter and meaning, and it is this thread I look to extend here. The visual economies of fair trade are more than mere marketing tools, 'as semiotic intermediaries situated between consumers and producers of fair trade goods, they are, in essence, *indispensible* in creating the meanings of fair trade' (ibid.: 209–10, original emphasis). As such, Goodman et al. point to the productive agentic capacity of discursive symbols and narrative that, I argue, can be taken even further if we start to consider how bodies and matter get drawn into, and constructed, through such assemblages.

In the first instance, Goodman et al. trace the multiple stages of fair trade's 'embodiment', although let us not get misled by their use of this term; in this context they are referring to material manifestations rather than accounting for the engagements of a sensate body in-the-world. Nonetheless, their historical tracing of fair trade discourse and how it has evolved demonstrates how pictures of growers' bodies appeared extensively in the imagery of fair trade in its earliest conceptions as a way of encouraging 'semiotic connectivity' (ibid.: 212) between consumers and fair trade farmers. This soon shifted, however. As quality and taste became paramount, romantic landscapes and touristic reflections of place displaced the bodies of farmers, which were regarded as out-of-place and 'too fair trade' for a premium product (ibid.: 214). Bodies of celebrities then came to the fore, forming aspirational connections, followed by images of the tools of a growers' labour, which suggest connections with bodies of growers but in a manner that 'maintains the dis-embodiment of fair trade farmers' (ibid.: 218). Finally, the bodies of growers became visible once more through new technologies, as consumers are encouraged to click on farmers' faces and enter their world through thick description. Examples of such narratives from producers include 'we are the growers and you can *taste* it' and 'I like my work – I pick the tea and put it in my basket. Believe it or not, I can *smell* the quality of the tea leaves' (ibid.: 219, emphasis mine).

Although Goodman et al. take their discussion in a different direction, these snippets of text invoke an embodied shared connection between the grower who can *smell* their tea and the eater who will be able to *taste* it (and one assumes also smell it). These discourses draw on the sensory encounters that food presents to create an imagination of shared bodily experience, which is not too far removed from commensality and its attendant social proximities. Resonating with my arguments in the previous chapters, these marketing narratives point to the possibility of sharing substance and the kinning of bodies, but in this context across space and the hugely divergent bodies of producers and consumers. Yet it is not just growers' bodies that are drawn into these assemblages of alternative foods, non-human bodies also have a presence. Kneafsey et al. (2008), for example, discuss an 'Adopt-a-Sheep' programme. It is also worth noting here, however, that this process does not equate to a dynamic of parity and it does not produce bodies that are the same. The consumer can see and engage with producers' bodies, but this privilege of visibility is not accorded to producers (cf Goodman, DuPuis and Goodman 2011). Moreover, growers and eaters may share a sensory encounter with tea, but the embodied experiences of labouring to grow it and of drinking it, as well as the political economic and material conditions in which these experiences take place, are very different. Likewise, seeing and creating an affective tie to a well-cared-for sheep is one thing, but the sheep still gets milked and its wool acquired to fulfil the needs of the human eater. We have to remember that shared encounters, proximities and presences do not produce social sameness and political equity.

That being said, fair trade also centres on the embodied agency of the eating subject to affect social change and my second point is that, while much literature on fair trade suggests its potential to create a visceral affect in the eating body through its recourse to 'care', scant attention has been paid to the feelings in consumers that eating fair trade food stimulates, and in turn the types of bodies this produces. Fair trade, among other forms of 'ethical consumption', has been conceptualized as the commodification of distanced caring relations (cf Barnett et al. 2005a; Goodman, DuPuis and Goodman 2011; Goodman 2015; Lewis and Potter 2011; Morgan 2010) that take place in the domestic realm (Barnett el al. 2005b). Fair trade discourse thus tells us that caring for the world can be enacted through acts of (better) consumption and at the level of responsible and individual action (cf Brooks et al. 2013; Guthman 2003, 2007, 2008a). This form of caring implies an emotional affective entanglement; care can be abstracted but it is also a feeling (Lavis, Abbots and Attala 2015). Accounts of fair trade that are otherwise nuanced and thoughtfully analysed therefore beg the questions, 'how does fair trade feel?', 'and not just for the consumer, but also for the producer?', and 'what affective ties, if any, are produced through fair trade?'. As yet, these questions have, in the main, gone answered (and unasked) and I raise them here as possible future avenues that could be productive, given the visceral and embodied 'turn' within food studies, as illustrated by Hayes-Conroy and Hayes-Conroy's (2010a; also Hayes-Conroy 2014) accounts on alternative food networks, which I discuss below.

Third, and related to this second point, is the argument that fair trade products and representations thereof centre on taste, both in the corporeal and Bourdieusian sense (Brooks et al. 2013; Goodman, DuPuis and Goodman 2011). Yet much discussion to date has tended towards the Bourdieusian path of class distinction and construction of the ethical self (cf Barnett et al. 2005a) at the expense of the visceral experience of fair trade. In essence, we get told that producers and retailers place the flavour and quality of their product first and foremost, but we do not get told how consumers physically and subjectively experience these supposed material properties. Eating is thus rendered analytically invisible. I am not suggesting for a moment here the need for swathes of research that incorporate blind taste tests. But, given my arguments that taste is subjective and, at the very least in part, socially ascribed and learnt (see Chapters 2 and 3; see also Carolan 2011; Classen 1997; Hayes-Conroy 2014; Probyn 2000), the possibility that fair trade, as a mediating symbol for matter, can act upon the body to orientate it to experience the substance being ingested in a particular way could be more fully considered. To put it bluntly, if we are told that fair trade chocolate, for example, tastes better than other chocolate, do we experience it differently in our bodies?

What I am calling for here is the other side of Bourdieu – that which focuses on *habitus* and embodied practice (Bourdieu 1990) – to be given the same attention by scholars of fair trade as the side that focuses on *Distinction* (Bourdieu 1984). Fair trade food is, after all, eaten, and scholars would do well to remember this and place as much import on food on the plate and in the body as it has in the shopping basket. Finally, returning to care, questions remain as to the ways care-full eating produces creates care-full bodies (Abbots, Lavis and Attala 2015) and how eating as an embodied manifestation of caring relations informs the ways bodies engage in-the-world (cf Abbots 2015; Lavis, Abbots and Attala 2015). I return to this question in my discussion of eating for self and society in the following chapter, but now I expound some of these points by turning to Bennett's (2010) account of the vitality of Slow Food.

Bennett offers Slow Food, which was founded in 1986 with the aim of countering 'Global Food' and homogenization (Petrini 2001), especially in the form of fast food, as an example of 'artful consumption' (2010: 50). She briefly explores its capacity to become a 'particularly powerful assemblage' (ibid.: 50) in helping us shift towards a more sustainable way of living by celebrating an enhanced ecological and culturally sensitive way of eating. At its heart, she writes that the Slow Food movement provides visibility and insight into the stuff that goes into the food we are eating, not just in terms of the ingredients, but also labour relations, economic activity and political policies. Indeed, Slow Food has long argued that everyone benefits from 'good food' and the gastronomic, cultural and ecological diversity it protects. Nonetheless, this professed capacity to challenge global consumerism, food still remains somewhat passive in Slow Food discourse for Bennett, and she reflects on whether considering food as a more active agent could animate public awareness. In short, she presents Slow Food as a good model that could be made even more effective if it were to reframe food as a vital substance and active 'player' (ibid.: 51).

As should hopefully be evident from my arguments in earlier chapters, I am not disputing the material efficacy of food, slow or otherwise, that is found in Bennett's conceptualization, but I do want to question the inherent vitality to do good that is implied in Bennett's somewhat celebratory and uncritical rendering of the Slow Food movement. This is not to critique for the sake of critique, but to highlight the ways by which material vitality is intrinsically bound up in social vitality and political relations. My argument is that Slow Food is not inherently good or even more powerful than any other type of food, but is instead subjectively constructed as being so through the discourses in which it is embedded – a discourse that Bennett unreflexively reproduces. Its potential vitality to move us towards a more sustainable way of life is created through the interplays between matter and meaning that are shaped by bio-authorities that promote and valorize a particular type of food, deemed 'Slow', over others. This practice of valorization, as I have demonstrated in the previous chapter's account of heritage foods, is a political act – an argument that is further found in West and Domingos' (2012) account of a Slow Food Presidia in the Alentejo region of Portugal.

West and Domingos examine how a Slow Food sponsored project centred on Serpa cheese looked to reverse three production practices that had changed: the cessation of using milk from lower-yielding Merino sheep; the shift to ageing the cheese in refrigerated stores instead of on straw mats on rafters; and the sale of younger, softer cheeses. Offering a deep historical analysis, the authors trace the political and economic influences that led to these changes and argue that attempts by Slow Food to 'return' to previous production methods were ironically ahistorical, in that they glossed over the lived social histories of cheesemakers. As such, West and Domingos illuminate the elitist and romantic nature of the Slow Food movement, and the ways its celebrations and classifications of food that is 'good, clean and fair' (Petrini 2007) are informed by its own particular ideology, itself a product of class and aesthetic politics that are specific to its ethnographic and historical context. As Miele and Murdoch (2003) describe, the

Slow Food movement emerged from a group of elitist gastronomes in Italy and targeted middle- and upper-class consumers, and the exclusionist overtones of Slow Food's approach and deep ambivalence to the mass market and lower-class consumers (and paradoxically also producers) have been noted by a number of commentators (see, for example, Chrzan 2004; Lauden 2004; Leitch 2013; Parkins 2004; Pietrykowski 2004).

These critiques of Slow Food in no way deny that different methods of production can change the matter of the food in question. Indeed, on the contrary, West and Domingos show in detail how shifts in production created a very different Serpa cheese to the one promoted by Slow Food. And, for some eaters, food that is produced slowly and through artisan methods, however these may be defined, may even taste better than Carolan's 'Global Food'. In line with the questions raised above about fair trade, I query how this embodied experience of taste is informed by broader discourses and produced knowledges. But, whatever the answer to that question of corporeal and social taste, the key point here is to recognize that valuing a process of production that shapes a food's material characteristics as somehow 'better' than another, often more industrialized and complex, process, is in itself a political act. And it is those politics that help imbue a food with its social vitality.

In many ways, then, scholarship on fair trade and Slow Food typifies the two approaches I am attempting to reconcile. With fair trade, eating bodies, matter and substance are absented in favour of political economic structures. Whereas, in Bennett's brief account of Slow Food, we have matter and vitality to the fore, but a distinct absence of political economy. An approach that attempts to bring the visceral and the political together in the context of alternatives to 'Global Food', and which answers some of the questions above, can be found in the work of Allison and Jessica Hayes-Conroy, and I bring this chapter to a close by considering how this work can lead us to a better understanding of the interplays between food, bodies, knowledges and politics.

Active alternatives and visceral geographies

Hayes-Conroy and Hayes-Conroy (2010a) call for greater attention to be paid to the visceral feelings that alternative food movements, such as Slow Food, can provoke. Arguing that different bodies respond in different ways to such movements, and that this is an inhibiting factor for engagement, they highlight the ways in which the corporeal and the social intersect to produce varied feelings. It therefore follows that focusing on visceral responses and critically unpacking the social dynamics and categories shaping such bodily feelings and sensations can provide a route through which to counter boundaries to participation and the lack of diversity in alternative food movements, such as that discussed by West and Domingos. Involvement with alternative foods, then, is not just an intellectual or ideological 'choice', but one that is experienced and informed by the body. Eating thus becomes of paramount importance.

This is illustrated in Jessica Hayes-Conroy's (2014) exploration of the School Garden and Cooking Programmes (SGCP) in Berkeley, California and Nova Scotia. She engages with the criticism that 'alternative' food initiatives, as highlighted in reference to Slow Food above, are racially homogenous and elitist to the extent they can be defined as white, upper-middle-class spaces (see also Goodman, DuPuis and Goodman 2011; Guthman 2008c; Slocum 2007; Slocum and Saldanha 2013),[2] but moves beyond these discussions by asking what motivates people to engage with alternative foods. This question takes her to the body, affect and viscerality, and she allows for broader framings of identity by actively recognizing that social dynamics, such as race and gender, inform eating experiences. She writes, 'We must become attentive to the ways that sensory perceptions and visceral reactions both propel and betray social categories' and 'must struggle to understand how social disenfranchisement and physical tastes both reinforce and repel each other' (ibid.: 3).

Resonating with Carolan (2011), Hayes-Conroy treats the body as an active agent that can instigate social change, although she approaches bodies in an arguably more active manner than Carolan's framing allows. Moreover, she clearly demonstrates that not all bodies experience alternative foods equally, and while all and any food has the capacity to generate pleasant sensations, it can also be alienating and dislocating. An acknowledgement of these disparities and the ways they interface with identity politics is, for Hayes-Conroy, the key to unlocking levels of engagement with alternative foods and food activism. What she defines as visceral geographies, meaning 'the ways in which bodily human experiences are reproduced relationally and materially through complex interconnections with both social forces and other physical "bodies"' (ibid.: 7), is consequently placed front and centre (see also Hayes-Conroy and Hayes-Conroy 2008, 2010a,b).

Critical to this visceral geographies approach propounded by both Jessica Hayes-Conroy and Allison Hayes-Conroy is the tenet, which accords with my own perspective, that embodied responses are not passive and reactive, but are instead learned behaviours embedded in social dynamics. Paying close attention to eating, and the bodily sensations and feelings it invokes, can thus shed new light on political relations, as well as the ways in which bio-authorities and knowledge brokers look to manipulate them (cf Anderson 2011; Thrift 2004). Jessica Hayes-Conroy (2014) illustrates this through the reinforcement and blurring of racial boundaries that takes place in the alternative foods spaces of the SGCP. She notes that the programme's food is labelled as 'white food' by the children, despite it traversing a range of culinary traditions including Indian, Mexican, Southern/Soul and Chinese. The classification is not enacted purely through the symbolism and cultural meanings of the food being promoted, but is instead played out through more intangible and affective experiences. One teacher offers an explanation to Hayes-Conroy about why black students may be more uncomfortable with the SCGP experience, which highlights the situatedness of food's material substance within a broader assemblage of food practices, relations and knowledges:

> It is less about the food itself and more the other things connected with the gathering and the readying and the preparing and the cooking and the partaking of the food, that style is what I think that they truly perceive as 'white'. (ibid.: 116)

The teacher continues to draw attention to the visceral and affective experience of the food, 'it sounds a little bit different, and smells a little bit different, and feels a little bit different' (ibid.: 116). This does not mean, however, that such food spaces are rigidly 'white'. Rather, Hayes-Conroy demonstrates how children play with racial categories through their visceral experiences with the food being promoted by the programme, and explores how this can blur boundaries, disrupt stereotypes and create new understandings of identity. Embodied encounters with food, then, is a means of expressing individual agency just as much as it was an attempt by those in authority to promote their notions of 'good food'.

Food, Hayes-Conroy shows us, is known corporeally and intellectually. These processes, in which matter and meaning are drawn together, are further evident in the way privileged migrants encounter food in Ecuador. Yet, in this context, tensions emerge between 'knowing food' and the experience of eating it, and, although eating gives rise to knowledge and vice versa, my participants struggle to reconcile these two aspects. The 'alternative' to 'Global Food', in the form of simple, local food, was commonly identified not just by its semiotic markers, that is, sold unbagged and unwrapped by peasant women in local markets or from wheelbarrows on street corners, but also through the visceral experience of eating it. That experience is not always pleasant and can be extreme in terms of its effect on the body and its health (see Chapter 3). Furthermore, it may not be to the taste of the eater. Whether it is disliking the chewy, stringy texture of grass-fed beef or finding 'organic' strawberries 'watery', my participants sometimes found local food materially dissimilar to that to which they had been accustomed. As such, they have to refine their palates if they are to take any visceral pleasure in eating local, non-complex and non-industrial 'alternatives'.

At times, this 'retuning' (cf Carolan 2011) was neither manageable nor desirable, and migrants seek out food to which their bodies – both guts and palates – are more acclimatized. Others, however, remain wedded to the ideology of alternatives, even when they know, intellectually, that the foods they are eating as 'alternative' are, in fact, global and complex. Steve, for example, 'knew' that the oversized 'tasteless' strawberries he acquired from a street-seller as organic were not so, just as Quentin 'knew' that the local pears purchased from the market had been branded as 'Dole' before the merchant had removed the sticker, but they kept eating these foods although they did not enjoy them – telling themselves, while doing so, that the foods were 'simple'. Such is the efficacy of the dream of alternatives to 'Global Food' in this context, and the ways in which matter and meaning are entangled in the production of the self as an eating subject.

Concluding remarks

This chapter examined the ways in which connections are forged between human and non-human bodies that are geographically dispersed. As such, it has elucidated how relations of proximity and distance are enacted across the assemblages of 'Global Food' and its alternatives. It has been shown that intimacies and affective relations can be created and nurtured across distances, while localism can produce boundaries and distinctions. A myriad of mediators, which become greater in number as food's assemblages are stretched and become more complex, shape an eater's embodied encounters with their food, a process that can disconnect as much as it can be seen to be connected. With such disconnections come anxieties and fears of hidden dangers, as foods and their producers are rendered increasingly opaque. Eaters thus take action to reassert control of their foods and their bodies; they attempt to opt out of the system and change the nature of their relationship by seeking alternatives, either in the form of alternative food movements or, more radically, moving location. Such actions work to co-produce the networks of relatedness, of matter, bodies and meanings, through which bio-authority and the vitality of food are realized. Agency is thus enacted and distributed while concomitantly coalescing around key actors, who 'tune' (cf Carolan 2011) consumer tastes or promote a certain, exclusionist ideology.

Eating and the body are critical to a better understanding of globalized, complex food and that which is positioned as it alternatives. Whether it is fair trade discourse encouraging affective ties and shared embodied experience, established social relations informing the ways in which alternatives are viscerally felt, or bodies being tuned and trained towards certain tastes, eaters engage with food in and through their bodies. The questions of political economy and cultural politics are central, but they can only take us so far, just as assumptions of the inherent vitality of alternatives, such as Slow Food, are limited. One approach is not more productive than the other and both illuminate as much as they conceal, but both are somewhat removed from the subjective experience of eating.

I hoped to have demonstrated in this chapter how critical a focus eating is, as matter and the symbolic meaning of foods work together to create affect and effect in the eater. It is this process that binds the vitality of food's matter to a culturally salient meaning and informs eaters' food 'choices' and their engagement and participation in a food's assemblage – a process that dialectically shapes the form that assemblage takes. A greater recognition that food preferences are viscerally felt and sensed in the body – in sum, that food is eaten – as well as being abstracted intellectual 'choices', can enhance our comprehension of global and alternative food politics by seeking to experience them through the embodied subject position of the eater. And this, in turn, can bring deeper insights into the ways such politics are countered and the barriers that prohibit engagement and contestation.

Chapter 6

Eating for self and society: Responsible, acceptable and abject bodies

Introduction

This final ethnographic chapter extends the discussion of global foods and its alternatives by further examining how the self and 'other' are constituted by eating foods socially labelled as 'good' and 'bad'. My focus shifts here to the ways in which abject and responsible bodies are discursively produced, although I work to steer clear of fully adopting a social constructionist stance by stressing material engagements and embodied experiences that intersect with such discourses. Traversing the seemingly diverse topics of organic and GMO foods, waste, and obesity, which are drawn together by thread of 'responsibilized eating', I hence continue to ethnographically elucidate how matter and meaning are entangled and the vitalism of food, as made manifest by eating, is bound by social, cultural and political dynamics. I tease out the bio-authorities who identify and define abject and irresponsible eating and eating bodies, and show how this process oftentimes dialectically makes the self as responsible.

In short, in this chapter I drill down into notions of responsible and reflexive eating, both as a construction of the self and as a way of creating distance and proximity to other eating bodies. I am mindful here, however, not to construct a false dichotomy between eating a so-called 'responsible' diet – one that is framed as good for the individual body, social body and environment – as a form of care-full and reflexive eating loaded with political agency, and the consumption of its seeming opposite – commonly regarded as fast and global foods – as unreflexive and lacking in agency (cf Guthman 2003). Instead, I show how both, and neither, can be framed in this manner, as eating ostensibly for society is ultimately eating for the self. In so doing, I look to dissolve boundaries between good and bad eating, and acceptable and abject bodies, by highlighting how such classifications are produced through social and political relations.

The notion of care, which has been touched upon in all the chapters thus far, especially Chapters 4 and 5, is further developed in this chapter. And, not surprisingly given the subject matter, the themes of trust, risk and anxieties also re-emerge. Much has been written on the subjects of organic food and GMO, particularly from an agri-food studies and political economy perspective, which addresses questions of care, risk and responsibility. Likewise, obesity has been the subject of significant academic, popular and policy debate and waste is rapidly emerging as a productive avenue for examination in both the academy and beyond. I situate what follows within this literature, but I have no interest here in engaging with debates over which forms of food production are more sustainable, the consequences of commodifying care, or the potential effects of other environmental and social factors, such as climate and population change.

This is not to deny the critical importance of these discussions at academic, practice and policy levels, but I have chosen, as I hope has become evident throughout the course of the previous chapters, to take a different direction that stresses the need to treat food as food – a substance we eat – and attends to bodies and embodied practice first and foremost. Paying more attention to the sensations and affects created by organic food or waste, for instance, their social and material vitality, and the ways in which their broader assemblages are defined by both abstracted discourses and the embodied experiences of eating, facilitates deeper insights into the structural relations and political dynamics that have been the subject of so much attention to date.

Organic and GMO foods

Organic food emerged as a counterculture (Belasco 1989) and has not uncommonly been represented as situated in polar opposition to the industrialized, food system (cf Morgan and Murdoch 2000) in both academic and popular discourse (see previous chapter), although commentators have critiqued this oversimplification and drawn attention to the mainstreaming of organic and its misplaced association with the local and small scale (Clarke et al. 2008; Coles 2015; Goodman 2013; Guthman 2003). Like fair trade, among other food practices broadly labelled as 'alternative', eating organic food can be seen as the commodification of care and the enactment of caring relations at a distance, albeit for the environment rather than for growers. Studies of organic food have also, in a not dissimilar fashion to discussions of alternative food movements, drawn attention to how its consumption is performative of social hierarchies and class distinctions (Goodman 2013; Guthman 2003). These parallels and conflations are not surprising given the extent to which, in practice, many alternative food initiatives are based on organic provisioning, although this is not exclusively the case and, as I expound below, organic food has long been adopted by 'the mainstream' (cf Guthman 2003).

GMO food has arguably drawn more polarized debate in academic and policy circles, as well as in popular discourse, than any other contemporary food issue. As Müller writes, GMOs are 'global objects of contention, crystallizing some of today's major political and social controversies', which are 'alive and have agency' and provoke 'a culture of urgency' (2006: 3). They are intrinsically entangled with political economic questions of intellectual property and the associated institutionalized dynamics of power, such as international trade agreements, as well as the effectiveness of democratic institutions to regulate corporate interests. Moreover, GMOs raise social concerns over who is marginalized, heard and silenced, in addition to much broader issues of the nature of life itself and philosophical right for human action to intervene (ibid.: 4). GMO foods, particularly in the form of their popular avatar Monsanto, have also been a central lens through which broader contestations of neoliberalism and agri-industrial capitalism have been played out (Fitting 2014).

In the region of the Ecuadorian Andes where I conducted my fieldwork, GMO foods are less of an issue than in other Latin American contexts such as Colombia and Mexico (cf Fitting 2014), although this is not to state that modified foods are not produced in country or available.[1] There are concerns about GMO foods, as the scantest of glimpses at privileged migrant blogs will show (see for example gringosabroad.com), but, on the whole, there are greater anxieties over the non-human substances found in food produced through, what was framed as, conventional agriculture – although such discussions slide readily into GMO debates and the distinctions were, at times, blurred, primarily due to the obfuscation and fears I highlighted in the previous chapter. What was clear, however, is that worries over organic and GMO foods were far more prevalent among the privileged migrant community than my Ecuadorian research participants.

One of the most striking motifs in my discussions with privileged migrants was organic food, particularly the difficulties they had in acquiring it. The topic cropped up consistently in formalized interview situations and in focus group discussions, as well as during more informal chats and conversations, such as those that took place during 'Gringo Nights' in local restaurants and even upon meeting incidentally in the street or plaza. 'Is it organic?' was a common question my participants asked when ordering food, and I was not infrequently asked about ways that 'safe' organic food could be obtained from 'trusted' sources, as well as being party to a number of discussions on the topic. Snippets of information about possible suppliers were circulated among the community, and I was particularly struck when I heard one of my participants, Jimmy, asking a barman whether the mint in his *mojito* was organic. Moreover, a number of participants explained that one of the aspects of their new life they found hardest to negotiate was the scarce availability of organic food, which, considering the levels of bureaucracy involved in navigating residency, property, finance and taxation in Ecuador, is telling. The lack of certified, organic food was also a major disappointment for those seeking 'a simple life': Steve, for example, told me that his wife 'is finding it really hard. She wants to eat organic food and you just can't find it here. I'm OK, I'm finding ways of dealing with it but it's been really hard for her.'

I found this dominance of organic food – in discourse if not in practice – surprising in this context, given that over the course of the decade I had been visiting the region, I rarely, if ever, heard the term 'organic' when conducting research with small-scale producers and retailers. My astonishment at the time is reflected in my field journal, which I reproduce verbatim here:

> Just another thing reflecting on this whole organic / expat thing. I remember Linda waxing lyrical about the Peruvian restaurant and the K cafe, and the main selling point about them being that there were these 'organic' salads. I remember her saying that 'I had this great salad, it was all organic and fresh; it had everything in it – beets and carrots and corn and well, just everything' (or words to that effect). The fascination with organic food with the expats is remarkable – and doesn't really engage with local valorizations of food.

Moreover, I had infrequently seen food labelled as organic in higher-end restaurants or the supermarket, let alone in the local markets, although the restaurant scene had changed dramatically over my fieldwork period (see Abbots 2014a). In essence, I had never made associations between the region and 'organic' food in its labelled and categorized sense, although I knew some small-scale producers who preferred non-chemical fertilizers, had passed numerous bags of rotting fish and bonemeal waiting to be spread on agricultural plots, been taught about planting during moon cycles, and observed my Jimeño participants leaving their domestic produce to grow without any intervention. In short, while organic production methods may have been utilized by the smaller-scale producers I worked and lived with, it was rarely consciously constructed as such. In essence, 'organic' was just not in the local lexicon. So, I was perhaps even more surprised to hear the barman answer Jimmy's question with 'yes, of course it's organic, I know how to look after my customers', as I was when I was offered oversized fruit from a street vendor who told me without hesitation or prompting 'it's organic'. A shift had certainly occurred.

The extent and ways that 'organic' has moved into the Cuencano narrative of food gives some indication of the influence of the privileged migrant community on the local foodscape, as well as the ways that local retailers and producers are responding to the economic opportunities migrants bring. That, however, is a discussion for another time and place. What interests me here is questioning, following Jessica Hayes-Conroy's (2014) lead, what motivates this desire for organic food and the emotions and feelings that emerge as a result. My answer here, simply put, is fear. As I have indicated in previous chapters, privileged migrants are fearful of the unknown non-human and human bodies implicated in their food, and this extends to pesticides and chemicals, as much as it does obscured people and pathogens (see Chapter 5). In contrast to Jackson's (2015) findings that eaters are not consumed by anxieties in their quotidian food practices, my participants have a far more anxious approach to food that results in a ferocious policing of their bodily boundaries. This is compounded, in part, by being a migrant and the bodily dislocation this brings (see Chapter 3). But it is not the only factor as the desire for simple food was a motivation for privileged migrants' move in the first instance. As highlighted in the previous chapter, migrants themselves often cited the 'not knowing' that comes with complex food networks as a significant food issue. Yet I want to suggest that they did, in a fashion, know. They may not have liked what they knew in a general sense and were uncomfortable with their lack of awareness of the details, but they strongly felt they knew that 'something' undesirable was entering, or had a strong possibility of entering, their food. They did not know exactly what that something was, and that is part of the problem, but anxieties about this were strong enough to influence their decision to invest economically and emotionally in living in another country.

Privileged migrants look to their own bodies for this knowledge. While not all have been subject to life-threatening disease and health scares, those that had experienced such personal traumas and difficulties used their illnesses as evidence that eating industrial food laden with pesticides had damaged their body. In some cases, this had led to an epiphany and significant lifestyle change. One of my participants, for example, following his own treatment for a stress-related illness, was exploring the possibility of starting a medical tourism venture that would potentially provide nutritional education and cleansing programmes. While low healthcare costs were the primary factor, seemingly easy access to cheap, healthful and 'clean' food was also an attraction. Privileged migrants consequently sought to rectify and minimize corporeal damage by now eating organic foods. Moreover, others looked to the 'damaged' bodies of their peers and the possibility of disease, and sought to take preventative action. Eating organic was thus a mechanism for maintaining their bodily integrity.

The issue privileged migrants then face is they feel they cannot trust the local growers, retailers and markets, which resulted in them seeking out formally certified food in the sterile spaces of the supermarket.[2] This, in turn, gives rise to another tension, as they are engaging with the globalized foods and foodspaces they were intending to avoid. They are thus caught in a paradox: their bodies require 'simple food', but the fears and embodied experiences of this simple food push them back to more complex foods. On one hand, some, like Steve, attempt to navigate this by forcing himself, in an act of Cartesian will, to eat the foods (mis)sold by local vendors, even though he knew 'in my heart that it isn't organic' and his embodied experience of eating watery, tasteless strawberries supported that knowledge. On the other hand, others actively do all they can to seek out organic food. Recognizing the corporeal tensions they experience gives some clarity to such motivations. Labelled and certified organic food is, in this context, if not a happy, at least a more comfortable medium: it maintains bodily boundaries, can still be justified and defined as simple, despite often being acquired through supermarkets, and can be trusted.

Another aspect motivating organic eating that I wish to raise here is the way in which, in this ethnographic context, it is centred on the self and care for the self. There was little recourse in my participants' commentaries on organic food on the broader ecological impact or any sense of eating for the greater good. In essence, there was no hint of broader environmental concerns or ideologies in their discussions, as may have been expected, given the discourses of sustainability in which organic production is situated, although these did emerge a little more in discussions of food waste as I discuss below. There is some sense of organic food being positioned as an 'alternative' to 'Global Food' (cf Carolan 2011) that stemmed from the ways privileged migrants constructed it as 'simple', but this is less driven by broader ideological principles about industrial capitalism and more centred on the ways these complex and obscured political dynamics played out in the individual body, especially in the form of its health. In short, any discourse of caring for the planet or society was subsumed by caring for the self – or more specifically the body of the self, which, in turn, helped construct the social identity of the self (Bourdieu 1984; Guthman 2003).

Care for self and society are not antithetical, however. Eating for the self (in terms of bodily care and expression of social position), as I expound below and have also suggested in my discussion of fair trade in the previous chapter, can neatly align with and be reflective of broader societal concerns, and this, I suggest, is the case with privileged migrants' preference for organic. The self comes first, but the consequences of eating in their preferred manner removes them (or is an attempt to remove them) from a food system and political economic structure they find problematic. This further shows why eating as a material practice is critical to these broader debates, as it is through the eating body that these political economic dynamics are experienced and contested, albeit sometimes incidentally.

The way in which care for the self, albeit in a different guise, motivates organic consumption is also evident in Guthman's (2003) account of the 'mainstreaming' of organic food in California specifically and the United States more widely. Guthman traces the evolution of organic food from 'counter-cuisine' (cf Belasco 1989) to its appropriation and adoption by large-scale retailers, thus questioning the simplistic dichotomy between organic/alternative/small-scale and conventional/industrial/large-scale (see also Coles 2015; Goodman 2013). She does this by centring on salad mix (or *mesclun*), which she argues 'jump-started' the sector as higher-end trendsetting restaurants and then larger retailers started marketing the product to an upwardly mobile eater. Restaurants initially created a taste for *mesclun* and retailers followed by establishing a market and high volume sales. Salad mix thereby became an aspirational food, or 'yuppie chow' in Guthman's terms, but these elitist leanings and its mainstreaming did not result in the foodstuff becoming disembedded entirely from its alternative roots. Rather, it came to epitomize social awareness and class position. Guthman concludes:

> Eating organic salad mix was in some sense performative of an elite sensibility, albeit a rather unusual one. Organic salad mix was strongly coupled with – indeed helped to animate – the figure of the 'yuppie', the San Francisco Bay area of which was not wholly devoid of social conscience … but not shorn of gentrified aspirations either. (ibid.: 52)

What interests me the most in Guthman's account is the notion that the substance of food matters, which is implied in her discussion of how salad mix as an enabler of yuppie identity dovetailed neatly with dominant political and body image ideals. For the privileged migrants in Cuenca, Ecuador, what matters is that the food they are eating is organic and therefore, in a sense, it does not matter what food it is – whether it is mint leaves in a cocktail, strawberries, beef, milk or grain, food is a carrier for other substances that act upon migrants' bodies in positive or damaging ways. Or more accurately, organic food, whatever form it takes, is constructed as having an absence of harmful bodies more than a presence of potentially beneficial ones. Whereas in Guthman's account, the fact that salad mix *is* salad mix is not incidental – it is absolutely critical to its consumer appeal. This is, in part, attributable to the ways it can be grown and distributed – there is a production aspect here that is instrumental to its popularity and market take-up – but it also has a paucity of calories that makes it particularly attractive to eaters concerned with having a thin body.

Thinness was the desired body shape for yuppie consumers, and salad mix aligns perfectly with this aesthetic as it 'was a good option for mediating body anxiety' (Guthman 2003: 54). A convergence emerges, then, between salad's popularity and prevalent body ideals among this group of 'yuppie' eaters. This, coupled with its symbolic capacity for political consciousness and class mobility, propelled organic salad. In short, it became a food through which yuppies could express their social position, demonstrate their ecological and political conscience, *and* be thin. The substance of salad thus neatly fitted into a broader assemblage of discourses about healthful, reflexive eating and the construction of the self. Matter, bodies (and ideals about bodies) and political ideologies thus interacted in one potent encounter. As Guthman surmises, salad mix played 'into yuppie sensibilities, including the desire to control one's body shape' (ibid.: 54).

Salad was not just deemed 'healthy', but also tasty. Moreover, its taste was not just derived from its substance, but also its social and political dynamics, with one of Guthman's commentators explaining that 'when you choose to buy and eat organic and sustainably raised produce, a little bit of this karma rubs off on you, which makes everything taste better. A lot of this local, organic stuff does taste better' (Unterman 2000 in Guthman 2003: 54). Likewise, Goodman (2013: 119) notes that the 'better tasting' nature of organic milk influenced his family's purchasing preferences. I have addressed the cultural construction of taste in earlier chapters and do not wish to retread this ground, so I merely note here the prevalence of the embodied experience and how it is through eating that these judgements are made. The veracity of claims that organic food tastes better is not my concern and the question is one that is ultimately redundant, given the ways in which taste is subjectively experienced and socially acquired (Carolan 2011; Classen 1997; Hayes-Conroy 2014; Probyn 2000). What does come to the fore here, nonetheless, is the way in which corporeal and social tastes entwine and imbue each other with specific characteristics. In Unterman's quote above, social relations, in the form of karma, *make* the food taste better. The sociality of the food, its symbolic meaning, is thereby seen to inform its matter, and this is fully manifested and experienced upon its encounter with the eating body.

The body is absented in Fitting's (2014) political economic account of GMO activism in Colombia and Mexico, but we can still see how the matter of food is critical. Fitting describes how anti-GMO campaigners in both countries have strategically mobilized narratives of corn as a means of forging solidarity with multiple organizations that extend beyond agriculture and environment. Although the narratives differ a little, corn is an important cultural symbol of place in both Colombia and Mexico, as it is in Ecuador. In Colombia, it is firmly associated with indigeneity while in Mexico it has come to stand for indigeneity and the *mestizo* (mixed-race) nation (see also Pilcher 1998). As such, it has a cultural and social vitality rooted in contemporary politics and historical processes. Activists animate and draw upon these discourses in slogans such as 'We are a people of corn' and 'Without corn there is no country' (Fitting 2014: 175), thereby emphasizing the centrality of the crop to cultural identity, place-based belonging and livelihoods. Corn is also a key component of diet to the extent that a meal is not considered complete in rural Mexico without corn *tortillas* (Fitting 2014: 177). Like those of my Jimeño research participants, Mexican *campesino* (peasantry) bodies are thus, in part, made of corn.

This cultural vitality of corn is key as it enables anti-GMO activists to galvanize support in ways that would not be possible if their campaigns centred on other foods. Indeed, Fitting writes that other transgenic crops, such as cotton, have been produced in Mexico without the levels of concern that corn engenders, and she attributes this to corn's social and cultural significance in this ethnographic context, stressing that activists 'strategically focused on maize as a powerful symbol of *their* region, its peoples, and its cultures' (ibid.: 187, original emphasis). In so doing, she follows Schurman (2003) in indicating the differences between anti-GMO campaigns in the Global North, which focus on ethical concerns around inter-species boundaries, playing God and food safety, and those in the Global South that coalesce around neoliberal and neo-imperialist issues affecting farmers' livelihoods, the environment and society. This may be a somewhat oversimplified binary depiction but, nevertheless, what emerges from Fitting's account is the centrality of a particular foodstuff to the campaigns she discusses, rather than abstracted ideological concerns shaping contestations to GMO elsewhere. Put crudely, Franken*food* is less of an issue here than Franken*corn*. It is corn that has the capacity to generate affect and attachment because of its social and cultural positioning. Invoking Douglas' (2002) body as metaphor model, to infringe upon corn is to infringe upon the social body.

Fitting's corn resonates with Guthman's organic salad mix in indicating that it is the substance of the food in question, rather than food per se, that is of import. The factors behind the foods' appeal may be very different – thinness and yuppie class aspirations versus cultural belonging and indigenous and national identity – but the foundations are the same. It is the matter, the specificities of the food, not food as a general category, which counts. Matter does not stand in isolation, however: it generates and is folded into multiple social knowledges and symbolic meanings and, as both corn and salad mix demonstrate, it is these assemblages and interplays that confer its agentic capacity to create new consumer markets or lead campaigns. As Müller concludes, 'GMOs have agency because they are alive, but they cannot assume responsibility for their actions, as this in an inherently human quality' (2006: 4–5).

The matter of waste

Notions of responsible and reflexive eating, especially in relation to the environment, further coalesce around the theme of food waste. This emergent topic, which is giving rise to a small yet critically important and theoretically innovative body of interdisciplinary literature (Evans, Campbell and Murcott 2013; see, for example, Alexander, Gregson and Gille 2013; Evans 2014), is proving to be a fertile lens through which to explore questions of materiality and the agency of 'stuff'. Food waste was not a topic I actively pursued over the course of my fieldwork in Ecuador as my Ecuadorian participants rarely raised it as an issue. In Jima, food scraps from household consumption go to the pigs, while other food-related rubbish, of which there was little, as grain staples are bought in large sacks and fruit and vegetables acquired without wrapping, are burnt. Privileged migrants living in Cuenca city and its environs did broach the subject, often in the context of broader discussions of globalized food and their preferred eating preferences. As such, they tended to direct the conversation towards waste, even when it was not a key question on the agenda. This is exemplified by Angela who gave her opinion about the food choices of the local Ecuadorian population during a small group discussion:

> They don't know what they're doing; they're eating all this junk food and just don't realize what they're doing to their bodies – how bad it is for them. And the waste as well: the amount of rubbish that gets produced and just gets thrown all over the landscape – this beautiful landscape! It's being ruined.

One of the most striking aspects of Angela's comment is the way in which she casts waste as an inevitable by-product of industrial food and global capitalism. The 'junk' food she is referring to here is that which is obtained from global fast food outlets, along with other processed and complex foods that she, along with her peers, diametrically counterposes to local and simple food. Her definition of food waste centres on the material packaging through which this food travels to the consumer, which may seem a commonsensical and self-evident definition, but there are multiple ways food waste can be framed (cf Evans, Campbell and Murcott 2013). While I am not denying that the fast food industry, among other globalized food actors, produce packaging that needs to be discarded, I do want to stress that the waste-complex food association is just one of many possibilities and thereby warrants attention. The way Angela then situates waste within the landscape further indicates her broader political sensibilities and suggests how these may be mediating her eating, although environmental concerns are certainly not the only factor influencing migrant eating practices, as I have demonstrated in earlier chapters.

Privileged migrant attitudes to fast food chains are particularly ambivalent, not only because they are regarded as the epitome of complex food, but also because migrants view them as symbol of North American cultural imperialism (see Abbots 2013). It is not surprising, then, that Angela's comments slipped easily from the damage being done to the landscape to the damage being done to the local culture, as she talked about the erosion to local and 'traditional' food practices. In making these connections, Angela is replaying a common refrain found in both popular and activist (and some academic) discourse – that complex food, and the fast food industry in particular, is a homogenizing entity from which local food heritages need protecting (cf Ritzer 2010).[3] These connections were made through recourse to the landscape, which reflects the hegemonic discourse that occurs in this specific ethnographic context, where natural environment and cultural practices tend to be drawn together and represented as one under the rubric of 'heritage'. This interplay between nature and culture is embodied in the female peasant figure of the *Chola Cuencana*, who is deeply embedded in romantic and timeless pastoral scenes and has come to stand for the 'blending' of indigenous and Spanish traditions. Living reflections of this folkloric figure tend to perform the labour of upholding rural food culture while also lacking the bio-authority to politically represent it (Abbots 2014b).

Privileged migrants did not, however, seek to draw my attention to any food waste that was produced in and of the countryside, such as burning piles of toxic plastic sacks or stacks of slaughtered and rotting animal bodies, or any material that could be a by-product of small-scale agricultural production. The countryside only featured, somewhat passively, in relation to what was being done to it by the forces of complex 'Global Food' and there was no accounting for any waste produced within a landscape that was constructed as a rural idyll.[4]

Moreover, food did not feature explicitly in migrants' framings of food waste. Rather, food packaging was the problem. But packaging does not throw itself over the landscape, however much agency it has attributed to it, and Angela's comment also suggests that human action is at play here. One can surmise from the tone of her narrative that those who are throwing the rubbish of fast food are those who are eating fast food. This accords with other comments from privileged migrants that disparaged the local population's perceived tendency to publicly litter, despite the number of municipal workers employed to keep the city centre spotless. The way they regarded littering as problematic behaviour stems partly from migrant norms and their environmental concerns, but it is further compounded as a problem, I suggest, because it runs counter to the idealized image, which circulates prevalently among this group, of the local 'other' as guardians of the landscape.

What this account illustrates is the inherently relational and contingent properties of waste (cf Evans, Campbell and Murcott 2013; Evans 2014; Gille 2007), and the ways in which the classification of what constitutes food waste is entangled in social relations, knowledges and ideologies. But just as the matter of waste is enmeshed in social relations, so are social relations shaped by waste's materialities. The shifting assemblages of food waste are teased out particularly cogently in Evans, Campbell and Murcott's (2013) edited collection *Waste Matters*, with the editors noting, alongside Shilling's (2013) *Forward*, how studies of food waste align with and can be productively informed by new materialism perspectives, to the extent that contributors to the volume who start from a political economy or cultural turn approach ultimately arrive at a 'post-humanist' reading that stresses the agency of matter (Evans, Campbell and Murcott 2013: 11). The microorganisms involved in food decomposition lend themselves neatly to accounts of material vitality and, indeed, Bennett asks how 'would patterns of consumption change if we faced not litter, rubbish, trash, or "the recycling," but an accumulating pile of lively and potentially dangerous matter?' (2010: viii). In accord, Alexander and Reno (2012) show us that the matter of waste needs to be taken seriously, as objects are recycled, reused, re-formed and re-traded in ways that produce new forms of identities, economic activities and social and political networks, and Gregson and Crang (2010) call for a focus on the stuff of waste and a recognition that waste is not 'stuff that "just is"', but is instead stuff that 'becomes' (ibid.: 1028). They too argue that materiality is central to the understanding of waste.

A new materialist-post-human approach that is in line with my own in propounding the performativity of matter while also arguing that matter's agency is not inherent but derived from its articulation with social, economic and political dynamics can be found in Hawkins's (2013) discussion of food packaging. Her starting point is that

> packaging has agency in both food markets *and* political processes; that aspects of its materiality participate in assembling consumers and recyclers in both productive and problematic ways. This agency, however, has to be enacted; it is not inherent in the material but emerges in the force field of relations in which packaging acquires the capacity to effect actions or prompt changed practices. (ibid.: 67)

Hawkins elucidates this perspective by interrogating how food packaging acquires the capacity to facilitate the construction of new political subjectivities through the recycling of empty food containers. Arguing that such objects are 'political devices' (ibid.: 68), she describes how the decision to rinse and put an empty food tin in a specially allocated container for recycling, instead of just throwing it in the general waste bin, affords the consumer with the opportunity to enact new forms of engagement that helps constitute them as a 'recycler'. The tin's very material presence gives rise to questions about what should be done with it once it no longer has a place within the household. But the tin does not work in isolation. Rather it is entangled in wider discourses of ethical concern for the environment, the 'afterlife' of objects and notions of consumer responsibility. The tin, therefore, forms part of an assemblage of matter and meaning and, as such, is 'a device for materializing new forms of political participation and citizenship' (ibid.: 80). Moreover, the tin does not just generate forms of political participation in humans – as part of waste's assemblage with the capacity to create a/effect, it *is* a political participant.

Hawkins continues to show how packaging can be economic as well as political matter through the lens of a PET water bottle, which, she explains, shaped new ways of marketing water drinking, and also prompted different forms of waste management systems that were disrupted by the new meanings of disposability its material properties presented. The PET bottle did not just act as a substitute for other forms of packaging, but also worked to create new market realities and consumer behaviour, in addition to making new meanings and practices around shifting notions of disposability and single-use items. In essence, it assembled new meanings for water that extended beyond the market and reached into environmental and political frames. Hawkins thus concludes that while packaging has had significant economic effects, such capacity 'cannot be separated out from its impacts on mediating and reordering the economy of qualities of what we eat or drink and the way we do it' (ibid.: 81).

Hawkins's account highlights how matter is embedded within and animates social life, and we see this in privileged migrant discourse as exemplified by Angela. I wish to suggest here that the material presence of the litter privileged migrants saw strewn across the landscape forms part of an assemblage of fast food and articulates with, and charges, their social concerns about cultural imperialism, complex food systems and environmental pollution. Recognizing the agentic capacity of this waste helps us understand that it was not just viewed through this lens of discourse, but is its own intrinsic element that dialectically is part of, and makes, this discourse. The litter is not an empty vessel that is merely attributed social meaning and thereby becomes symbolic of wider concerns, instead, as a mediating agent it helps constitute such concerns. In so doing, following Hawkins, it informs the making of privileged migrant political subjectivity as responsible eaters.

Fast-food-generated rubbish does not just prompt the making of the self, but it further facilitates the construction of 'the other' – the other being, in this Ecuadorian context, the irresponsible eating bodies who are consuming complex food and throwing its packaging across the landscape. When Angela opines, 'They don't know what they're doing; they're eating all this junk food and just don't realize what they're doing to their bodies – how bad it is for them,' she is constructing a group of eaters as lacking in education, awareness and self-reflection, in contrast to her own and peers' subject position as reflexive and politically sensitive eaters. The 'they' in question are consequently, in this privileged migrant commentary, represented as fast-food-consuming 'dupes' who do not know any better (cf Guthman 2003; Phillipov 2013). As Guthman (2003) duly notes, these dichotomous constructions strip 'irresponsible' eaters of agency, while according reflexive eaters with the political agency to co-produce food systems. One group are passive eaters, represented as mindlessly consuming that which is offered without question and subjected to the political economic forces of complex food – in Carolan's (2011) terms, eaters that have been tuned to 'Global Food' – whereas the others are consciously eating and retuning their tastes to effect social change. The former are thereby constructed as a problem that requires the intervention and bio-authority of the latter group to teach them the error of their ways (cf Foucault 1978, 1980) and to eat in a more responsible manner (cf Guthman 2011).

Waste-full and waist-less bodies

This (false) dichotomy of eaters emerges even more strongly when we consider the bodies – and body ideals – of the two groups. Angela's comment slips readily from rubbish to unhealthy eating, and the conversation thread across the focus group rapidly moved to the average larger body size of the local Cuencano population and diet they supposedly consumed. The dangers of complex food and irresponsible eating were made manifest to my privileged migrant participants not solely in the packaging spread across the landscape, but also in the embodied forms of the local populace. These two visual markers – fast food waste and bigger bodies – each reinforced the other in migrants' narratives of local care-less eaters. There is an easy, yet highly problematic, association here between larger body size and rubbish that hints that unreflexive eaters are constructed as wastefully consuming calories as much as they are creating waste through their food packaging. The 'junk food' to which Angela refers can be seen as literally and metaphorically junk – unwanted, unnecessary and ultimately disposable.[5] Resonating with Guthman's (2003) account of yuppie subjectivities, notions of responsible eating and political citizenship among privileged migrants, as mediated through food waste and care for the environment, are inherently bound up with body shape ideals: Waist-full is waste-full, and waist-less, waste-less.

Junk food did not just create waste in terms of packaging, then, but also created surplus in the body in the form of fat. The seeming agentic capacity of 'junk food' to act upon the body is demonstrated in commentaries, like Angela's, which make simplistic cause-and-effect associations between eating complex globalized food and larger body sizes. Such bodies, as Guthman (2011) shows, are as undesirable as the foods that are understood to produce them. Eating abject foods, the narrative goes, makes abject bodies (Phillipov 2013, see also Forth 2014). Such narratives have been subject to critique, especially in literature that sits under the umbrella term of obesity studies or critical fat studies (see for example *Antipode* 2009; Aphramor, Brady and Gringas 2013; Colls 2007; Colls and Evans 2008, 2013; Eli and Lavis 2016; Lupton 2015), and I wish to close this chapter by unpacking the ways in which bio-authorities are created through such discourses, while also highlighting the importance of recognizing the mediated embodied experience and material encounters of eating that can often be glossed over in social constructionist frames.

The way that fat as matter can be regarded as waste is drawn out by Ehlers (2014), who writes that 'while not routinely expelled from the body, it [fat] is *designated* as that which *should* be expelled and as corporeal tissue that can be wasted' (2014: 110, original emphasis). Fat thus joins pus, faeces and urine as repugnant and surplus tissue, as framed within the biomedical economy of value, as it is not essential to the body's functioning. It is this very status as waste, Ehlers argues, that enables fat to be revalued as matter that can be productively deployed in plastic surgery. This brief example suggests that fat is not inherently abject, but rather its social value is entangled with its material form and the ways in which the substance is then put to use. The extent to which fat is constituted as waste, and the amount of fat that is deemed surplus, is clearly socially contingent as scholarship on the discursive construction of fat bodies shows (*Antipode* 2009; Aphramor, Brady and Gringas 2013; Colls 2007; Colls and Evans 2008, 2013; Guthman 2011; Longhurst 2012; Wright and Harwood 2009). Indeed, returning briefly to Jima, larger body sizes were favoured by my *campesina* participants, who often valued bigger female bodies through the lens of fertility and their perceived capacity to produce healthy children. The approving call of '*que esbelta!*' (what a figure!) often accompanied women with ample hips, while those on the slimmer side were a cause for concern as they were 'too thin'. Hence I was party to many a discussion about what constituted 'a good weight' and experienced my own body, and those of my visiting European friends, being surveyed from various angles as my Ecuadorian friends sought to determine our potential to bear children. In sum, fat is seen as a waste in some contexts but valued as a resource in others, and the size of eaters who embody fatness is relational and contingent.

Nonetheless, fat bodies, whatever size they may need to be to be labelled 'abject' or even 'fat', are not uncommonly socially constructed as problematic. As Colls and Evans argue, fatness is an 'inherently political issue' (2009: 1011), and a number of scholars have worked to expound the social dynamics and assumptions informing much anti-obesity rhetoric and interventions (see, for example, *Antipode* 2009; Colls and Evans 2013; Gard and Wright 2005; Lupton 2015), stressing, in the process, how fatness becomes equated with individual irresponsibility (Colls and Evans 2008; Evans 2006; Guthman 2011) and the counterproductive ways the visceral and emotional are overlooked in public health initiatives (Aphramor, Brady and Gringas 2013). This latter point is picked up by Forth (2014), who notes that fat generates strong emotional responses and, while these are varied across cultural contexts, disgust is the most prevalent in popular discourse and has been the recipient of most academic attention (see also Lupton 2015). He stresses that responses to fat and fat bodies are not just visual, but are synesthetic reactions that may 'rely on tactile, olfactory, and auditory impressions as well as visual ones' (ibid.: 4).

Firth thus calls for a focus on the material and experiential properties of fat that have evaded social constructionist approaches that, in privileging the visual and the abstract discursive representation of fatness and the body, reproduce Cartesian mind/body dualisms. In so doing he extends Colls's (2007) call for Fat Studies scholarship to move beyond questions of representation and take the matter of fat seriously as 'it has its own capacities to act and be active' (Colls 2007: 358). This is not to extricate materiality from knowledge and representation entirely, with Colls (ibid.) writing that both matter and discourse are so mutually entangled that one cannot privilege the other. Fatness is thus socially created as a moral issue (Colls and Evans 2009; Guthman 2011) and its representations should not be separated from its material capacity to evoke visceral and affective responses (Forth 2014).

The question of how fatness is discursively produced as a problem – a topic that has preoccupied those coming from a more social constructionist perspective – does help us understand the ways in which bio-authority is made and upheld. As fat bodies come to be treated as sites requiring intervention, the themes of governance, discipline, surveillance and regulation come to the fore and anti-obesity initiatives have comfortably leant themselves to Foucauldian analysis and critique. The collection *Biopolitics and the 'Obesity Epidemic'* (2009), edited by Wright and Harwood, is one such example. Wright and Harwood, as I discussed in Chapter 1, frame this collection through the lens of biopedagogies – which are defined as 'normalising and regulating practices' that 'not only place individuals under constant surveillance, but also press them towards increasingly monitoring themselves' (Wright 2009: 1). As such, the contributors to the volume look to 'make visible the ways the ideas or discourse associated with the obesity epidemic work to govern bodies and to provide the social meanings by which individuals come to know themselves' (Wright 2009: 5).

This is exemplified by Murray (2009) who explores how fatness is read and pathologized by the medical profession in a manner that results in an individual 'confessing' to being 'a deficient self residing in a fat body' (ibid.: 79). Drawing on autoethnographic insights of being subjected to the medical gaze, she describes the process by which the visibility of her fat not only led to her being labelled as 'obese' and classified as a problematic body by various doctors, despite her good health, but also how such labelling requires and results in her own recognition and 'admission' of her own pathology. Framing this process as a Foucauldian confessional, Murray thus elucidates how obesity is co-constitutively discursively produced between medic and patient. This is not a symmetrical dynamic, however, but one mediated by the medic confessee, who has the greater authority. The 'confession' of fatness 'is only legitimized and validated if the confessee is positioned as a subject of authority who holds the power to forgive, correct, alter or transform the newly purged confessor' (ibid.: 84). This interaction, then, simultaneously constructs 'obesity' by privileging the visual gaze and fatness, pathologizes obesity as a problem, imbues the authority of the medic, and encourages the fat body to self-discipline through a reflexive process of admission. The embodiment of the fat self is thus valued, and found wanting, through the reflected gaze of medical discourse.

This gaze of 'confessors' and anti-obesity bio-authorities is not limited to the medical profession or to state and market interventions in the form of public health campaigns and the diet industry. The media, in the form of reality television (cf Eli and Lavis 2016), celebrity chefs (cf Abbots 2015b; Bell and Hollows 2011; Barnes 2014; *Food, Culture and Society* 2015; Hollows and Jones 2010; Piper 2015) and social media (cf Abbots and Attala 2014; Lavis 2016; Rousseau 2012a,b, 2015) can all be seen as public pedagogical mechanisms that inform and look to shape knowledges of what constitutes morally acceptable and 'healthy' bodies. Eli and Lavis (2016), for instance, argue that the reality show *Supersize vs Superskinny*, which pairs underweight and overweight participants in a diet-swapping practice, presents viewers with a 'stark and supposedly educative' (n.p.) take on food choices framed as 'public pedagogy'. Underpinning such discourses, they argue, is a classed and gendered dynamic, invoking models of responsibilized, middle-class motherhood and moral citizenship, which construct obese women as abject bodies through the lens of their fitness to mother. The dynamics between media (in its many divergent forms) and eating preferences is an emergent area of study through which shifting notions of abject and acceptable foods and bodies can be traced, and it offers a particularly promising route through which to examine the circulation, (re)production and potential democratization of food/body knowledges (cf Abbots and Attala 2014; Rousseau 2012a, 2015). The challenge, I suggest, for future research is to bring corporeality and embodied encounters with food into a subject area that is seemingly dominated by the visual (cf Goodman and Abbots 2015; Lavis 2016).

Embodiment has been drawn together with a Foucauldian interest in mediation, authority and knowledge in Truninger and Tiexera's (2015) account of school meals in Portugal. Bringing Carolan (2011) and Wright and Harwood's (2009) notion of biopedagogies into dialogue, they demonstrate how the practices of school meals, state authorities, and educational and kitchen staff all regulate and discipline childrens' individual and collective bodies. Yet they also show how these ordering mechanisms do not go uncontested but are instead negotiated and co-produced through childrens' embodied encounters with food. Although school meals are shaped by state policy and expert nutritional advice, state representatives reported that they adapted their guidelines to childrens' taste preferences, as well as family budgets and consumption habits. These negotiations continue at school canteens and coffee shops, with children expressing their agency by requesting second helpings, rejecting food by piling up plates to hide it or throwing it on the floor, swapping food with friends and even forced vomiting. Such visceral displays of taste and embodied performances of rejection, Truninger and Teixeira conclude, show how childrens' bodies and material constraints 'collide' with biopedagogical mechanisms and they elucidate the ways these interactions between knowledges, bodies and matter mediate everyday encounters with food.

Truninger and Teixeira's discussion indicates how political sensibilities, knowledge and embodied experience do not always neatly align but can, instead, give rise to tensions, a theme also evident in Longhurst's (2012) influential account of *'Becoming Smaller'*. Centred on her own personal journey of weight loss dieting, Longhurst examines the paradoxes of being a feminist writer critiquing discourses of thinness while desiring a smaller body, supporting the *Health at Every Size* movement publicly while personally placing losing weight over fitness, and eating in a simultaneously disciplined and disordered fashion. These paradoxes, she writes, 'felt uncomfortable'. As she cultivated the self, she reproduced and upheld the hegemonic ideal and knowledge of slim bodies in relation to, and at the expense of, othered fat bodies (ibid.: 884). Becoming smaller, then, was 'both enabling and repressive, dominant and resisting, about the social and the individual, and about the self and the Other' (ibid.: 884). It was also an inherently embodied experience, with Longhurst becoming aware of the spaces through which her increasingly slimmer body moved, monitoring the food and drink that went into her mouth, and having a greater sense of well-being as she began to socially and corporeally 'fit into' spaces of consumption, became more energetic and had less body aches and chafing. Her personal reflections consequently illuminate how interrogating the tensions between being and knowing can bring a deeper understanding of how food/body knowledges are upheld and contested – in short mediated – through the everyday visceral experiences of the eating body. She further, like Murray (2009), offers some intriguing methodological prospects for developing insights into eating through recourse to our own embodied encounters with food and autoethnography (see also Sexton 2016), the possibilities for which I reflect upon in the following concluding chapter.

Concluding remarks

This chapter has focused on the topics of organic and GMO foods, waste and obesity in order to tease out the ways in which bodies and eating practices are variously constructed as responsible, acceptable and abject, a process that dialectically produces sameness and otherness. While drawing heavily on scholarship influenced by social constructionist perspectives, I have also sought to highlight the subjective, lived experience of being and living in such bodies and the ways in which the matter of organic and GMO foods, food waste in the form of packaging, and fat have a vitality that acts upon eaters in myriad ways. I have thus continued to emphasize how matter and meaning intersect and are drawn together through the body by eating, in addition to elucidating how these processes are enacted through recourse to ethnography. In so doing, I have indicated how the vitalism of the material discussed is bound by (constructed) knowledge and its embeddedness within broader assemblages that can incorporate political discourse and ideology, notions of landscape and heritage, and biomedical understandings of the body, as well as the substances of other human and non-human bodies. From within these assemblages, bio-authorities, in the form of responsible eaters, medical professionals, media celebrities, to name a few examples, emerge.

In indicating ways that bio-authorities claim their authority through politically loaded, socially constructed knowledges that create 'the other' as irresponsible and abject and, in turn, present themselves as responsible, in addition to highlighting the contingencies and relationalities of such processes, I have worked to destabilize the (false) dichotomy between reflexive eating bodies that have the agentic capacity to make social and political change and those deemed to be unreflexive and lacking in agency. Placing bodies, in both their abstract forms and in the sense of subjective embodied encounters, at the forefront of my analysis, I have further looked to draw attention to the ways in which a focus on visceral sensations and affects can promote a deeper, more eater-orientated, insight into the structural relations and political dynamics that have been subject to so much discussion to date, especially in relation to organic and GMO foods. The materiality of such foods and the ways eaters subjectively experience them, as well as waste and fat, are critical to analysis. This does not negate the need to take political relations into account. Rather, it requires us attending to the ways in which such dynamics inform how we come to regard and treat these substances (and the bodies that incorporate, contain and discharge them), and inscribe them with social efficacy and meaning.

Chapter 7

Eating futures: Reflections and directions

In the preceding chapters I have worked to interrogate how the embodied act of eating draws together human and non-human bodies, material objects and cultural knowledge – all of which I have treated as mediators – into networks of relatedness. These interactions, between matter, meaning and bodies, shape a food's assemblage's form and charge each mediating actant with vitality – both social and material. Matter, as I have demonstrated, is made to matter through socially constructed knowledges and symbolic meanings. It does not have an inherent vitality, as Bennett (2010) writes, but instead a latent vitality that is brought to life and attributed meaning through human engagement and assembled interactions. Vitalism is thus bounded by social relations and practice. Embodied engagements, such as eating, make the matter of matter manifest by co-producing knowledges relating to the efficacy, affects and effects of that substance.

This is not to state that matter cannot act upon the body in an unmediated fashion (cf Mol 2008). Rather, the ways in which these bodily responses are understood to be provoked by certain substances and are then, in turn, projected onto and seen to be indicative of social relations and situations is, I have argued, a political process. Knowledge is thus constructed through bodily experience and also used to interpret and give meaning to such experiences. In short, I have looked to show that just as material is made to matter through symbolic meaning, meaning is made meaningful through matter. Thus, food has the agentic capacity to produce a/effect in the body not only because of its substance, but also because of the social meaning that humans give to that substance and the agency they bestow to it. These charged meanings, however, are enabled by the material substance through which meanings are carried and are made manifest. Matter and meaning are thereby intrinsically entangled.

In exploring how these entanglements are crystallized by eating, I have looked to highlight the commonsensical yet oft-forgotten fact that we eat food, and have worked to demonstrate that the materiality of food is worthy of more considered and systematic attention by food studies scholars. Following Holtzman (2009), I have argued for food to be treated as food, instead of just as a lens through which we can view 'society'. Food should be treated as an object of enquiry in its own right and eating considered as a moment through which discourse, social dynamics and substance are realized. This focus on the material facticity of food is not to deny its symbolic efficacy; on the contrary, I have elucidated how food is laden with knowledge and its very substance situated in assemblages of cultural knowledge and social and political dynamics. But this is just a part of the story, and here I continue the call I have previously made with Anna Lavis (Abbots and Lavis 2013; Abbots et al. 2015) – that we need to develop conceptual frameworks of eating that allow for food's multifaceted nature and recognize that it is simultaneously material, social, political and symbolic. There are many ways to do this, and what I have offered in this book is just one possible take on the subject. My approach has centred on interrogating how matter and meaning are folded into each other and interrelate, and I suggest that exploring these complex dynamics in multiple food and eating contexts can be a way forward through which to build the conceptual tools required to better understand food's multifaceted nature. What I am propounding, therefore, is a multidimensional approach that is not wedded to one particular theoretical school or paradigm, but instead draws elements of multiple perspectives together. I am thus urging food studies scholars to work across disciplines and bodies of literature even when – or especially when – they do not neatly align. It is at these jagged intersections that new and creative ways of concomitantly accounting for the materiality, the cultural meaning *and* the political economy of food can be forged (cf Abbots and Lavis 2013).

Foregrounding the body

The body comes to the fore in these new renderings of materiality, as the focus shifts towards the ways in which eating bodies subjectively and viscerally experience food. Adopting a phenomenological approach by considering how bodies-in-the-world encounter the substances of food can give us deeper insights into the ways in which social and political relations are not just intellectually experienced but are also corporeally *felt*. The experience of the eater thus becomes central, as we pay greater attention to how it feels, both physically and emotionally, to share the food of those we love even though they may be geographically distanced, or be fearful of drawing a unknown substance into our bodies, or be excited by the multisensory buzz of a food festival, or be transported to a place and time in our personal histories – to name but a few examples cited in the previous chapters. When we consider food and eating through this lens, the answer to the question 'why we should think about this body?' is self-evident: while eating can take many forms, it is an embodied and affective experience, and to ignore or 'gloss over' this is to bypass the critical moment when food – and all its attendant knowledges, meanings and political dynamics – becomes realized through the body of the individual eater.

Eating encounters are deeply personal and individual, and how we experience each encounter is informed by our own affective background of social relations, intimacies, values, memories and histories. We do not come to each eating experience as an empty vessel that absorbs the cultural meanings of a food and upon which political relations can be inscribed. Instead, the eating body is an active agent, which co-produces and mediates food knowledges and gives meaning to the matter being eaten. In so doing, the eating body (re)makes itself and a food's assemblage in which it is situated. It is a co-constitutive actor. The body, therefore, is not a fully malleable, plastic entity that has things done to it and can be moulded in a certain manner, as more passive representations suggest (cf Carolan 2011), but is instead fully active and involved. This activity is not completely governable, as Mol (2008) shows us, as the physical substances within the body interact with the substances of food in sometimes unpredictable ways, and in a manner that cannot be controlled by the thinking subject and willpower. As the experience of privileged migrants eating Ecuadorian food illustrates, the body can, at times, act in undesirable ways and produce unpleasant experiences. Agency is thus dispersed throughout the eating body: At times it can be (partially) subjected to the sheer will of the eater as Steve's determination to enjoy 'tasteless' strawberries suggests; but on other occasions, as Josie's experience of her body going into a 'tailspin' shows, no amount of will can control the internal workings of the body or the ways in which it interacts with the substance being ingested.

Agency is not just dispersed throughout the eating body, but is further located in the substances being ingested, or more accurately in the interactions between this material substance of food and the eating body. As my experience of eating cuy elucidates (Chapter 2), this matter can start to act upon the eating body to the extent that it does not just become incorporated into it, but can also be seen to be acquiring that body. Through repeated eating, I shifted from a position of disliking the meat to the point of desiring, even craving, it. There is a dual process occurring here; on one hand, cuy was colonizing my body as I became increasingly familiar with the meat, while on the other hand, my body was also domesticating cuy by making it more familiar. Eating bodies are therefore active, but this does not equate to them being fully in control. In this way, the matter of food can be seen as training bodies – whether it is Latour's (2004) perfumers having a 'trained' nose, Coles's (2013) coffee experts training their palates, or even Carolan's (2011) consumers being tuned to 'Global Food', repeated experiences of eating can be understood as directing and orientating an eater, and priming their bodies to experience that food in a certain manner.

The matter of food, however, while having the agentic capacity to prime bodies does not work in isolation, but instead comes to us with attendant meanings and cultural knowledge. Knowledge is, in itself, constructed through social relations and political dynamics, of which the eating body is mutually a part. It is these knowledges that give understanding and efficacy to the matter being eaten. A festivalgoer at Gilroy, for example, is not just viscerally experiencing garlic, but is doing so through a 'frame' (cf Adema 2009) that charges the garlic with social import. Likewise, Coles's experts can assess coffee beans through a rubric of abstracted knowledges based on what a coffee from a particular geographical location should taste like, and my Jimeño friends can determine whether a cuy is good or not, or is even cuy, through evaluating whether it has been raised, prepared and cooked in accordance with cultural norms. These knowledges emerge through repeated visceral interactions with the food in question, but they also come to the eater through other bio-authorial mechanisms, such as food festivals and history lessons. It is bio-authorities – in the forms of, for example, cooks, festival organizers, food industry actors, the media, other eaters, restaurateurs and grocery store owners – that help prime and orientate an eating body towards a food and shape the ways it is viscerally and subjectively received (by that body). This is not, as I have repeatedly stressed, a one-way dynamic through which bodies are subjected to and they passively absorb such bio-lessons – a process of mediation and contestation occurs.

Knowledge-power thus flows through and is produced through interactions between bio-authorities, the matter of food and the eating body. This thesis gives us greater insight into the political relations as they play out in the microsite of the eating body, and thereby deepens understandings of the ways in which power dynamics are experienced and felt. What I am encouraging here, building on the work of Hayes-Conroy and Hayes-Conroy (2008, 2010a,b) and Carolan (2011), is a more visceral and affective approach to the cultural politics of food that views political economic structures from the perspective of the individual eater and his or her embodied experience. This is not to deny the importance of studying such structures and relations, as the macro- and meso-level views are also critical to our comprehension of contemporary food systems. Rather, I am calling for greater attention to be paid to the micro-experiences of the individual eater, who is both situated within and co-produces such networks of political relations. In so doing, we can move to a more holistic understanding of food and eating by attending to the ways in which broader structures and dynamics play out in lived realities and filter down and into the body.

Rich ethnographic description becomes critical here, in that it can tease out the minutiae of how individuals feel and encounter the food they are eating, how they relate to what others are (or are not) eating, and the ways in which they engage with those actors who value (or not) and provide knowledge and cultural meanings about the food being eaten. And while anthropology does not have exclusive rights over ethnography, it arguably remains the lynchpin of the discipline and has been subject to much discussion and reflection, both in terms of methodology and representation, over the years (cf Clifford and Marcus 2010). The lessons learnt from such discussions and the qualitative approach commonly utilized by anthropologists can offer much to cross-interdisciplinary scholarship within food studies. Capturing the voices and experiences of eaters, as I hope to have illuminated here, helps ensure that potentially abstract concepts and debates, such as those around the agency of the non-human and new materialisms, are grounded in everyday lived reality, thereby minimizing the risk of them existing solely in an imaginary abstracted realm of academic thought. Applying conceptual tools and frameworks to the messy realities of quotidian life, and letting theoretical paradigms emerge from such realities, helps us assess the limitations and benefits of particular perspectives. Scholarship is thus enhanced and, perhaps, most importantly, building upon Goodman's (2015) foundational observation, agency and political dynamics are not just consigned to the realm of the ontological, but they are also considered through the lens of the political realities to which individuals are subjected and have to negotiate in their daily lives.

In some respects, then, this book and the ethnography contained within can be seen as my response to the question of 'what do I bring as an anthropologist?' What I bring from my discipline is a rich appreciation of ethnography and a desire to focus on individual micro-experiences of food. Ethnography can only be partial and subjective, and it is but one piece of the jigsaw through which to understand the political dynamics of food networks. I am not suggesting that ethnography is just 'grafted on' to structural analysis and scholarship that focuses more on macro-level questions. Instead, I am calling for a constantly shifting gaze between the micro, meso and macro, and have aimed to offer in the preceding pages a way in which this can be achieved. My focus has been on the myriad ways in which matter and meaning are entangled, and it is through ethnography that these subtle and nuanced entanglements can be teased out.

Methodological challenges

A focus on embodied experience, subjective encounters, and the affects and effects of matter presents methodological challenges to the study of eating specifically, and food more generally. As Murcott has noted (2013), one of the problems with researching eating is that the object of investigation quite literally disappears. Eating is also a momentary act, and we have to consider how we draw boundaries around eating or even if this is desirable. Do we focus on one mouth- or fork-full? Or an entire plate or meal? Moreover, do we focus on the moment of eating, of food being in the mouth, being chewed, swallowed and digested? Or should we be attending to the whole eating process – of sitting down in front of a plate of food, smelling its aromas and looking at it? If we are to argue that eating is synesthetic, then does it not follow that we need to take all of the senses into account, and not just the moment when food enters the body?, especially as recent work, for example Lavis (2016), has broadened our ideas of what eating is by attending to the visual and its visceral affects (see also Holtzman 2016). However, eating is different exactly because it transgresses bodily boundaries, it takes that which is outside and draws it into the body through the mouth. This process is one, moreover, through which matter is incorporated and makes the eating body (Fischer 1988). But there again, can we regard smelling or visually gazing at food also a bodily transgression? They may not be material substances as we intuitively perceive them to be, but images and aromas can also be imprinted onto the body, as work on food and memory shows us (cf Ben Ze'ev 2004; Serematakis 1994; Sutton 2001). They may not make a body in its physical sense, but they can still provoke an embodied response.

There is a danger that such questions result in nothing but an entangled researcher chasing his or her tail in a futile attempt to fix and frame a practice that cannot be fixed, and I advocate a fluid approach that does not attempt to do so. Eating does not need to be neatly and rigidly modelled in order to be analysed. On the contrary, a more fertile perspective may be to use a looser frame of reference that allows for the fact that eating can be many different practices that invokes a multiplicity of responses. Eating means different things to different people and animates myriad relations and practices. As such, definitions of what constitutes eating run the risk of being ethnocentric and deterministic. Instead, asking 'what is eating?', as Lavis (2016) does in the context of anorexia, allows for research participants' voices and understandings to be incorporated, in addition to productively directing us away from our own assumptions and preconceptions.

If we are to return to the more established notion of eating, of food entering the body and of that which is external becoming internal, we are faced with further challenges. As social scientists and humanities scholars, even those among us with a more 'scientific' leaning, we have tended not to follow food into the body – we do not have the analytical tools to do so. Meanwhile, the human sciences have the wherewithal and knowledges to understand how food interacts at a molecular level, but are less equipped to comprehend political economic structures, cultural meanings and social relations. Eating is, then, perhaps, a space for radical interdisciplinary dialogue between the natural and social sciences, in which a food can be followed through its social and political networks deep into the body. I have started to map such an approach with colleagues through the concept we have termed 'affective political ecology', and we are considering the interplays between external environmental factors and the internal workings of the microbiome in the context of obesity discourses (Abbots et al. n.d.). Interdisciplinary teams that can trace a food's affects and effects from the macro level of the 'Global Food' industry to the micropolitics of the gut (and back again) could be a fruitful area of future research that broadens and deepens the scope of what I have presented here.

Another issue we face as food studies scholars is how to observe and record, and then analyse, the visceral and subjective eating experiences of our research participants. I may be eating the same cuy as one of my participants, and the meat might even come from the same carcass, but I do not know if we are experiencing the same matter in the same way, let alone what emotional responses, memories or previous experiences the meat could be privately triggering in others. In some contexts bodily reactions may be explicit and self-evident, although care has to be taken not to attribute our own reading of facial expressions, for example, especially in cross-cultural contexts. That being said, if an individual spits out a mouthful of food with an emotive 'urgh!', we are most likely safe in assuming the sensation has not been to his or her pleasure. But observation can only take us so far, and we remain reliant on our participants' narratives and words to describe their embodied experience. And however nuanced and sophisticated our methods are for recording the thoughts and commentaries of our research participants, the issue remains that a subjective embodied, multisensory experience is still being abstracted and codified into language that cannot fully account for that phenomenological encounter. A level of abstraction between embodiment and the body necessarily occurs, which can give rise to analytical tensions that require reconciling.

Autoethnography may be one way forward here. This approach has been successfully utilized at times, whereas on other occasions writers have slipped into self-indulgent navel-gazing or seemingly used their own experiences to counter a lack of data. This is, of course, a matter of perspective, and I do not intend to cite examples of what I consider to be poor use of autoethnography here. I do wish, however, to highlight the lessons we can learn from those who have made productive use of their own eating experiences. Longhurst's (2012) *Becoming Smaller* is such as case, as she traces the tensions that arise between her own desire to be thin and her political and academic aspirations and values. Writing about her own experience of weight loss, she draws out the paradoxes of being a feminist scholar critiquing socially constructed discourses of fatness while also feeling societal pressures to be thin – and feeling better for being so. She states:

> Simply reclaiming the word 'fat' as a positive signifier and outing myself as a fat woman was not enough to make me forget the dominant discourses that surround fat bodies. I felt, therefore, societal pressure to become thinner despite wanting to resist and disrupt the dominant discourses around fat. (ibid.: 880)

Longhurst's commentary raises important questions about the extent a scholar of food and the body has to embody, or *feels* they have to embody, their own arguments. As Longhurst herself notes, is she less of a feminist role model for being thinner? If the answer to this is in the affirmative, we have to reflect, I suggest, upon the discourses circulating within the academy and the ways in which they, perhaps, inform our own eating and bodily practices. To elucidate, if Fat Studies writers feel they have to have larger bodies in order make their intellectual case, is this not, in itself, also a constraining discourse, albeit one that appears to run counter to hegemonic discourses of slimness? Similarly, do we expect food scholars to be appreciative of 'good food' or advocates for 'alternatives', even when we understand such definitions as constructs? These are not facile questions as our own eating practices can arguably shape both our intellectual insights and our academic identities, not to mention the gender and generational dynamics that are potentially at play here. I have witnessed vegetarian academics eat meat at a food studies conference, for example, in order to 'fit in' with a prevailing ethos that celebrated being a omnivore, and others purposefully select 'junk food' to help ensure that they are not seen as a gastronome, but rather a serious food scholar. And I too have to admit a reticence to 'admit' my veganism to food studies colleagues. I am not propounding an approach here that requires each writer to detail his or her own subject position vis-à-vis their eating and their body, and, for me, the value of knowing the writer as eater is very much dependent on the discussion being presented – otherwise there is a danger that we slide once more into navel-gazing territory. But, Longhurst's personal account, alongside paradoxes and tensions clearly experienced by some scholars, does give us pause to think about the potentially constraining discourses within food studies and the ways in which this possibly shapes our own eating and the ways in which we approach that of others.

Longhurst's account, much like that of Murray (2009, see chapter 6), further gives us a route into comprehending how an individual embodied subject interrelates with broader political dynamics and bio-authorial actors, such as medics in the case of Murray. Thus, their own bodies are lenses through which to view wider cultural and societal relations. Autoethnography here is not just writing about the self, but is writing from the position of the self with a constantly shifting gaze that looks outwards towards society and then returns inwards back towards personal experience. In so doing, the personal and the political are connected. This process of reflection can also yield valuable insights through which 'society', as it relates to the body, can be better understood. Sexton (2016), for example, uses autoethnography as both a method and a way of narrating and analysing her findings in her account of *Beyond Meat*, a plant-based meat substitute. Reflecting on the visceral processes of buying, preparing, cooking with and eating, *Beyond Meat*, she 'gets at' those aspects of food-body relations that are often invisible, as she uses her embodied encounter to consider how such experiences shaped the way in which she made sense of the 'non-meat' as meat. Stressing the partiality of her findings, Sexton is careful to situate her personal experiences alongside the voices of others in order to draw out wider connections and conclusions. Furthermore, in treating her own body as a research instrument, her own subject position and experiences open up new avenues for investigation. Hurn (2013) adopts a related approach in her account of being a vegan anthropologist, as she uses her own eating preferences to solicit her participants' perspectives on meat eating and the effects of not eating meat on human bodies, and I too (2015b) had used insights gained from reflecting upon my own embodied experiences with the 'stuff' of my kitchen to inform the questions I asked of my participants. In this manner, then, autoethnography can be mobilized as a method for collecting data, as well as an analytical tool and a narrative form.

The final methodological challenge posed by attending to the materiality of food, and which emerges from ANT-inspired approaches more generally, is: 'if we are to take the agency of the non-human seriously, how do we research the non-human – especially as the social sciences and humanities are essentially human-centric?' This question may again, at first glance, seem rather facile, but it is not when we consider that such disciplines have developed methodologies in accord with their human-centrism – broader ontological questions aside about how foregrounding the non-human impacts human-based disciplines. And to state the somewhat obvious, you cannot interview or conduct a focus group with non-human matter. We can observe such matter, of course, and, within reason, observe its effects on the body, notwithstanding the extent to which these effects are subjectively experienced by an individual. And individual bodies can record the affects and effects of the non-human in words and images, and we may even be able to go into those bodies, with the help of the biological sciences, to observe such effects. Nevertheless, observing the agency of the non-human, even when using, as I have done throughout the preceding pages, a Latourian (2005)/Bennet (2010) definition that agency is the capacity to cause affect and effect and is not associated with intent, still involves a conceptual leap. I have argued that ethnography and thick description can play a key role here in minimizing such leaps and abstractions by grounding the discussion in lived reality, but there is still much opportunity and scope for the development of new methodological instruments. The methods required to fully unpack and engage with new materialisms have not yet caught up with the theoretical advances and it may require considerable innovation to do so. Yet, it is critical that we develop these methodological approaches, otherwise we run the risk that, while creative conceptual models may inspire us to think differently, they remain in the ontological abstract and are not tested and stretched by everyday lived experience.

Bio-authority and bounded vitalism: Future themes and directions

Throughout the book I have mobilized two concepts through which to interrogate the interplays between matter and meaning and the ways in which agency is distributed and enacted through eating, as well as to better understand the ways in which food-body knowledges are mediated, contested, performed and shaped – bio-authority and bounded vitalism. These concepts are tools that have helped me think through and analyse the ethnography in a way that draws both new materialist and political economic approaches into dialogue. As such, they have enabled me to pick my way through ANT approaches to agency, mediation and the non-human, Foucauldian thought on biopower, and Bourdieusian perspectives to cultural intermediaries. They are not, however, conceptual tools that I have looked to apply wholesale to ethnographic data, but are instead merely ways of making sense of lived experience in a manner that aids their comparison to other case studies and contribution to wider debates on the politics of food and the body. Hence, they offer a mechanism for shifting my analytical gaze between the micro and the macro and back again. With this in mind, I have resisted the temptation to close with a discussion of how these core concepts can be applied to other topics and discussions. Rather, I prefer to indicate themes that have emerged as potential directions and opportunities for future research as a result of my use of bio-authority and bounded vitalism.

I have already highlighted the space that is opened up for interdisciplinary engagements between the natural and social sciences, as well as new methodologies, and there are further subject-specific areas that could be extended and developed. First, as I have briefly noted in the previous chapter, considering the media, or more accurately specific actors within the media, as bio-authorities that act upon the bodies of viewers may open up a fertile avenue of investigation. As definitions of eating are opened up to include the visual (Holtzman 2016; Lavis 2016), and this is coupled with work that emphasizes the synesthetic quality of food (cf Sutton 2001), possibilities to consider eaters' engagements with myriad forms of media as visceral experiences emerge. This can help take us beyond 'the gaze' by attending to ways in which food media encounters produce effects and affects in the 'eating' body, which, in turn, can foster a deeper understanding of how intimacies between eaters and particular media actors are established (cf Abbots 2015b). It can also enhance our comprehension of the ways in which media outlets can shape eating preferences, as well as the manner in which these dynamics are contested by eaters. Considering media as actively entering bodies and producing (possibly ungovernable) feelings, emotions and senses may also be a way of building upon scholarship that has addressed media influence largely through a Foucauldian frame, especially in relation to notions of ideal body types. A greater focus on emotions per se could also yield deeper insights into the ways in which eaters relate to specific media forms and actors.

A more thorough and systematic focus on emotions more widely could be productive in food studies, as indicated by scholarship on fears and anxieties – which could, in itself, pay more explicit attention to emotion. In Chapters 5 and 6, I have indicated how care as a concept has been used in relation to fair trade, organic, and GMO food, and more work could be done in considering care as an emotion and feeling, and the ways in which affective bonds are fostered with such foods and their associated human actors. Thinking through affect takes us back to the body, and I have argued that the body could be far more prevalent in discussions of fair trade and alternative foods, which have, with some notable exceptions (cf Guthman 2003; Hayes-Conroy and Hayes-Conroy 2010a,b), tended to take lesser account of embodied experience than they have structural dynamics. Taste, in its haptic corporeal sense, and the ways in which these foods feel in the body are also of import here, especially given contemporary marketing practices that focus on the quality of such foods. This approach can be further extended to heritage foods, whether they are local, regional or national, and to food festivals more widely, and in Chapter 4 I have suggested ways in which visceral experiences of food festivals, which have mainly to date been glossed over in favour of economic development questions, could be a productive area of research. As with the media, a focus on the visceral and emotive, and the bio-authorities involved in orchestrating such affective experiences, could provide greater illumination as to the ways in which political dynamics are enacted in and through bodies. Labour relations are also critical here, and the different forms of food labour and the relative extent of bio-authority of these forms, as well as its gendered, classed, racialized and generational dynamics, are worthy of greater investigation.

In my discussion of food festivals, I further drew attention to the need to consider food as part of a broader material and discursive assemblage. Too often, food studies scholars have taken a foodstuff in isolation. We have been exceptionally good at using food as a lens through which to view social relations and cultural knowledges, and have therefore excelled at situating a food within its broader social and political context. Indeed, an entrenched strength of existing scholarship is the way in which food is analysed in relation to the myriad practices surrounding it. But if we have given little attention to food as food (cf Abbots and Lavis 2013; Holtzman 2009), we have paid even less notice to other material components that charge food with meaning, such as the array of Indian goods in Mankekar's (2002) grocery store (see Chapter 3). I have argued throughout the preceding pages that it is the other material objects within a food's assemblage – as well as symbolic meanings and cultural knowledges – that dialectically imbue a food's matter with its vitality. It therefore follows that instead of solely focusing on the food being eaten, we could be paying more attention to the other 'stuff' that enables a food to be eaten in a particular way, as well as tracing the ways in which this stuff can potentially change the meaning of the food – as I have done when discussing cuy in Chapters 2 and 3. In short,

I am encouraging a greater level of assemblage thinking here; this should not just be in a manner that notices semiotic markers that charge a food, but also in a manner that interrogates the embodied experience such collections of objects provoke. This, in turn, enables a greater consideration of the ways in which the vitalism of a food is bound by its social assemblage – of objects and meanings – and how bio-authorial relations take shape.

Finally, I conclude where I have started – with a call for greater attention to be paid to the materiality of food, the body, and the embodied experience of eating. And I repeat the necessity for food studies scholars to treat food as food, and not just as a mechanism through which to understand 'society'. That food is good to think with is indisputable, but it is also good (or sometimes bad) to eat. It is symbolic, political and economic, but it is also a material substance that we feel within our bodies, that stimulates our senses, produces embodied responses and invokes emotions. Paying greater heed to this, as I hope to have demonstrated, can only serve to deepen our understandings of the political dynamics of food and eating, and enhance the theoretical contribution of food studies to emergent cross-disciplinary debates on cultural politics, new materialisms and the body.

Notes

Introduction

1. For detailed discussion of migration and the rural economy of the area, see Jokisch (2007), Jokisch and Pribilsky (2002), Miles (2004), Pribilsky (2007) and Weismantel (2003).
2. It is worth making a brief note of language here: when using the term Jimeño, I am referring to both men and women, while with Jimeña I refer solely to women.
3. Class in the region intersects culture and ethnicity, with class position being shaped by factors such as education, level of culture, degrees of whiteness and indigeneity, surname, country or city dwelling, mannerisms, sources of income, dress, and food practices – to name but a few. See Abbots (2011, 2012b, 2014a,b, 2015a), Miles (2004) and Weismantel (2003).

Chapter 1

1. 'That is, sites that have the power to teach, to engage "learners" in meaning-making practices that they use to make sense of their worlds and their selves' (Wright 2009: 7).

Chapter 2

1. I am not looking to create a false dichotomy here between nature and culture, but am merely representing how my participants construct the difference between Pablito's and my hunger for *cuy*.
2. Such collectives, known colloquially as *mingas*, were leisurely occasions when members of the, sometimes extended, household would come together to make large quantities of labour-intensive foods, such as *empanadas*, *humitas* and cuy. Such events in Jima took place for fun and leisure. The term *minga* has historically been used in the region to define a collective work party borne out of necessity, such as agricultural and construction work, but has been adapted in circumstances of waged labour and increased wealth to refer to any collective activity that involves manual labour, however enjoyable or not it may be.

Chapter 3

1. The correct use of terminology and the possible distinctions between an anthropology of the senses and sensory anthropology, among other possible terms, have been subject to some discussion. See Pink (2010) and the response by Howes (2010) for an overview.

2. Ray's (2004) account of middle-class Bengali-Americans offers a slightly different perspective. He writes that some elements of the gendered division of food labour have been reconfigured, and that although cooking remains a largely feminized task, men's participant rates are slowly increasing with 10 per cent cooking regularly and 40 per cent occasionally (ibid.: 116–17). Men are also heavily involved with gardening, while women take on the majority of grocery shopping work. Moreover, the general level of cooking work is decreasing, with most households only consuming one hot meal a day instead of three (ibid.: 121).

3. Following Fechter (2007), I prefer to use the term 'privileged migrants' here to better account for the subject position and privileged social and economic situation of those with whom I conducted research, instead of the more politically loaded term 'expat'. The term also differentiates these individuals from the migrant kin of my Jimeño participants who are in far more economically and socially precarious positions than those migrating from the North to the South.

Chapter 4

1. See Abbots (2011, 2012a, 2014a) for a fuller discussion of *comida típica* in this context.

2. It is tempting here to draw attention to the symbolic salience of using the school as the site for a community 'lesson' about food, but I am tentative about making such associations based on the material layout of the village, as it was arguably the only location in which such a gathering could take place.

3. See Abbots (2014a, 2015a) for additional analysis of the Jima Health Fair and the foods that were deemed acceptable or not.

4. This process can be seen a part of a much broader process of pluriculturalism and the associated celebration and reinvention of the pre-Hispanic past across Ecuador and the Andean countries. See Andolina (2003), Cadena (2000), Espinosa (2000) and Whitten (2003) for further discussion.

Chapter 5

1. There is an added irony here that a proportion of the food sold by 'peasant sellers' and in local markets is acquired through large-scale, global producers such as Dole and Del Monte (Abbots 2014b).

2. See Lockie (2013) for a discussion of this literature and the ways in which this framing can overlook the participation of ethnic and marginalized groups in AFNs.

Chapter 6

1. In 2008, an amendment to the Ecuadorian constitution banned GMO foods. Anecdotal evidence, in the form of comments by privileged migrants and Ecuadorian friends, as well as personal experience in the country, suggest that this is not 100 per cent foolproof.
2. I have discussed elsewhere why the supermarket is trusted in comparison to the foodspaces that migrants deem as 'more local' (see Abbots 2013).
3. There are a number of critiques to this argument that show that global foods, and its avatar fast food, interplay rather than takeover local 'traditional' foods in complex and nuanced ways (see for example Abbots 2012a, 2014a; Caldwell 2004; Lozada 2000; Watson 1997).
4. See Domingos, Sobral and West (2014) for further discussion of the framings of the relationship between the country and the city.
5. I am not stretching this argument so far as to argue that some bodies are regarded as more disposable and surplus than others as this did not emerge from my data, although there is literature in other contexts outside the topic of food that has convincingly demonstrated this to be the case (see, for example, Scheper-Hughes 2000).

Bibliography

Abbots, E-J. (2011), '"It doesn't taste as good from the pet shop"; Guinea pig consumption and the performance of class and kinship in Highland Ecuador and New York City', *Food, Culture and Society*, 14(2): 205–24.

Abbots, E-J. (2012a), 'The celebratory and the everyday: Guinea pigs, hamburgers and the performance of food heritage in Highland Ecuador', in M. McWilliams (ed.), *Celebrations: The Proceedings of the Oxford Symposium on Food and Cookery 2011*, London: Prospect Books, 12–23.

Abbots, E-J. (2012b), 'In the absence of men? Gender, migration and domestic labour in the southern Ecuadorean Andes', *Journal of Latin American Studies*, 44(1): 71–96.

Abbots, E-J. (2013), 'Negotiating foreign bodies: Migration, trust and the risky business of eating in Highland Ecuador', in E-J. Abbots and A. Lavis (eds), *Why We Eat, How We Eat: Contemporary Encounters Between Foods and Bodies*, Farnham: Ashgate, 119–38.

Abbots, E-J. (2014a), 'The Fast and the fusion: Class, creolization and the remaking of *comida típica* in Highland Ecuador', in J. Klein and A. Murcott (eds), *Food Consumption in Global Perspective. Essays in the Anthropology of Food in Honour of Jack Goody*, London: Palgrave Macmillan, 87–107.

Abbots, E-J. (2014b), 'Embodying country-city relations: The figure of the *Chola Cuencana* in Highland Ecuador', in N. Domingos, J. Sobral and H. G. West (eds), *Food Between the Country and the City: Ethnographies of a Changing Global Foodscape*, London: Bloomsbury, 41–57.

Abbots, E-J (2015a), 'Caring about care-less Eating: Class politics, governance and the production of otherness in Highland Ecuador' in E-J. Abbots, A. Lavis and L. Attala (eds), *Careful Eating: The Embodied Entanglements of Food and Care*, Farnham: Ashgate, 69–87.

Abbots, E-J. (2015b), 'The intimacies of industry: Consumer interactions with the "stuff" of celebrity chefs', *Food, Culture and Society*, 18(2): 223–43.

Abbots, E-J. (2015c), 'Buying the ties that bind: Consumption, care and investment among transnational households in Highland Ecuador', in E. Casey and Y. Taylor (eds), *Intimacies, Families and the Practices of Consumption*, Basingstoke: Palgrave Macmillan, 36–59.

Abbots, E-J. (2016a), 'Introducing a special issue on food stuffs: Materialities, meanings and embodied encounters', *Gastronomica: The Journal of Critical Food Studies*, 16(3): 1–4.

Abbots, E-J. (2016b), 'Approaches to food and migration: Rootedness, belonging and exchange', in J. Klein and J. Watson (eds), *Handbook of Food and Anthropology*, London: Bloomsbury, 115–32.

Abbots, E-J. and Attala, L. (2014), 'It's not what you eat but how and that you eat: Social media, counter-discourses and disciplined ingestion among amateur competitive eaters', *Geoforum*. Available online before print, doi:10.1016/j.geoforum.2014.11.004.

Abbots, E-J. and Coles, B. (2013), 'Horsemeat-gate: The production of a neoliberal food "scandal"', *Food, Culture and Society*, 16(4): 435–550.

Abbots, E-J. and Lavis, A. (2013), 'Contours of eating: Mapping the terrain of body/food encounters', in E-J Abbots and A. Lavis (eds), *Why We Eat, How We Eat: Contemporary Encounters between Foods and Bodies*, Farnham: Ashgate, 1–14.

Abbots, E-J., Lavis, A. and Attala, L., eds (2015), *Careful Eating: Bodies, Food and Care*, Farnham: Ashgate.

Adema, P. (2009), *Garlic Capital of the World: Gilroy, Garlic and the Making of the Festive Foodscape*, Jackson: University Press of Mississippi.

Aguilar Vázquez, C. (1944), *Obras Completas: Prosa, Vol 5, Xima*, Cuenca: Ministerio de Educación Públic.

Alexander, C., Gregson, N. and Gille, Z. (2013), 'Food waste', in A. Murcott, W. Belasco and P. Jackson (eds), *The Handbook of Food Research*, London: Bloomsbury, 471–84.

Alexander, C. and Reno, J., eds (2012), *Economies of Recycling: The Global Transformation of Materials, Values and Social Relations*, London: Zed Books.

Anderson, B. (2011), 'Affect and biopower: Towards a politics of life', *Transactions of the Institute of British Geographers*, 37: 28–43.

Anderson, B., Keanes, M., McFarlane, C. and Swanton, D. (2012), 'On assemblages and geography', *Dialogues in Human Geography*, 2(2): 171–18.

Andolina, R. (2003), 'The sovereign and its shadow: Constituent assembly and the indigenous movement in Ecuador', *Journal of Latin American Studies*, 35(4): 721–50.

Antipode (2009), Special Issue, Critical geographies of fat/bigness/corpulence, 41(5).

Aphramor, L., Brady, J. and Gringas, J. (2013), 'Advancing critical dietetics: Theorizing Health at Every Size', in E-J Abbots and A. Lavis (eds), *Why We Eat, How We Eat: Contemporary Encounters Between Foods and Bodies*, Aldershot: Ashgate, 85–102.

Appadurai, A. (1988), 'How to make a national cuisine: Cookbooks in contemporary India', *Comparative Studies in Society and History*, 30(1): 3–24.

Archetti, Eduardo P. (1997), *Guinea-pigs: Food, Symbol and Conflict of Knowledge in Ecuador*, Oxford: Berg.

Aull Davies, C. (2008), *Reflexive Ethnography: A Guide to Researching Selves and Others*, 2nd edn. London and New York: Routledge.

Avieli, N. (2005), 'Roasted pigs and bao dumplings: Festive food and imagined transnational identity in Chinese-Vietnamese' *Asia Pacific Viewpoint*, 46(3): 281–93.

Avieli, N. (2016), 'The hummus wars revisited: Israeli-Arab food politics and gastro-
    mediation', *Gastronomica: The Journal of Critical Food Studies*, 16(3): 18–28.

Ayora-Diaz, S. I. and Vargas-Cetina, G. (2005), 'Romantic moods: Food, beer, music
    and the Yucatecan soul', in T. M. Wilson (ed.), *Drinking Cultures: Alcohol and Identity*,
    Oxford and New York: Berg, 155–78.

Barham, E. (2003), 'Translating terroir: The global challenge of French AOC labelling',
    Journal of Rural Studies, 19(1): 127–38.

Barnes, C. (2014), 'Mediating good food and moments of possibility with Jamie Oliver:
    Problematising celebrity chefs as talking labels', *Geoforum*. Available online before
    print, doi:10.1016/j.geoforum.2014.09.004.

Barnett, C., Clarke, N., Cloke, P. and Malpass, A. (2005a), 'The political ethics of
    consumerism', *Consumer Policy Review*, 15(2): 45–51.

Barnett, C., Clarke, N., Cloke, P. and Malpass, A. (2005b), 'Consuming ethic: Articulating
    the subjects and spaces of ethical consumption', *Antipode*, 37, 23–45.

Batsell, W. R., Brown, A., Ansfield, M. and G. Paschell (2002), 'You will eat all of that!:
    A retrospective analysis of forced consumption episodes', *Appetite*, 38: 211–19.

Belasco, W. J. (1989), *Appetite for Change: How the Counterculture Took on the Food
    Industry, 1966–1988*, New York: Pantheon Books.

Bell, D. and Hollows, J. (2011), 'From *River Cottage* to *Chicken Run*: Hugh Fearnley-
    Whittingstall and the class politics of ethical consumption', *Celebrity Studies*, 2(2):
    178–91.

Bell, D. and Valentine, G. (1997), *Consuming Geographies: We Are Where We Eat*,
    London: Routledge.

Bennett, J. (2005), 'The agency of assemblages and the North American blackout',
    Public Culture, 17(3): 445–65.

Bennett, J. (2007), 'Edible matter,' *New Left Review*, 45, 133–45.

Bennett, J. (2010), *Vibrant Matter: A Political Ecology of Things*, Durham, NC: Duke
    University Press.

Ben-Ze'ev, E. (2004), 'The politics of taste and smell: Palestinian rights of return', in
    M. Lien and B. Nerlich (eds), *The Politics of Food*, Oxford: Berg, 141–60.

Bessiere, J. (1998), 'Local development and heritage: Traditional food and cuisine as
    tourist attractions in rural Areas', *Sociologia Ruralis*, 38(1): 21–34.

Blay-Palmer, A. (2008), *Food Fears: From Industrial to Sustainable Food Systems*,
    Aldershot: Ashgate.

Bohannan, P. and Bohannan, L. (1968), *Tiv Economy*, Harlow: Longmans.

Bond, G. and Gillam, A., eds (1994), *Social Construction of the Past: Representation as
    Power* London: Routledge.

Boniface, P. (2003), *Tasting Tourism: Travelling for Food and Drink*, Burlington, VT:
    Ashgate.

Bourdieu, P. (1984), *Distinction: A Social Critique of the Judgement of Taste*, New York
    and London: Routledge.

Bourdieu, P (1990), *The Logic of Practice*, translated by R. Nice, Stanford: Stanford University Press.

Bourque, N. (2001), 'Eating your words: Communicating with food in the Ecuadorian Andes', in J. Hendry and C. W. Watson (eds), *An Anthropology of Indirect Communication*, London: Routledge, 85–100.

Bowen, S. and Zapata, A. (2009), 'Geographical Indications, terroir, and socioeconomic and ecological sustainability: The case of tequila', *Journal of Rural Studies*, 25(1): 108–19.

Brooks, S., Burges Watson, D., Draper, A., Goodman, M. K., Kvaalvag, H. and Wills, W. (2013), 'Chewing on choice', in E-J. Abbots and A. Lavis (eds), *Why We Eat, How We Eat: Contemporary Encounters Between Foods and Bodies*, Farnham: Ashgate, 149–68.

Butler, J. (1993), *Bodies That Matter: On the Discursive Limits of 'Sex'*, London: Routledge.

Cadena, de la M. (2000), *Indigenous Mestizos: The Politics of Race and Culture in Cuzco, Peru, 1919-1991*, Durham, NC: Duke University Press.

Cairns, K. and Johnston, J. (2015), *Food and Femininity*, London: Bloomsbury.

Caldwell, M. L. (2004), 'Domesticating the french fry: McDonald's and consumerism in Moscow', *Journal of Consumer Culture*, 4(1), 5–26.

Caldwell, R. (2007), 'Agency and change: Re-evaluating Foucault's legacy', *Organization*, 14(6): 769–91.

Callon, M. (2005), 'Let's put an end on uncertainties', *Sociologie du Travail*, 47: 94–100.

Campbell, K. F. (2014), 'Enemy cuisine: Claiming agency, seeking humanity and renegotiating identity through consumption', in P. Collinson and H. Macbeth (eds), *Food in Zones of Conflict: Cross-Disciplinary Perspectives*, New York: Berghan, 145–54.

Caplan, P. (1997), 'Approaches to the study of food, health and identity', in P. Caplan (ed.), *Food, Health and Identity*, London: Routledge, 1–31.

Carolan, M. (2011), *Embodied Food Politics*, Farnham: Ashgate.

Carrier, J. and Leutchford, P., eds (2012), *Ethical Consumption: Social Value and Economic Practice*, New York and Oxford: Berghahn.

Carsten, J. (1989), 'Cooking money: Gender and the symbolic transformation of means of exchange in a Malay fishing community', in J. Parry and M. Bloch (eds), *Money and the Morality of Exchange,* Cambridge: Cambridge University Press, 117–41.

Carsten, J. (1995), 'The substance of kinship and the heat of the hearth: Feeding, personhood and relatedness among Malays in Pulau Langwaki', *American Ethnologist*, 22(2): 223–41.

Carsten, J. (1997), *The Heat of the Hearth: The Process of Kinship in a Malay Fishing Community*, Oxford: Clarendon Press.

Carsten, J. (2004), *After Kinship*, Cambridge: Cambridge University Press.

Cavanagh, J. (2007), 'Making salami, producing Bergamo: The transformation of value', *Ethnos*, 72(2): 149–72.

Chapman, G. E. and Beagan, B. L. (2013), 'Food practices and transnational identities: Case studies of two Punjabi-Canadian families', *Food, Culture and Society*, 16(3): 367–86.

Chrzan, J. (2004), 'Slow Food – what, why, and to where', *Food, Culture and Society* 7(2): 118–31.

Clarke, N., Cloke, P., Barnett, C. and Malpass, A. (2008), 'The spaces and ethics of organic food', *Journal of Rural Studies*, 24: 210–30.

Classen, C. (1997), 'Foundations for an anthropology of the senses', *International Social Science Journal*, 49(153): 401–12.

Clifford, J. and Marcus, G. (2010), *Writing Culture: The Poetics and Politics of Ethnography*, 2nd edn, Berkeley: University of California Press.

Coles, B. (2013), 'Ingesting places: Embodied geographies of coffee', in E-J Abbots and A. Lavis (eds), *Why We Eat, How We Eat: Contemporary Encounters Between Foods and Bodies*, Aldershot: Ashgate, 255–70.

Coles, B. (2014), 'Making the market place: A topography of Borough Market', *Cultural Geographies*, 21(3): 515–23.

Coles, B. (2015), 'Placing security: Food, geographical knowledge(s) and the reproduction of place(less-ness)', in E-J. Abbots, A. Lavis and L. Attala (eds), *Careful Eating: The Embodied Entanglements of Food and Care*, Farnham: Ashgate, 151–72.

Coles, B. (2016), 'The shocking materialities and temporalities of agri-capitalism', *Gastronomica: The Journal of Critical Food Studies*, 16(3): 5–11.

Collier, S. J. and Ong, A. (2005), 'Global assemblages, anthropological problems', in J. Collier and A. Ong (eds), *Global Assemblages: Technology, Politics and Ethics as Anthropological Problems*, Oxford: Blackwell Publishing, 3–21.

Collins, E. L. (2008), 'Of kimchi and coffee: Globalisation, transnationalism and familiarity in culinary consumption', *Social and Cultural Geography*, 9: 151–69.

Colls, R. (2007), 'Materialising bodily matter: Intra-action and the embodiment of "fat"', *Geoforum*, 38: 353–65.

Colls, R. (2012). 'Big girls having fun: Reflections on a 'fat accepting space', *Somatechnics*, 2(1): 18–37.

Colls, R. and Evans, B. (2008), 'Embodying responsibility: Children's health and supermarket responsibility', *Environment and Planning A*, 40: 615–31.

Colls, R. and Evans, B. (2009), 'Critical geographies of fat/bigness/corpulence: Introduction, questioning obesity politics', *Antipode*, 41(5): 1011–20.

Colls, R. and Evans, B. (2013), 'Making space for fat Bodies? A critical account of the "obesogenic environment"', *Progress in Human Geography*, 1–21.

Cook, I., Crang, P. and Thorpe, M. (1999), 'Eating into Britishness: Multicultural imaginaries and the identity politics of food', in S. Roseneil and J. Seymour (eds), *Practising Identities: Power and Resistance*, Basingstoke: Macmillan, 223–48.

Counihan, C. (1988), 'Female identity, Food and power in contemporary Florence', *Anthropological Quarterly*, 61(2): 51–62.

Counihan, C. (1998), 'Food and gender: Identity and power', in C. Counihan and
S. L. Kaplan (eds), *Food and Gender: Identity and Power*, London: Routledge, 1–10.

Coveney, J. (2006), *Food, Morals and Meaning: The Pleasure and Anxiety of Eating*,
London: Routledge.

Csordas, T. J. (1990), 'Embodiment as a paradigm for anthropology', *Ethos*, 18(1):
5–47.

Csordas, T. J. (1994), 'Introduction: The body as representation and being-in-the-world',
in T. J. Csordas (ed.), *Embodiment and Experience: The Existential Ground of Culture
and Self*, Cambridge: Cambridge University Press, 1–26.

Cusack, I. (2000), 'African cuisines: Recipes for nation-building?', *Journal of African
Cultural Studies*, 13(2): 207–25.

DeFrance, S. D. (2006), 'The sixth toe: The modern culinary role of the guinea pig in
Southern Peru', *Food and Foodways*, 14: 3–34.

Deleuze, G. and Guitarri, F. (2004), *A Thousand Plateaus: Capitalism and Schizophrenia*,
London and New York: Continuum.

Demossier, M. (2011), 'Beyond terroir: territorial construction, hegemonic discourses,
and French wine culture', *Journal of the Royal Anthropological Institute* (N.S.) 17:
685–705.

DeVault, M. L. (1991), *Feeding the Family: The Social Organisation of Caring as
Gendered Work*, Chicago: Chicago University Press.

Domingos, N. (2016), 'The market as mediator: The corporate creation of Portuguese
wine', *Gastronomica: The Journal of Critical Food Studies*, 16(3): 29–41.

Domingos, N., Sobral, J. and West, H., eds (2014), *Food Between the Country and the
City: Changing Ethnographies of a Global Foodscape*, London: Bloomsbury.

Douglas, M., 2002 [1966], *Purity and Danger: An Analysis of Concepts of Pollution and
Taboo*, London: Routledge and K. Paul.

DuPuis, E. M. (2000), 'Not in my Body: rBGH and the rise of organic milk', *Agriculture
and Human Values*, 17(3): 285–95.

Earle, R. (2012), *The Body of the Conquistador: Food, Race and the Colonial Experience
in Spanish America, 1492–1700*, Cambridge: Cambridge University Press.

Ehlers, N. (2014), 'Fat is the future: Bioprospecting, fat stem cells, and emergent
breasted materialities', in C. Forth and A. Leitch (eds), *Fat: Culture and Materiality*,
London: Bloomsbury, 109–22.

Eli, K. and Lavis, A. (2016), 'Becoming fit to be a mother: Class, learning and redemption
in Supersize vs Superskinny', *Journal of Gender Studies*, available online before print,
doi:10.1080/09589236.2016.1178630.

Espinosa, M. F. (2000), 'Ethnic politics and state reform in Ecuador', in W. Assies, G. van
der Haar and A. Hoekema (eds), *The Challenge of Diversity: Indigenous Peoples and
Reform of the State in Latin America*, Amsterdam: Thela Thesis, 47–56.

Evans, A. B. and Miele, M. (2012), 'Between food and flesh: How animals are made
to matter (and not matter) within food consumption practices', *Environment and
Planning D*, 30: 298–314.

Evans, D. (2014), *Food Waste: Home Consumption, Material Culture and Everyday Life*, London: Bloomsbury.

Evans, D., Campbell, H. and Murcott, A. (2013), 'A brief pre-history of food waste and the social sciences', in D. Evans, H. Campbell and A. Murcott (eds), *Waste Matters: New Perspectives on Food and Society*. Oxford: Wiley-Blackwell/The Sociological Review, 5–26.

Falk, P. (1994), *The Consuming Body*, London: Sage.

Fechter, A-M. (2007), *Transnational Lives: Expatriates in Indonesia*, Farnham: Ashgate.

Fischler, C. (1988), 'Food, self and identity', *Social Science Information*, 27: 275–92.

Fitting, E. (2014), 'Cultures of corn and anti-GMO activism in Mexico and Colombia', in C. Counihan and V. Siniscalchi (eds), *Food Activism: Agency, Democracy and Economy*, London: Bloomsbury, 175–92.

Flowers, R. and Swan, E. (2012), 'Eating the Asian other? Pedagogies of food multiculturalism in Australia', *PORTAL Journal of Multidisciplinary International Studies*, 9(2): 1–30.

Flowers, R. and Swan, E. (2015a), 'Food pedagogies: Histories, definitions and moralities', in R. Flowers and E. Swan (eds), *Food Pedagogies*, Farnham: Ashgate, 1–27.

Flowers, R. and Swan, E. (2015b), 'Multiculturalism as work: The emotional labour of ethnic food tour guides', in E-J. Abbots, A. Lavis and L. Attala (eds), *Careful Eating: The Embodied Entanglements of Food and Care*, Farnham: Ashgate, 25–44.

Fock, N. (1981), 'Ethnicity and alternative identification: An example from Cañar', in N. E. Whitten (ed.), *Cultural Transformations and Ethnicity in Modern Ecuador*, Urbana: University of Illinois Press, 402–19.

Food, Culture and Society (2015), Special Issue on food celebrities and the politics of lifestyle mediation 18:2.

Forth, C. (2014), 'Introduction: Materializing fat', in C. Forth and A. Leitch (eds), *Fat: Culture and Materiality*, London: Bloomsbury, 109–22.

Foucault, M. (1977), *Discipline and Punish: The Birth of the Prison*, London: Allen Lane.

Foucault, M. (1978), *The History of Sexuality: An Introduction*. New York: Pantheon.

Foucault, M. (1980), *Power/Knowledge: Selected Interviews and Other Writings 1972–1977*, translated by C. Gordon, L. Marshall, J. Mepham and K. Soper, New York: Pantheon Books.

Foucault, M. (2001), *Madness and Civilisation: A History of Insanity in the Age of Reason*, translated by R. Howard, London: Routledge Classics.

Foucault, M. (2002a), *Power: The Essential Works of Michel Foucault 1954–1984. Volume 3*, translated by R. Hurley et al., London: Penguin.

Foucault M. (2002b), *The Archaeology of Knowledge*, translated by A. M. Sheriden Smith, London: Routledge Classics.

Foucault, M. (2002c), *The Order of Things: An Archaeology of the Human Sciences*. London: Routledge Classics.

Foucault, M. (2003), *The Birth of the Clinic: An Archaeology of Medical Perception*, London: Routledge Classics.

Frost, N. (2008), '"Strange people but they sure can cook!": An Indonesian women's group in Sydney', *Food, Culture and Society*, 11(2): 173–89.

Frøystad, K. (2003), 'Master-servant relations and the domestic reproduction of caste in Northern India', *Ethnos*, 68(1): 73–94.

Gade, D. (2004), 'Tradition, territory, and terroir in French viticulture: Cassis, France, and Appellation Contrôlée', *Annals of the Association of American Geographers*, 94(4): 848–67.

Garcilaso, de la Vega. (1966), *Royal Commentaries of the Incas, and General History of Peru*, translated with an introduction by Harold, H. Livermore, Austin: University of Texas Press.

Gard, M. and Wright, J. (2005), *The Obesity Epidemic: Science, Morality, and Ideology*, London: Routledge.

Gill, L. (1990), 'Painted faces: Conflict and ambiguity in domestic servant-employer relations in La Paz 1930–1988', *Latin American Research Review*, 25(1): 119–36.

Gille, Z. (2007), *From the Cult of Waste to the Trash Heap of History: The Politics of Waste in Socialist and Postsocialist Hungary*, Bloomington: University of Indiana Press.

Giroux, H. (2004), 'Cultural Studies and the politics of public pedagogy: Making the political more pedagogical', *Parallax*, 10(2): 73–89.

Goodman, D. (1999), 'Agro-food studies in the 'age of ecology': Nature, corporeality, bio-Politics', *Sociologia Ruralis*, 39(1), 17–38.

Goodman, D. and Dupuis, M. (2002), 'Knowing food and growing food: Beyond the production-consumption debate in the sociology of agriculture', *Sociologia Ruralis*, 42(1): 5–22.

Goodman, D., DuPuis, E. M. and Goodman, M. K. (2011), *Alternative Food Networks: Knowledge, Practice and Politics*, Oxford: Routledge.

Goodman, M. K. (2013), 'Eating powerful transgressions: (Re)assessing the spaces and ethics of organic food in the UK', in M. K. Goodman and C. Sage (eds), *Food Transgressions: Making Sense of Contemporary Food Politics*, Farnham: Ashgate, 109–30.

Goodman, M. K. (2015), 'Of dialectical food pedagogies and political economies: Taking debates forward in an afterword', in R. Flowers and E. Swan (eds), *Food Pedagogies*, Farnham: Ashgate, 229–40.

Goodman, M. K. (2016), 'Food geographies 1: Relational foodscapes and the busy-ness of being more-than-food', *Progress in Human Geography*, 40(2): 257–66.

Goodman, M.K. and E-J. Abbots (2015), *Affective Austerity: Virtual Food Mediation in the Anthropocene*, paper presented at AAG Conference, Chicago.

Goody, J. (1982), *Cooking, Cuisine and Class: A Study in Comparative Sociology*, Cambridge and New York: Cambridge University Press.

Gregg, M. and Siegworth, J. (2010), *The Affect Theory Reader*, Durham: Duke University Press.

Gregson, N. and Crang, P. (2010), 'Guest editorial, materiality and waste: Inorganic vitality in a networked world', *Environment and Planning A*, 40: 1026–32.

Guthman, J. (2003), 'Fast food/organic food: Reflexive tastes and the making of the "Yuppie Chow"', *Social and Cultural Geography*, 4: 45–58.

Guthman, J. (2004), *Agrarian Dreams: The Paradox of Organic Farming in California*, California: The University of California Press.

Guthman, J. (2008a), 'Neoliberalism and the making of food politics in California', *Geoforum*, 39(3): 1171–83.

Guthman, J. (2008b), 'Bringing good food to others: Investigating the subjects of alternative food practice', *Cultural Geographies*, 15(4): 431–47.

Guthman, J. (2008c), '"If only they knew": Color blindness and universalism in California alternative food institutions', *Professional Geographer*, 60(3): 687–97.

Guthman, J. (2011), *Weighing In: Obesity, Food Justice and the Limits of Capitalism*. Berkeley, CA: University of California Press.

Guy, K. M. (2001), 'Wine, champagne, and the making of French identity in the Belle Epoque', in P. Scholliers (ed.), *Food, Drink and Identity: Cooking, Eating and Drinking in Europe since the Middle Ages*, Oxford and New York: Berg, 163–78.

Hall, C. M., Sharples, L., Mitchell, R., Macionis, N. and Cambourne, B (2003), *Food Tourism Around the World: Development, Management and Markets*, Oxford: Butterworth-Heinemann.

Haraway, D. (1990), 'A manifesto for cyborgs: Science, technology, and socialist feminism in the 1980s', in J. L. Nicholson (ed.), *Feminism/Postmodernism (Thinking Gender)* London: Routledge, 190–233.

Harbottle, L. (2000), *Food for Health, Food for Wealth: The Performance of Ethnic and Gender Identities by Iranian Settlers in Britain*, New York and Oxford: Berghahn Books.

Hage, G. (1997), 'At Home in the entrails of the West: Multiculturalism, ethnic food and migrant home-building', in H. Grace, G. Hage, L. Johnson, J. Langsworth and M. Symonds (eds), *Home/World: Space, Community and Marginality in Sydney's West*, Annandale NSW: Pluto Press, 99–153.

Harris, O. (2000), *To Make the Earth Bear Fruit: Essays on Fertility, Work and Gender in Highland Bolivia*, London: Institute of Latin American Studies.

Harwood, J. (2009), 'Theorizing biopedagogies', in J. Wright and V. Harwood (eds), *Biopolitics and the 'Obesity Epidemic': Governing Bodies*, New York: Routledge, 15–30.

Hawkins, G. (2013), 'The performativity of food packaging: market devices, waste crisis and recycling', in D. Evans, H. Campbell and A. Murcott (eds), *Waste Matters: New Perspectives on Food and Society*, Oxford: Wiley-Blackwell/The Sociological Review, 66–84.

Hayes-Conroy, J. (2014), *Savoring Alternative Food: School Gardens, Healthy Eating and Visceral Difference*, Abingdon: Routledge.

Hayes-Conroy, A. and Hayes-Conroy, J. (2008), 'Taking back taste: Feminism, food and visceral politics', *Gender, Place and Culture: A Journal of Feminist Geography*, 15(5): 461–73.

Hayes-Conroy, A. and Hayes-Conroy, J. (2010a), 'Visceral difference: variations in feeling (slow) food', *Environment and Planning* A, 42: 2956–71.

Hayes-Conroy, J. and Hayes-Conroy, A. (2010b), 'Visceral geographies: Mattering, relating and defying', *Geography Compass*, 4(9): 1273–82.

Hayes-Conroy, J. and Hayes-Conroy, A. (2013), 'Veggies and visceralities: A political ecology of food and feeling', *Emotion, Space and Society*, 6, 81–90.

Heldke, L. (2003), *Exotic Appetites: Ruminations of a Food Adventurer*, New York: Routledge.

Hickey-Moody, A., Savage, G. and Windle, J. (2010), 'Pedagogy writ large: Public, popular and cultural pedagogies in motion', *Critical Studies in Education*, 51(3): 227–36.

Hobsbawn, E. and Ranger, T., eds (1983), *The Invention of Tradition*, Cambridge: Cambridge University Press.

Hollows, J. and Jones, S. (2010), '"At least he's doing something about it": Moral entrepreneurship and individual responsibility in Jamie's Ministry of Food', *European Journal of Cultural Studies*, 13(3): 307–22.

Holtzman, J. (2009), *Uncertain Tastes: Memory, Ambivalence and the Politics of Eating in Samburu, Northern Kenya*, Berkeley: University of California Press.

Holtzman, J. (2013), 'Reflections on fraught food', in E-J. Abbots and A. Lavis (eds), *Why We Eat, How We Eat: Contemporary Encounters Between Foods and Bodies*, Farnham: Ashgate, 139–46.

Holtzman, J. (2016), 'To love sugar one does not have to eat it', *Gastronomica: The Journal of Critical Food Studies*, 16(3): 42–53.

hooks, b. (1992), *black looks: race and representation*, London: Routledge.

Howes, D., ed. (1995), *Empire of the Senses: The Sensual Cultural Reader*, London: Berg.

Howes, D. (2003), *Sensual Relations: Engaging the Senses in Culture and Social Theory*, University of Michigan Press.

Howes, D. (2010), 'Response to Sarah Pink', *Social Anthropology*, 18(3): 333–36.

Hurn, S. (2013), 'Confessions of a vegan anthropologist: Exploring the trans-biopolitics of eating in the field', in E-J. Abbots and A. Lavis (eds), *Why We Eat, How We Eat: Contemporary Encounters Between Foods and Bodies*, Aldershot: Ashgate, 219–35.

International Living 'Why Ecuador' [online]. Available at: http://www.internationalliving. com/Countries/Ecuador/Why-Ecuador [accessed 18 March 2010].

Jackson, M. (1989), *Paths Towards a Clearing: Radical Empiricism and Ethnographic Enquiry*, Bloomington: Indiana University Press.

Jackson, P. (2015), *Anxious Appetites: Food and Consumer Culture*, London: Bloomsbury.

Jenkins, T. (1994), 'Fieldwork and the experience of everyday life', *Man*, 29: 433–56.

Johnston, L. and Longhurst, R. (2012), 'Embodied geographies of food, belonging and hope in multicultural Hamilton, Aotearoa, New Zealand', *Geoforum*, 43: 325–31

Jokisch, B. (2007), 'Ecuador: Diversity in migration', in *Migration Information Source*
Migration Policy Institute (ed) available at http://www.migrationinformation.org/
USfocus/display.cfm?ID=575 (accessed 5 April 2007).

Jokisch, B. and Pribilsky, J. (2002), 'The panic to leave: Economic crisis and the "new
emigration" from Ecuador', *International Migration*, 40(4): 75–102.

Klein, J. (2007), 'Redefining Cantonese cuisine in post-Mao Guangzhou', *Bulletin of
SOAS*, 70 (3): 511–37.

Kneafsey, M., Cox, R., Holloway, L., Dowler, E., Venn, L. and Tuomainen, H. (2008),
Reconnecting Consumers, Producers and Food: Exploring Alternatives,
Oxford: Berg.

Korsmeyer, C. (2005), 'Introduction: Perspectives on taste', in C. Korsmeyer (ed.), *Taste
Culture Reader: Experiencing Food and Drink*, London: Berg, 1–9.

Latour, B. (2004), 'How to talk about the body?: The normative dimension of Science
Studies', *Body and Society*, 10(2–3): 205–29.

Latour, B. (2005), *Reassembling the Social: An Introduction to Actor Network Theory*,
Oxford: Oxford University Press.

Laudan, R. (2004), 'Slow Food: The French terroir strategy and culinary modernism',
Food, Culture & Society, 7(2): 134–44.

Lavis, A. (2016), 'Food, bodies and the "stuff" of (not) eating in anorexia', *Gastronomica:
The Journal of Critical Food Studies*, 16(3): 54–63.

Lavis, A., Abbots, E-J. and Attala, L. (2015), 'Introduction: Reflecting on the embodied
intersections of eating and caring', in E-J. Abbots, A. Lavis and L. Attala (eds),
Careful Eating: Bodies, Food and Care, Farnham: Ashgate, 1–21.

Law, J. and Hassard, J. (2004), *Actor Network Theory and After*, Oxford: Blackwell.

LeHeron, R. (2014), 'From embodied to enacting – further igniting new food politics',
Journal of Rural Studies, 34: 277–8.

Leitch, A. (2013 [2009]), '"Slow Food and the politics of "virtuous globalization"', in
C. Counihan and P. Van Esterik (eds), *Food and Culture: A Reader*, London:
Routledge, 409–25.

Levi-Strauss, C. (1969), *Totemism*, translated by Rodney Needham, London: Penguin
Books.

Lewis, G. H. (1997), 'Celebrating asparagus: Community and the rationally constructed
food festival', *Journal of American Culture*, 20: 73–8.

Lewis, T. and Potter, A., eds (2011), *Ethical Consumption: A Critical Introduction*, London:
Routledge.

Long, L. M., ed. (2004), *Culinary Tourism*, Lexington: The University Press of Kentucky.

Longhurst, R. (2012), 'Becoming smaller: Autobiographical spaces of weight loss',
Antipode, 44(3), 871–88.

Longhurst, R., Johnston, L. and Ho, E. (2009), 'A visceral approach: Cooking "at home"
with migrant women in Hamilton, New Zealand', *Transactions of the Institute of British
Geographers*, 34, 333–45.

Lockie, S. (2013), 'Bastions of white privilege? Reflections on the racialization of alternative food networks', *International Journal of Sociology of Agriculture and Food*, 23(3): 409–18.

Lowenthal, D. (1985), *The Past in a Foreign Country*, Cambridge: Cambridge University Press.

Lozada Jr., E. P. (2000), 'Globalized childhood? Kentucky Fried Chicken in Beijing', in J. Jing (ed.), *Feeding China's Little Emperors: Food, Children and Social Change*, Stanford, CA: Stanford University Press, 114–34.

Lupton, D. (1996), *Food, the Body and the Self*, London: Sage.

Lupton, D. (2015), 'The pedagogy of disgust: The ethical, moral and political implications of using disgust in public health campaigns', *Critical Public Health*, 25(1): 4–14.

Lyon, S. (2010), *Coffee and Community: Maya Farmers and Fair-Trade Markets*, Boulder, CO: University Press of Colorado.

Mankekar, P. (2002), '"Indian shopping": India grocery stores and transnational configurations of belonging', *Ethnos*, 67(1): 75–98.

Marx, K. (1995 [1867]), *Capital: An Abridged Edition*, Oxford: Oxford University Press.

Matthews, J. and Smith Maguire, J. (2014), 'Introduction: Thinking with cultural intermediaries', in J. Smith Maguire and J. Matthews (eds), *The Cultural Intermediaries Reader*, London: Sage, 1–12.

Mauss, M. (n.d [1934]), *Techniques of the Body* https://monoskop.org/images/c/c4/Mauss_Marcel_1935_1973_Techniques_of_the_Body.pdf [accessed 13 Jun 2016].

McClintock, A. (1995), *Imperial Leather: Race, Gender and Sexuality in the Colonial Contest*, London: Routledge.

McFall, L. (2014), 'The problem of cultural Intermediaries in the economy of qualities', in J. Smith Maguire and J. Matthews (eds), *The Cultural Intermediaries Reader*, London: Sage, 42–51.

McIntosh, A. and Zey, M. (1998), 'Women as gatekeepers', in C. Counihan and S. L. Kaplan (eds), *Food and Gender: Identity and Power*, London: Routledge, 125–44.

Mennell, S. (1996), *All Manners of Food: Eating and Taste in England and France from the Middle Ages to the Present*, Springfield, IL: Illini Books.

Miele, M. and Murdoch, J. (2003), 'Fast food/slow food: standardising and differentiating cultures of food', in R. Almas and G. Lawrence (eds), *Globalisation, Localisation and Sustainable Livelihoods*, Farnham: Ashgate, 25–41.

Miles, A. (2004), *From Cuenca to Queens: An Anthropological Story of Transnational Migration*, Austin: University of Texas Press.

Mol, A. (2002), *The Body Multiple: Ontology in Medical Practice*, Durham and London: Duke University Press.

Mol, A. (2008), 'I eat an apple: On theorizing subjectivities', *Subjectivity*, 22: 28–37.

Molz, J. (2007), 'The cosmopolitan mobilities of culinary tourism', *Space and Culture* 10(1): 77–93.

Morales, E. (1995), *The Guinea Pig: Healing, Food and Rituals in the Andes*, Tucson: University of Arizona.

Morgan, K. (2010), 'Local and green, global and fair: The ethical foodscape and the politics of care', *Environment and Planning A*, 42(8): 1852–67.

Morgan, K. and Murdoch, J. (2000), 'Organic vs conventional agriculture: Knowledge, power and innovation in the Food Chain', *Geoforum*, 31: 159–73.

Morris, B. (1994), *The Anthropology of the Self: The Individual in Cultural Perspective*, London: Pluto Press.

Müller, B. (2006), 'Introduction: GMOs – global objects of contention', *Focaal: European Journal of Anthropology*, 48: 3–16.

Murcott, A. (1983), '"It's a pleasure to cook for him": Food, mealtimes and gender in some South Wales households', in E. Garmanikow, D. Morgan, J. Purvis and D. Taylorson (eds), *The Public and the Private: Social Patterns of Gender Relations*, London: Heinemann, 78–90.

Murcott, A. (2013), 'Interlude: Reflections on the elusiveness of eating', in E-J Abbots and A. Lavis (eds), *Why We Eat, How We Eat: Contemporary Encounters between Foods and Bodies*, Farnham: Ashgate, 209–18.

Murray, S. (2009), 'Marked as "pathological": "Fat" bodies as virtual confessors', in J. Wright and V. Harwood (eds), *Biopolitics and the 'Obesity Epidemic': Governing Bodies*, New York: Routledge, 78–90.

Nixon, S. and du Gay, P. (2002), 'Who needs cultural intermediaries?', *Cultural Studies*, 16(4): 495–500.

Ohnuki-Tierney, E. (1993), *Rice as Self: Japanese Identities Through Time*, Princeton, NJ: Princeton University Press.

Ormond, J. (2013), 'The transition to low carbon milk: Dairy consumption and the changing politics of human-animal relations', in E-J Abbots and A. Lavis (eds), *Why We Eat, How We Eat: Contemporary Encounters between Foods and Bodies*, Farnham: Ashgate, 187–208.

Parascoli, F. and Tasaki, A. (2011), 'Shared meals and food fights: Geographical Indications, rural development, and the environment', *Environment and Society: Advances in Research*, 2: 106–123.

Parkins, W. (2004), 'Out of time: Fast subjects and slow living'. *Time & Society*, 13(2/3): 363–82.

Parry, J. and Bloch, M. (1989), 'Introduction: Money and the morality of exchange', in J. Parry and M. Bloch (eds), *Money and the Morality of Exchange*, Cambridge: Cambridge University Press, 1–32.

Petrini, C. (2001), *Slow Food: The Case for Taste*, New York: Columbia University Press.

Petrini, C. (2007), *Slow Food Nation: Why Our Food Should be Good, Clean, and Fair*, translated by C. Furlan, New York: Rizzoli Ex Libris.

Pietrykowski, B. (2004), 'You are what you eat: The social economy of the Slow Food Movement', *Review of Social Economy*, 62(3): 307–321.

Phillipov, M. (2013), 'Resisting health: Extreme food and the culinary abject', *Critical Studies in Media Communication*: 1–14.

Pilcher, J. M. (1998), *Que Vivan Los Tamales!: Food and the Making of Mexican Identity*, Albuquerque: University of New Mexico Press.

Pink, S. (2010), 'The future of sensory anthropology/the anthropology of the senses', *Social Anthropology*, 18(3): 331–33.

Piper, N. (2015), 'Jamie Oliver and cultural intermediation', *Food, Culture and Society*, 18(2): 245–64.

Pribilsky, J. (2007), *La Chulla Vida: Gender, Migration and the Family in Andean Ecuador & New York City*, Syracuse, NY: Syracuse University Press.

Probyn, E. (2000), *Carnal Appetites: FoodSexIdentities*, London and New York: Routledge.

Rabinow, P. and Rose, N. (2006), 'Biopower today', *BioSocieties*, 1: 195–217.

Ray, K. (2004), *The Migrant's Table: Meals and Memories in Bengali-American Households*, Philadelphia: University of Pennsylvania Press.

Reed-Danahay, D., ed. (1997). *Auto/ethnography: Rewriting the Self and the Social*, Oxford: Berg.

Ritzer, G. (2010), *McDonaldization: The Reader*, LA: Pine Forge Press.

Rose, N. (2001), 'The Politics of life itself', *Theory, Culture and Society*, 18(6): 1–30.

Rose, N. (2007), *The Politics of Life Itself: Biomedicine, Power, and Subjectivity in the Twenty-First Century*, Princeton, NJ: Princeton University Press.

Roseberry, W. (1996), 'The rise of yuppie coffees and the reimagination of class in the United States', *American Anthropologist*, 98(4): 762–775.

Rousseau, S. (2012a), *Food media: Celebrity Chefs and the Politics of Everyday Interference*, London: Berg.

Rousseau, S. (2012b), *Food and Social Media: You Are What You Tweet*, Lanham, MA: Altamira.

Rousseau, S. (2015), 'Is sharing caring: Social media and discourses of healthful eating', in E-J. Abbots, A. Lavis and L. Attala (eds), *Careful Eating: Embodied Entanglements Between Food and Care*, Farnham: Ashgate, 45–67.

Saber, G. and Posner, R. (2013), 'Remembering the past and constructing the future over a communal plate', *Food, Culture and Society*, 16(2), 197–222.

Samuel, R. (2012 [1995]), *Theatres of Memory: The Past and the Present in Contemporary Society*, London: Verso.

Scheper-Hughes, N. (2000), 'The global traffic in human organs', *Current Anthropology*, 41: 191–224.

Scheper-Hughes, N. and Lock, M (1987), 'The mindful body: A prolegomenon to future work in Medical Anthropology', *Medical Anthropology Quarterly*, 1(1): 6–41.

Schurman, R. (2003), 'Introduction: Biotechnology in the new millennium', in R. Schurman and D. Doyle Takahashi Kelso (eds), *Engineering Trouble: Biotechnology and Its Discontents*, Berkeley: University of California Press, 1–23.

Sedgwick, E. K. (2003), *Touching Feeling: Affect, Pedagogy, Performativity*, Durham: Duke University Press.

Serematakis, C. N. (1994), 'The memory of the senses, part 1: Marks of the transitory', in C. N Serematakis (ed.), *The Senses Still: Perception and Memory as Material Culture in Modernity*, Chicago: University of Chicago Press, 1–18.

Sexton, A. (2016), 'Alternative proteins and the (non)stuff of "meat"', *Gastronomica: The Journal of Critical Food Studies*, 16(3): 64–73.

Shilling, C. (1993), *The Body and Social Theory*, London: Sage.

Shilling, C. (2013), 'Series editor's introduction', in D. Evans, H. Campbell and A. Murcott (eds), *Waste Matters: New Perspectives on Food and Society*, Oxford: Wiley-Blackwell/ The Sociological Review, 1–4.

Slocum, R. (2007), 'Whiteness, space and alternative food practice', *Geoforum*, 38: 520–33.

Slocum, R. and Saldanha, A., eds (2013), *Geographies of Race and Food: Fields, Bodies, Markets*, Farnham: Ashgate.

Smith Maguire, J. (2014), 'Bourdieu on cultural intermediaries', in J. Smith Maguire and J. Matthews (eds), *The Cultural Intermediaries Reader*, London: Sage, 15–24.

Stockhammer, P. (2016), 'Past food for thought: The potential for archaeology', *Gastronomica: The Journal of Critical Food Studies*, 16(3): 89–99.

Stoller, D. (1989), *The Taste of Ethnographic Things: The Senses in Anthropology*, Philadelphia: University of Pennsylvania Press.

Strathern, M. (1988), *The Gender of the Gift: Problems with Women and Problems with Society in Melanesia*, Berkeley: University of California Press.

Sutton, D. (2001), *Remembrance of Repasts: An Anthropology of Food and Memory*, Oxford: Berg.

Thrift, N. (2004), 'Intensities of feeling: Towards a spatial politics of affect', *Geografiska Annaler, Series B, Human Geography*, 86(1): 57–78.

Trubek, A., Guy, M. K. and Bowen, S. (2010), 'Terroir: A French conversation with a transnational future', *Contemporary French and Francophone Studies*, 14(2): 139–48.

Truninger, M. and Teixera, J. (2015), 'Children's engagements with food: An embodied politics of care through school meals', in E-J. Abbots, A. Lavis and L. Attala (eds), *Careful Eating: Bodies, Food and Care*, Farnham: Ashgate, 195–212.

Tuomainen, H. M. (2009), 'Ethnic identity, (post)colonialism and foodways: Ghanaians in London', *Food, Culture and Society*, 12(4): 525–54.

Turner, B. S. (1996), *The Body and Society: Explorations in Social Theory*, 2nd edn, London: Sage Publications.

Vallianatos, H. and Raine, K. (2008), 'Consuming food and constructing identities among Arabic and South Asian immigrant Women', *Food, Culture and Society*, 11(3): 355–373.

Van Otterloo, A. H. (1987), 'Foreign immigrants and the Dutch at table, 1945–1985: Bridging or Widening the Gap?', *Netherlands Journal of Sociology*, 23: 126–143.

Watson, J. L., ed. (1997), *Golden Arches East: McDonalds in East Asia*, Stanford, CA: Stanford University Press.

Weismantel, M. J. (1988), *Food, Gender and Poverty in the Ecuadorian Andes*, Philadelphia: University of Pennsylvania Press.

Weismantel, M. J. (1995), 'Making kin; Kinship theory and Zumbugua adoptions', *American Ethnologist*, 22(4): 685–704.

Weismantel, M. J. (2003), 'Mothers of the *Patria*: La Chola Cuencana and La Mama Negra', in N. E. Whitten (ed.), *Millennial Ecuador: Critical Essays on Cultural Transformations and Social Dynamics*, Iowa City: University of Iowa Press, 325–54.

West, H. G. (2013), 'Appellations and indications of origin, terroir, and the social construction and contestation of place-named foods', in A. Murcott, W. Belasco and P. Jackson (eds), *The Handbook of Food Research*, London: Bloomsbury, 209–28.

West, H. G. (2016), 'Artisanal foods and the cultural economy: Perspectives on craft, heritage, authenticity and reconnection', in J. Klein and J. Watson (eds), *Handbook of Food and Anthropology*, London: Bloomsbury, 406–34.

West, H. G. and Domingos, N. (2012), 'Gourmandizing poverty food: The Serpa cheese slow food presidium', *Journal of Agrarian Change*, 12(1): 120–43.

Whitten, N. E. (2003), 'Introduction', in N. E. Whitten (ed.), *Millennial Ecuador: Critical Essays on Cultural Transformations and Social Dynamics*, Iowa City: University of Iowa Press, 1–45.

Wilk, R. (2002), 'Food and nationalism: the origins of "Belizean" food', in W. Belasco and P. Scranton (eds), *Food Nations: Selling Taste to Consumer Societies*, New York and London: Routledge, 67–89.

Wilk, R. (2006), *Home Cooking in the Global Village: Caribbean Food from Buccaneers to Ecotourists*, Oxford and New York: Berg.

Wilk, R. (2010), 'Power at the table. Food fights and happy meals', *Cultural Studies: Critical Methodologies*, 10: 428–36.

Wright, J. (2009), 'Biopower, biopedagogies and the obesity Epidemic', in J. Wright and V. Harwood (eds), *Biopolitics and the 'Obesity Epidemic': Governing Bodies*, New York: Routledge, 1–14.

Wright, J. and Harwood, V., eds (2009), *Biopolitics and the 'Obesity Epidemic': Governing Bodies*, New York: Routledge.

Yotova, M. (2013), 'It is the bacillus that makes our milk', in E-J. Abbots and A. Lavis (eds), *Why We Eat, How We Eat: Contemporary Encounters Between Foods and Bodies*, Farnham: Ashgate, 187–208.

Index

actor network theory 1, 21–2, 24–7, 49, 152–3, *see also* Latour, Bruno

adoption 37–8, *see also* kinship and relatedness

affect 3–4, 11, 20, 35, 42–3, 46–50, 62–7, 80, 83, 85–9, 92, 97–8, 110–12, 114, 118–19, 121, 124, 139, 146, 148–9, 152–4, *see also* embodiment and senses

affective background 45, 49, 57, 80, 85–9, 110–11, 145, *see also* buzz

affective relations 20, 29, 36–8, 53, 112, 114, 120–1, 154, *see also* intimacies of migrants 57–67

agency, definition of 21–2

agri-business, *see* agri-industry

agriculture 8–9, 125, 131
  community supported 103, 107
  small-scale 8–9, 104, 126, 129, 133

agri-food, *see* agri-industry

agri-industry 20, 102, 104–9, 112, 124–5, *see also* Global Food and industrial food

alternative food(s) 101–2, 106, *see also* fair trade and Slow Food
  alternative food networks 32, 112–20

amerindian 92–3

anorexia 15, 149

anxiety 101–6, 120, 124–5, 127–8, 130, 145, 153

assemblage 10–12, 22–3, 27, 29, 31–2, 34, 35, 38–9, 42–3, 45–9, 54–5, 57–8, 64–7, 86–7, 89–91, 94–5, 101–2, 106, 108, 110–11, 113–15, 119–21, 130, 132, 134–6, 142–5, 154–5
  definition of 25–6

asylum seekers 60, *see also* migrants and refugees

Australia 71–2, 76

authorities, cultural 19, 22–3, 28–9, 31–2, 89, 108–9, *see also* bio-authority

autoethnography 7, 12, 35, 43–4, 139, 141, 150–1

beef 67, 73, 119, 129

Bennett, Jane 1, 5, 16, 21–4, 46–8, 50, 65–6, 88–9, 111, 115–17, 134, 143

bio-authority 10–13, 31–3, 35–6, 42, 45, 49, 50–1, 53–5, 58, 67, 69, 72, 79–80, 94–5, 98, 101–2, 106–9, 116, 118, 120, 123, 133, 136–7, 139–40, 142, 146, 152–4

biomedicine 18, 137, 142
  medical gaze 139–40

biopedagogy 28–31, 94, 140–1

biopower 3, 10, 13, 18, 27–8, 31, 34, 88, 153

blood 35–7, 40–1, 43

boundaries 3, 11–12, 15, 18–20, 26–27, 33, 35–6, 39, 42, 52, 55, 58–62, 68–77, 79, 91, 94, 96, 99, 102, 106, 118–20, 123, 127–8, 131, 148
  bodily 11–12, 18, 57–8, 60, 68–9, 71–2, 75, 76–7, 99, 102, 106, 127–8, 148
  gustatory 10, 57–9, 61, 69, 72, 75, 77, 83, 94

bounded vitalism 10, 12–13, 26–7, 31, 33, 54, 66, 143, 152–5, *see also* vitalism, definition of 22–4

Bourdieu, Pierre 24–7, 30–1, 115

buzz 80, 86–8, 98, 145, *see also* affective background

California 83–6, 96, 118, 146 129, *see also* United States of America

Canada 61, 69

care 49, 114–15, 123–4, 128–9, 137, 153–4
  commodification of 112, 114, 124

Carolan, Michael 20, 24, 45, 48, 102, 106–9, 111–12, 117–18, 136, 140, 145–6, *see also* embodied food politics

cheese   63, 84, 95–6, 116–17
chef(s)   51, 86, 140
Chola Cuencana   143
citizenship   11, 79–80, 92–5, 135, 137, 140
class relations   9, 24, 38, 54, 58–9, 61,
      71–2, 94, 103, 112, 115–18, 125,
      129–30, 132, 140, 154, 157
coffee   42, 109–11, 146
cohesion, social   10–11, 83–5, 92
Colombia   125, 131
comfort foods   49
comida típica   80, 90
commensality   10, 35–6, 41, 46, 49, 58, 72,
      75, 114
commodification   84, 91, 96, 112, 114, 124
control   12, 17–18, 21–2, 49–50, 70, 72–3,
      75, 101, 103–6, 120, 130, 145–6
   of food supply   52–4, 68
cook, the   10, 35–6, 39–43, 45–6, 49–53,
      55, 59, 146
cookbook(s)   80, 94, 96–8
cooking   14, 35–6, 39, 45, 49–53, 60, 63,
      68, 72, 86, 97, 107, 119, 151, 158
   competitions   81, 85
   programmes   118–19
corn   39, 59, 82, 90, 131–2
cosmopolitanism   9, 58, 76, 96
coterminous bodies   10, 16, 41, 57, 80,
      92–8
culinary safe havens   60, 62–7
cuy   10, 35, 38–48, 50–1, 54–5, 59–60,
      68–9, 73–4, 81–2, 90–1, 93–6, 98,
      103, 145–6, 149, 154, 157
   preparation of   39–41

desire   10, 36, 46–8, 50, 55, 59, 64, 72, 74,
      76, 104, 106, 127, 130, 150
discipline   17, 31, 50, 67, 74, 88, 139,
      140–1
distributed agency   5, 10–11, 21–2, 24–7,
      33, 35, 38, 54–5, 66, 89, 101, 120,
      152
doctors, *see* Medical profession
domestic labour   41, 50–4, 69, 72, 90–1,
      see also kitchen, staff and labour
domestication   73, 146

eating, definitions of   14–16
eating body, the   16–21

Ecuador   37–41, 50–2, 69–71, 74, 90–5,
      103–6, 119, 125–6, 129, 131–8, 145,
      158–9
   Greater Cuenca Region of   8–9, 103–5,
      127, 129, 132–3, 136–7
   Jima village   8, 41, 44–7, 50, 54, 59, 68,
      80–3, 85, 90–5, 132, 138, 157–8
embodied food politics   19–21, 48–9, 73,
      107–9, *see also* Carolan, Michael
embodiment   3–7, 10–11, 13–16, 23,
      30, 35–6, 38–46, 55, 57–8, 62–72,
      76–7, 85–9, 92, 96–8, 102, 107–15,
      117–21, 123–4, 128, 130, 140–51,
      154–5, *see also* affect and senses
encounters   27, 31–4, 42–5, 47–50, 62–6,
      70, 73, 76–7, 85–89, 92, 110–14,
      119–20, 137, 140–8, 150–1, 153
   bio-authorial   11, 31–2, 79–80, 83,
      88–9, 92, 97–9
enemy cuisine   74–5
ethical consumption   112, 114–15
ethnicity   58, 60–1, 69, 76, 82–4, 94, 96–7,
      112, 157, 158
experts   24, 110–11, 146, *see also*
      intermediaries, cultural

fair trade   12, 102–3, 112–15, 117, 121,
      124, 153–4
fast food   9, 81, 115, 123, 132–4, 136–7,
      159, *see also* hamburgers
fat   22, 43, 88, 137–42, 150
fear, *see* anxiety
festivals, food   11, 31–2, 79–92, 94–9
Foucault, Michel   3, 27–8, 31, 89, 98, 136
frankenfood   131, *see also* genetically
      modified foods

garlic   83–4, 86, 96, 146
gender   18, 20, 36, 48, 50–5, 61, 67–9,
      103, 118, 140, 150, 154, 158
genetically modified food(s)   12, 123–5,
      131–2, 141–2, 154, 159, *see also*
      Frankenfood
Ghana   60–1
gift(s)   52, 60, 67
'Global Food'   9, 20, 81, 101–22, 128,
      132–3, 136–7, 146, 149, *see also*
      fast food
GMO, *see* genetically modified food

governance   21, 29, 45, 50, 108, 139, 145,
      153
grass   39, 41–2, 44–5, 73, 90, 95, 119
Greece   63–4, *see also* Sutton, David
grocery store(s)   65–7, 71, 86, 146, 154
guinea pig, *see* Cuy
Guthman, Julie   18, 29, 106–7, 112, 114,
      123–5, 128–31, 136–9, 154

hamburgers   81, 91, 93, *see also* fast food
Hayes-Conroy, Jessica   16, 20, 22, 45–6,
      108, 119, 127, 130, *see also* visceral
      geographies
   and Hayes-Conroy, Allison   4, 14, 20,
      102, 114–15, 117–18, 146, 154
health   18, 28–9, 52, 104, 119, 127–8, 130,
      138–41,
   health Fair   80–3, 85, 90, 94, 97, 158
   scare(s)   104, 127
heritage   8, 11, 79–85, 96, 99, 107, 116,
      133, 142, 154
Holtzman, Jon   2, 15, 36, 38, 41, 48–9, 52,
      144, 148, 153–4
home   10, 39, 46, 57–61, 64–5, 67–70,
      77–8, 90, 104
   homeland   90
home-cooked   44–5, 90
homogenisation   115, 133
hybridization   11, 61, 69, 91
   hybridized identities   11, 58, 60–2, 74

incorporation   15, 46–7, 74–7
India   65–7, 86, 96, 119, 154
Indonesia   71–2, 110
industrial food   96, 103–7, 109, 117,
      124–5, 127–9, 132, *see also* agri-
      industry and 'Global Food'
intermediaries
   cultural   10, 24–5, 29–30, 33–4, 153
      (*see also* experts)
   semiotic   113
intimacies   10–11, 35, 44, 49, 53, 91, 101,
      120, 145, 153, *see also* proximities
      and sameness
Iraq   74–6
Italy   84, 86, 92, 117

junk   137, *see also* rubbish and waste
   food   132, 136–7, 150

kinship   10, 35–8, 46–7, 54, 59, 62, *see
      also* adoption and relatedness
kitchen   40, 50–1, 54
   equipment   90, 151
   staff   140, *see also* domestic labour
knowledge   1–3, 7, 10–11, 13–14, 24–35,
      38, 45–6, 48–50, 52, 54–5, 63–4,
      66–7, 71–2, 79, 87–9, 91, 94, 96–9,
      102, 105, 107–12, 117, 119, 127–8,
      132, 134, 139–47, 149, 152, 154
   -power   16, 29, 98, 146

labelling   79, 81, 119, 123–4, 126, 128,
      138–9
labour   37, 39, 48, 94, 103, 107, 113–14,
      116, 154, 157, *see also* domestic
      labour
   gendered   50–4, 67–9, 133, 158
   waged   91
Latour, Bruno   1, 13, 21, 24–5, 27, 31, 42,
      110, 146, 152.
Lavis, Anna   2, 5, 14–16, 20, 32, 41–2, 49,
      114–15, 137, 140, 144, 148–9, 153–4

Malay   36–7, 41
marketing   109, 113–14, 129, 135, 154
   market interventions   140
   new markets   132, 135
market(s)   73, 88, 105–6, 119–20, 126,
      128, 158–9, *see also* supermarkets
   Borough Market, London   42, 86–7
materialities   2, 10, 13–14, 20–1, 23, 35,
      41, 58, 61–3, 77, 85–8, 96, 103, 109,
      132, 134–5, 139, 142, 144, 152, 155,
      see also new materialisms
meals,   32, 59, 63, 131, 148, 158
   family   49
   school   107, 140–1
   shared   37–8
meat   59, 150, *see also* beef, cuy and
      salami
   extender   107
   substitutes   151
media   140, 142, 146, 153–4
mediation   3, 10, 13, 20, 24–5, 27, 29–32,
      34, 87, 97, 109, 140, 146, 153
mediators   24–5, 27, 31, 34–5, 42–3, 45,
      47–9, 55, 64, 66, 98, 120, 143, *see
      also* Latour, Bruno

medical profession 1, 139–40, 142
medicine, *see* Biomedicine
memory 44, 49–50, 62–4, 89, 145, 148–9
methodology 6–7, 12, 14, 19, 31, 62, 141, 147–53, *see also* autoethnography
Mexico 96, 125, 131
migrants 9–11, 32, 55, 57–78, 82, 84, 103–6, 109, 119–20, 125, 127–9, 132–4, 136–7, 145, 158–9, *see also* asylum seekers and refugees
  bodies of 57–8, 62, 65–74, 77, 105–6, 127–9
  migrant-peasantry 9
  privileged migrants 9, 69–74, 103–6, 109, 119, 125, 127–9, 132–7, 145, 158–9
migration 8–9, 11, 57–8, 62, 67–9, 157
milk 22, 36–7, 48–9, 63, 103, 106, 114, 116, 129–30
Mol, Annemarie 14–17, 19–21, 36, 39, 42, 45, 50, 66, 68, 70, 143, 145
multiculturalism 60, 75–6

nationalism 75, 92–3, 95, 99, *see also* transnationalism
  national food 11, 79, 80, 82, 95–7, 99
  national identities 58, 60, 63, 80
new materialisms 1, 5, 147, 152, 155
non-human, the 1, 3, 5, 10, 12–13, 19, 21–2, 24–7, 30, 33–5, 47, 54, 88–9, 91, 103, 105, 111–14, 120, 125, 127, 142–3, 147, 152–3
Not-in-my-Body 22, 48–9, 72

obesity 12, 18, 29, 123–4, 138–41, 149
  'epidemic' 139
organic food(s) 12, 22, 48, 73, 88, 103, 106, 119–20, 123–31, 141–2, 153–4
otherness 10–11, 55, 74–80, 91, 101, 141

packaging 68, 133–7, 142
Palestine 64, 97
pathogens 73, 104, 127
peasantry 9, 82, 119, 131, 133, 158
pedagogy 30, 80, 140, *see also* biopower, biopedagogies
pesticides 73, 104, 127
place 5, 8, 10–11, 39, 41, 45, 51, 55, 57–60, 62–4, 68, 71–2, 77–8, 79, 83, 87, 92, 95–6, 98–9, 109–11, 113, 131, 145

placelessness 101–3
plastic 133
  PET 135
plastic surgery 138
pleasure 44–8, 120, 149
Portugal 84, 116–17, 140–1
proximities 10–12, 35, 38, 47, 57–8, 60, 75, 77, 79, 93, 101, 114, 120, 123, *see also* intimacies and sameness

race 20, 75, 81–2, 112, 118–19, 131, 154, 171
recycling 134–5
reflexive eating 12, 49, 123, 130, 132, 136–7, 142, *see also* responsiblization
refugees 64, *see also* asylum seekers and migrants
refusal of food 10, 36, 46, 48–9, 55, 73, 106, 141
rejection of food, *see* refusal of food
relatedness 33, 35–7, 39. 41, 46–8, 54, 59, 78, 91–2, 95, 101, 106, 109, 120, 143, *see also* adoption and kinship
remittances 9, 60
responsibility 12, 28–9, 52, 69, 123–4, 132, 135, 138, 140
restaurant(s) 9, 60, 65, 70–2, 125–6, 129
risk 12, 18, 48, 57–8, 68, 70–2, 74, 76–7, 84, 101–5, 124,
rubbish 132, 134, 136–7, *see also* junk and waste

safety 70–1, 101–3, 131
salad 126, 129–32
salami 84, 86, 92, *see also* meat
sameness 10–11, 55, 57–8, 66, 78–80, 91–4, 99, 101, 114, 141, *see also* intimacies and proximities
school(s) 118–20
  meals (*see* Meals, school)
senses 3–5, 10–11, 20, 57–8, 62–6, 77, 86–7, 89, 92, 97–9, 102, 113–14, 118, 121, 145, 148–9, 153, 155, *see also* affect and embodiment
  sensory anthropology 62–3, 158
Slow Food Movement, the 12, 73, 84, 102–3, 112, 115–18, 121
smell 20, 40, 62–6, 92, 99, 113, 119, 148
starvation 52

substance   3, 5, 10, 12, 15, 21–2, 36–9,
      41–9, 55, 58–60, 62–8, 72, 77, 79,
      91–4, 97, 101, 104, 110–11, 114–17,
      119, 124–5, 129–31, 128, 142–5,
      148, 155
supermarket   71, 103, 126, 128, 159
supply networks   39, 102–3, 105
Sutton, David   4, 62–6, 148, 153

taste   17, 20,   24, 36, 39, 40, 42–5, 48,
      50, 55, 60, 63–6, 73, 76, 86, 90, 99,
      109–11, 113, 115, 117–21, 128–30,
      136, 140–1, 145–6, 154
terroir   95–6
thinness   18, 130–1, 141
tourism   8, 76, 83, 127
tradition   8, 11, 17, 38, 51, 54, 59–62, 69,
      81–5, 90–1, 96, 119, 133, 159
transnationalism   59, 60–2, *see also*
      nationalism
transubstantiation   15
trust   12, 70, 72–3, 103, 106, 124, 126,
      128, 159
tuning   20, 45–6, 48, 102, 107–11, 120–1,
      136, 146

United States of America   8–9, 59, 70, 73,
      75, 104–6, 129, *see also* California

veganism   151
vegetarianism   150
Vietnam   76, 84–5
viscerality   3–4, 7, 10, 12–14, 16, 20–2,
      30–1, 33, 36, 41, 45, 54–5, 57,
      62–4, 70, 76–7, 87, 107–8, 114–15,
      117–20, 138–9, 141–2, 144, 146,
      148–9, 151, 153–4
   visceral geographies   102, 117–20 (*see
      also* Hayes-Conroy)
vitalism   10–13, 22–4, 26–7, 29, 31–3, 39,
      42, 47, 50, 54, 58–9, 62, 65–8, 70,
      73, 80, 85, 87–9, 93–5, 98, 101–2,
      112, 115–17, 120–1, 123–4, 131,
      134, 142–3, 152–5

waste   12, 105, 123–4, 128, 132–8, 141–2,
      see also junk and rubbish
Weismantel, Mary   35–8, 46, 48, 50, 52,
      82, 94, 157

yogurt   95

Lightning Source UK Ltd.
Milton Keynes UK
UKOW06n0359110917
308957UK00005B/55/P